ALL THE HOLY DAYS
AND HOLIDAYS

In the afternoon of time
A strenuous family dusted from its hands
The sand of granite, and beholding far
Along the sounding coast its pyramids
And tall memorials catch the dying sun,
Smiled well content, and to this childish task
Around the fire addressed its evening hours.

— Robert Louis Stevenson

ALL THE HOLY DAYS AND HOLIDAYS

or

SERMONS ON ALL NATIONAL AND RELIGIOUS MEMORIAL DAYS

by

DR. HERBERT LOCKYER, R.S.L.

ZONDERVAN PUBLISHING HOUSE

OF THE ZONDERVAN CORPORATION
GRAND RAPIDS, MICHIGAN 49506

ISBN 0-310-28060-5

Library of Congress Catalog Number: 68-27463

ACKNOWLEDGMENTS

Grateful acknowledgment is made to:

The Macmillan Company for permission to quote from *The New Testament in Modern English* by J. B. Phillips, copyright © 1958 by The Macmillan Company. Also to quote from *The Modern Reader's Bible* by Richard G. Moulton.

Dr. Oswald J. Smith for permission to quote three of his poems: "The Cry of the Lost" page 178; "Evangelize" page 252; "The King Is Dead" page 272.

83 84 85 86 87 88 — 20 19 18 17 16 15 14 13 12

Dedicated
to
Mrs. G. W. Cleveland,
Mrs. J. H. Moorehead and
Miss Grace Conklin *(now in Glory)*
all of
Reedsburg, Wisconsin
All sisters in Christ who ministered unto
Him of their substance.

CONTENTS

INTRODUCTION

ANCIENT ORIGIN
OF FESTIVAL DAYS

Where is the Land of Memory,
The Land of long ago?
Is it some isle on Love's deep sea
Where everlastings grow?
Are shining stars with twinkling light
The peep-holes in its floor?
And was the sunset of last night
Its brilliant, golden door?

I love the Land of Memory,
The bright thoughts of the past
Take shape tonight and come to me
From out the unknown vast.
The dear ones that have gone before
Are wakened from their sleep,
Whene'er I knock on mem'ry's door
They bid me not to weep.

For age and youth in memory
Are welded into one.
The dim shades of futurity
Reflect its setting sun.
No storm-king rules with tyrant hand;
No lightnings rift its sky;
Its outskirts border Heaven's land,
And God is ever nigh.

I've found the Land of Memory,
The fairest land of all,
The bluebirds flit from tree to tree;
I hear the linnet's call;
And lilies bloom so pure and white,
Sweet fragrance they impart.
Oh, Memory's Land is my delight;
I've found it in my heart.
— Charles Wagner

ANCIENT ORIGIN
OF FESTIVAL DAYS

We readily admit that there is a baneful, as well as a beneficent aspect to the art of remembering, or to the opposite art of forgetting. If we have a bad memory for what is beneficial, and a good memory for what is unworthy, we are in sad need of sanctification of the mind. When a memory expert offered to teach the Athenian philosopher, Themistocles, how to remember, he replied, "No, no, I want to find someone who can teach me to forget." But there are past events and experiences we should never forget. During World War I, my wife and I had the pleasure of entertaining Gipsy Smith, the renowned evangelist. As he came to leave our home, we asked him to kindly sign his name in our autograph album, and, taking his pen, he wrote the beautiful and expressive sentiment —

"Remembrance is a paradise from which we need not be driven."

As we are to discover, there is a heavenly inspiration associated with the remembrance of conspicuous days in the annals of the Church, and also in national and personal history. While Oliver Wendell Holmes would have us know that: "Memory is a crazy witch; she treasures up bits of rags and straw, and throws her jewels out of the window," the recognition of outstanding festival days is one way of appraising the treasures of truth, faith and freedom. Dante Gabriel Rossetti has the couplet —

"Thou fill'st from the winged chalice of the soul
Thy lamp, O Memory, fire-winged to its goal."

Turning to the Bible we find that days of remembrance are of ancient origin, and were in some instances prescribed by God. The Passover Feast, connected with the death of the Egyptian first-born, and which consummated the plagues was instituted as a commemoration of the Exodus of the Israelites from Egypt (Exodus 3:18; 12:21-27; Deuteronomy 16:1-18). Millenniums after the first Passover, our Lord engaged in the Feast of its remembrance (Luke 22:11), merged it into the Last Supper, and saints through the ages have observed it as an act of remembrance of His death (Luke 22:14-20; I Corinthians 11:23-26). As the proverb puts it, "The deed is gone, the memorial thereof remains."

Joshua was divinely instructed to institute two memorials to remind the people of their complete deliverance from the bondage of Egypt. Twelve stones were taken out of Jordan and erected by Joshua in Gilgal, and twelve stones were left in Jordan to be covered by its waters. For the Christian these stones are memorials marking the distinction between Christ's death under judgment in the sinner's place (Psalm 22:1-18; 42:7; 88:7; John 12:31-33), and of his perfect emancipation from sin. The divine injunction was, *"Remember the day* when thou camest forth out of the land of Egypt *all the days* of thy life" (Deuteronomy 16:3). We, too, like the Jews, must "remember the days of old" (Deuteronomy 32:7), and muse upon the greatness and goodness of God (Psalm 143:5). Our remembrances will not be ashes (Job 13:12), if we pause to praise God for all the blessings and advantages coming to us from the past. It is a most profitable exercise to glance over all the passages collated for us in a Bible concordance under the captions *remember* and *forget*.

The history of almost all nations is replete with calendar days when the deeds of men long dead are recalled and extolled afresh. Gradually, some of these memorial days have gathered traditions and customs around them, such as Guy Fawkes Day, observed particularly by English children every November 5.

Please to remember
The Fifth of November,
   Gunpowder treason and plot.
We know no reason
Why gunpowder treason
   Should ever be forgot.

In Brussels, where the British community likes to celebrate the Fifth of November, the wife of one businessman insisted that he must leave his office at 5:45 to take their children to the embassy fireworks party. He made a large note in his diary and asked his secretary to remind him.

At 5:45 she interrupted an important conference with an American executive. "Excuse me, sir," she said, "you have an appointment with a guy called Fawkes." — *Daily Telegraph.*

In our own personal history there are unforgettable days. Whenever December 10 comes around, instinctively my mind goes back to December 10, 1906, when I was a youth, the day God graciously met me and saved me. That was the day that fixed my choice on Him as my Saviour, and on my spiritual birthday I pause to magnify Him anew for His saving grace and mercy.

High Heaven that heard that solemn
   vow,
   That vow renewed shall daily hear,
Till in life's latest hour I bow,
   And bless in death a bond so dear.

Whatever memorial day a nation, the Church, or a person recalls, remembrance is an empty gesture unless it results in the rededication of life to those ideals for which many courageous souls were prepared to die, and whose memory history keeps green. It was James Barrie who wrote that, "God gave us memory that we might have roses in December."

ALL THE HOLY DAYS
AND HOLIDAYS

For Christmas Day

For Christmas Day

A Hymn on the Nativity
I sing the birth was born tonight,
The Author both of life and light;
   The angels so did sound it.
And like the ravished shepherds said,
Who saw the light and were afraid,
   Yet searched, and true they found
      it.

The Son of God, the eternal King,
That did us all salvation bring,
   And freed the soul from danger;
He whom the whole world could not
      take,
The Word which heaven and earth
      did make,
   Was now laid in a manger.

The Father's wisdom willed it so,
The Son's obedience knew no No,
   Both wills were in one stature:
And as that wisdom had decreed,
The Word was now made flesh indeed,
   And took on him our nature.

What comfort by Him do we win,
Who made himself the price of sin,
   To make us heirs of glory!
To see this babe all innocence,
A martyr born in our defence:
   Can man forget this story?
                           — Ben Jonson

MEDITATION FOR CHRISTMAS DAY

IF CHRIST HAD NOT COME
John 15:22

Have you ever paused to think what kind of a world ours would be if Jesus had stayed in glory? That He did turn aside from the ivory palaces and wrap Himself around with the garment of our humanity is one of the incontrovertible facts of history — Biblical and secular.

But suppose Christ had *not* come? He Himself hinted at the hopelessness of man had He not been born in Bethlehem when he said, "If I had not come" (John 15:22). The presence and glorious triumph of the Church through the centuries, however, as well as our own salvation, testify to the fact that Christ did come to put away sin by the sacrifice of Himself.

Yet, suppose Christ had not come, how spiritually and morally destitute the world would be. It may be a cesspool of iniquity still, but society would be more putrid if it were not for the influence of Christ's character and His Church.

Life without Christmas is, indeed, a life unthinkable. Looking at it from the material angle, what would our home life, social life, commercial life and religious life be without Christmas? Advertisements and commercials constantly remind us, as the month of December approaches us, that there are only so many days left before Christmas. Such a warning is a spur to business as well as a call to ourselves to purchase all our gifts and perfect our holiday plans.

But what would the world be like without the traditional Christmas trees, presents, cards and greetings, and all that is associated with the happy and welcome occasion we call Christmas? Has it ever impressed you that only free peoples of the earth are those who, in their own national way, celebrate Christmas.

In this meditation, however, we are not concerned with debatable matters such as Romish aspects of Christmas, or of the exact date of Christ's birth. The important thing is that, stripped of its trimmings, the most unbelieving concede that Christmas commemorates

17

the entrance of Christ into the world. And, surely, there must have been something unique about the One whose birth has claimed, through the centuries, universal and perpetual recognition!

True, there have been others whose advent has blessed mankind and whose birthdays are nationally remembered. But the birthday of Christ has gained increasing honor with the years.

Our Lord, Himself, in His rebuke of the Pharisees, pictured the desolation of mankind if He had not been born in Bethlehem's manger. For more than nineteen centuries the world has heard His teachings and has been subject to His influences, so much so that friend and foe alike testify to His uniqueness.

Coming from the Father, Christ transformed a dreary wilderness into a garden of roses. But suppose He had not come, then we would have been of all men most miserable. Over against, "If I had not come," we can place, "I am come," and we bless Him for His coming.

Have you ever stopped to consider what life would be like had there been no first Christmas morn? Revelation would have been without a climax, prophecy without a fulfillment, humanity without an ideal, men without a Saviour, eternity without a hope, and the world without a song.

A. *Had Christ Not Come on That First Christmas, We Would Have Had a God Without Honor.*

Because of His foreknowledge, God was able to look down the vista of the ages and know that man, after his creation, would sin and require a Saviour. Thus, in the dateless past, love drew salvation's plan, and in the fullness of time Jesus came as the promised One. The character of a person has much to do with the fulfillment of any prom-

ise he may make. Who promised that Christ should come according to the flesh and die as man's Saviour? It was God Himself, and He was not a man that He should lie.

Think how the honor of God would have suffered, and man's faith in His integrity been blighted, if the angelic announcement, "For unto you is born this day in the city of David a Saviour, which is Christ the Lord," (Luke 2:11) had not been realized. However, "He is faithful that promised," (Hebrews 10:23) and, for our sakes, He carried out to the very letter His declaration to send His Son to die in our stead.

Bethlehem, then, vindicated the honor of God. Ever true to His Word, He fashioned for His beloved One a body in which to die in order that we might be delivered from sin. Always before Christ was the thought that in His ways and work He was fulfilling a divine purpose and promise. "My meat is to do the will of him that sent me, and to finish his work," Christ declared (John 4:34). Had He not come, the character of God would have been revealed as imperfect.

B. *Had Christ Not Come, We Would Have Had a Revelation Without a Climax.*

Majestic as the Old Testament is, with its unfolding of the Person and purpose of God, without the New Testament it would have been but a broken arc of a divine revelation. The expectation of the Old Testament awaited the manifestation of the New.

If Jesus had not come, then a complete Bible would never have been ours. If the Ancient of Days had not become the Babe wrapped in swaddling clothes, there would never have been a New Testament. And what a tragic loss we would have suffered. The Old Testament without the New would have been as a bridge that went only half way over the chasm of human darkness.

The last word of the Old Testament is "curse" (Malachi 4:6). What a tragic ending to the first half of the Bible, beginning as it does with the sublime sentence, "In the beginning God." First, God's majestic creation — then a curse. This is the story of the Old Testament. The curse fell upon man because of sin and rebellion. "Cursed is every one that continueth not in all things which are written in the book of the law to do them" (Galatians 3:10).

How miserable man would have been if left under a curse! How then did God come? Did He descend in judgment to mete out the promised curse? The answer is found in Matthew 1:1. The first line of the New Testament is taken up with Christ! The curse — then Christ; yes, He came to deliver the sinner from the curse. "Cursed is every one that hangeth on a tree" (Galatians 3:13). That was where Jesus hung, and by dying that death He delivered all who believe on Him from the law's curse and condemnation.

Coming, then, as He did, the long expected One, Christ completed the divine revelation, climaxing thereby the unfolding of the mind of God. This is why the New Testament ends, not with a curse, but with a benediction, even with the grace of the Lord Jesus Christ (Revelation 22:21). If we had only the Old Testament, with all its yearnings, promises and prophecies, one would have said, "Where is the other half of the Book?" Something, no, Someone is missing. Christmas gave us the other half, the final crown of Revelation.

C. *Had Christ Not Come We Would*

Have Had Prophecy Without a Fulfillment.

The mercy of God was such that, with the entrance of sin into the world, the first prophecy of redemption immediately followed. And Satan, the one responsible for sin, was the first to hear that the Seed of the woman would bruise his head, that is, destroy his authority. It is no wonder that the devil tried to destroy the royal seed from which Christ was to come. Despite Satan's attempts Christ ultimately came, and at Calvary He fulfilled the prophecy first given at the scene of man's transgression.

God supplied an abundance of prophecies and types in the Old Testament to foreshadow Christ's life and ministry. In the Pentateuch alone we have Christ pictured in a sevenfold way, as the Seed of the woman (Genesis 3:15), the Salvation of Jehovah (Genesis 49:18), as the Sceptre (Genesis 49:10; Numbers 24:17), as Shiloh (Genesis 49:10), the Shepherd of Israel (Genesis 49:24), the Stone of Israel (Genesis 49:24) and the Star of Jacob (Numbers 24:17). How futile these predictions would have been if Christ had remained in heaven! The blessedness of Christmas, however, is the glorious truth that the Christ of prophecy became the Christ of history, and, by faith, He becomes the Christ of experience to those who receive Him.

D. *Another Loss to the World, If There Had Never Been a First Christmas, Would Have Been That of Its Only Perfect Man.*

In Christ we have the sum of all virtues, the flower of humanity. There is none like Him. In perfection He is supreme, unapproachable. The best among men are only men at the best and tainted with sin. But Christ came as God's perfect Man, as man's perfect God.

How poor the world would have been if Christ had not come! It was Christ who wrote the charter of emancipation for women, who taught us the value of the child, and who proclaimed the pricelessness of the human soul. Apart from the fact that this unique Person changed the world's calendar (for this is the year of our Lord 1968), all institutions beneficial to the human race owe their origin to His influence. Hospitals, homes for the aged and orphanages are with us today because of His teaching regarding the worth of the individual. There has never been another comparable to Him in world influence. The impact of His personality is stamped upon every phase of life, as this writer set out to prove in the two volume work entitled, *The Man Who Changed the World*.

Coming into the world, Christ found it a dark place in which to live, but, as the Light from heaven, He caused much of the darkness of sin, error and unbelief to disappear. How true it is that the Light of the world is Jesus!

What a hopeless, helpless life would have been ours if Jesus had not been born of a woman, for man would have been without a Saviour. All humanity, ruined by the Fall, would have remained ruined, with nothing but the blackness of darkness before it. But when Jesus came, the power of sin was broken. He was born a Saviour, and His name declared His willingness to save men and women from their sins. He came into the world, Paul reminds us, to save sinners (I Timothy 1:15a).

Vaughn Shoemaker's famous Christmas cartoon, "The first Christmas gift," which first appeared in 1934, has a most interesting background. Shoe-maker walked into the office of the Chicago *Daily News* with his rough sketch under his arm, a drawing of a star gleaming down upon a manger, with the words of John 3:16 pencilled across the sky above it. The editors, while praising the sketch, argued that a Scripture reference might offend some readers. Shoemaker held his ground, however, and said that John 3:16 must be retained or he would not submit the sketch. Colonel Frank Knox, the publisher, said to his editors, "Let's be sensible. If it weren't for John 3:16 there wouldn't be any Christmas. It's a good cartoon. Run it. We need more like it in the *News*." Thereafter it was repeated every Christmas.

However, unless the Christ born in Bethlehem is born within our hearts as Saviour and Lord, the event of Christ's coming will avail us nothing.

E. *Had Christ Not Come, Man Would Be Forced To Face Eternity Without Hope.*

While the Old Testament saints knew that the grave did not end all, their conception of the future was dim and partial. But Christ, having lived before He was born, brought with Him not only the great fragrance of heaven, but also a fuller, more complete revelation of eternal bliss.

Without the New Testament, we could never have the unmistakable understanding which is ours today of the two destinies awaiting all travelers to eternity, namely, heaven and hell. It is to Christ we turn for the certainty of "the damnation of hell" for the sinner and "the Father's house," with its many mansions, for the saint. Had Christ not come, what gloom, despair and anguish would have been our portion. But coming as the Eternal One, He brought life and immortality to light through the Gospel.

F. *Had Christ Not Come, the World Would Have Been Without a Song.*

Heathenism has no songs. Singing is characteristic of Christianity alone. It was fitting, therefore, that the angels sang as Christ was born. What a sad, songless life ours would be, if Jesus had not made possible the Song of the Lamb! His condescension, crucifixion, resurrection and ascension have given us something about which to sing. If there had never been that first Christmas, there would never have been any churches, Sunday schools, missions, hymn books, and spiritual classics! How His wondrous birth has enriched the world, turning its night into day, its sighs into songs, its despair into delight. Thus, as we sing our carols anew, let us bless Him who has put a new song into our mouth, a song we will never tire of singing through the unending ages of eternity.

EPILOGUE

But Christmas is not only the milemark of another year, moving us to thoughts of self-examination — it is a season, from all its associations, whether domestic or religious, suggesting thoughts of joy. A man dissatisfied with his endeavors is a man tempted to sadness. And in the midst of winter, when his life runs lowest and he is reminded of the empty chairs of his beloved, it is well that he should be condemned to this fashion of the smiling face.

— Robert Louis Stevenson.

For a Watch Night Service

For A Watch Night Service

A Prayer From Christian Seasons,
A.D. *1900*

Almighty and most merciful Father, who hast given us grace in times past, and hast mercifully brought us to see the end of another year, grant that we may continue to grow in grace and in the knowledge of Thy dear Son. Lead us forward by Thy Spirit from strength to strength, that we may more perfectly serve Thee and attain a more lively hope of Thy mercy in Christ Jesus. Quicken our dull hearts, inspire us with warmer affections for Thee, O God, and for Thy heavenly truth. Stir up the gift that is in us, and pour down from above more abundant gifts of grace, that we may make progress in heavenly things. Increase our faith as Thou dost increase our years, and the longer we are suffered to abide on earth, the better may our service be, the more willing our obedience, the more consistent our daily lives, the more complete our devotion to Thee. Grant this our prayer, O gracious Father, which we humbly offer at the throne of grace, in the name and for the sake of Jesus Christ Thy Son, our Lord and Saviour.

Amen

SERMON FOR A WATCH NIGHT SERVICE

AN INDELIBLE RECORD
John 19:22

It is hard to trace just when the custom of having a watch night service to mark the last hour of the old year and the beginning of another year had its origin. One authority states that the custom had its rise in Bristol, England, but owes its general use to John Wesley, who included it in the yearly church calendar. Southey, in his biography of the founder of Methodism, denounced the watch night service as another of Wesley's objectionable institutions. The Christian Church for many centuries has made full use of the midnight hour of December 31st to review the past with gratitude to God, to repent of former sins and failures, and as the bells ring out the old year, rededicate life to Him whose years have no end.

In Scotland the passing of the old year and the dawn of the new year is known as "Hogmanay" — a term of doubtful origin — when there is a national holiday and rejoicing and the exchange of gifts. Both in American and British cities and towns, the last night of the year is accompanied with much revelry, but churches use the hour for prayer, praise and consecration. The Wesleys discovered that many of their converts had formed the habit in their unregenerate days of spending such a night in drunkenness and sin, and for their benefit instituted the watch night service. A significant hymn the Wesleys wrote for this occasion reads —

How many pass the guilty night
    In revellings and mirth!
The creature is their sole delight
    Their happiness the things of earth:
For us suffice the season past;
We choose the better part at last.

A fitting meditation for the ending of the year is to be found in the decree of Pilate. It was the custom, in the days when crucifixion was the form of capital punishment, to inscribe the crime and name of the criminal on a board, and affix the board to the cross, so that the passers-by might know who was being crucified and for what reason.

So Jesus, the supposed felon, died upon His cross. Pilate wrote the title

25

and put it on the cross, *Jesus of Naza-
reth* (His name) *the King of the Jews*
(His crime). Such a title was in the
chief languages of that day, and this
guaranteed that all spectators should
be able to read it. Hebrew was the
language of the Jews, Greek the current language of the Gentiles, and Latin
was the official language.

The Jews, protesting, urged Pilate to
alter the title so as to express not
Christ's real dignity, but His false claim
to it. Jewish ecclesiastics wanted to
make His crime more specific. "Write
not, The King of the Jews; but that he
said, I am King of the Jews" (John
19:21). In Pilate's reply we have his
contempt of the Jews, for his answer
carries the sting of impatience and also
the assumption of authority, "What I
have written I have written" (John
19:22). Having yielded enough to the
Jews, and having intended expressly to
spite and insult them by the title for
having forced him to act against his
own sense of justice, he flatly refused
them.

As the words, "What I have written
I have written" left Pilate's lips, they
were the peevish words of an ill-
tempered man on bad terms with himself and with those about him. Pilate
had forfeited the self-respect of his
fellowmen. His jurisdiction of Judea
had made him hated by the Jews. In
turn, Pilate hated them and was ready
to quarrel with them. It was thus that,
in the spirit of spiteful triumph, he
caused the superscription, so offensive
to the Jews, to remain. Pilate had surrendered Christ to the angry mob
against his better judgment, but was
unwilling to concede a mere detail,
when no principle was involved.

Pilate's declaration was prophetic of
a sad end. What he had written, he
had written. His own life story had

been written with the pen of expediency and the ink of cowardice, and
such a shameful story could not be cut
out nor rewritten. His writing remains
against him, for the world points a
finger of scorn at this weak-minded
man who should have written over the
middle cross, "Barabbas, the Murderer."
And if legend be true, Pilate reaped
what he had sown, for seeing that he
was disgraced, he committed suicide.

Let us note the various applications
of Pilate's harsh and authoritative reply,
"What I have written I have written."

A. *True Description of the Past — What
I have written I have written!*

There is a fatefully significant ring
about these words as we apply them to
a faded year with its story to which all
of us have contributed. A deeper and
more solemn truth than we can imagine
is resident in Pilate's declaration, for
the past is beyond recall. All of us
think of what we would do if only we
could live our lives over again. We
think of kind words we should have
spoken, but it is too late, for those who
should have heard them are gone forever. If only they could return for
five minutes, we might try to make
amends. We think of kind deeds we
might have performed, but the opportunity has gone. We think of the holy
life we might have lived, but the
door is closed upon the past with its
heaps of broken vows and blighted
resolutions.

We cannot undo what we have done,
or erase what we have written. It may
be possible to unravel a sock one is
knitting, if a mistake must be rectified,
but we cannot do this with our past
faults. Our past has turned its back
upon us forever, and departed into
eternity. We may cry, "O return, and
let me make amends!" but there will be
no response to our appeal. When David

heard of the death of his child he said, "I shall go to him, but he shall not return to me" (II Samuel 12:23). And this is true of our past. It will not return to us, but we must go out to meet our past. God grant that it will not rise up in condemnation against us!

B. *The Unalterable Character of God — What I have written I have written!*

There is a sense in which we can apply these words to God and His Word. Everywhere in the Bible the fixed, unchanging, immutable, eternal character of God is extolled. He is never sorry for anything He does — never retrieves any step — never takes anything back. His unalterableness runs like a golden thread through the Scriptures. "God is not a man, that he should lie; neither the son of man, that he should repent: hath he said, and shall he not do it? or hath he spoken, and shall he not make it good?" (Numbers 23:19). "I know that, whatsoever God doeth, it shall be for ever: nothing can be put to it, nor any thing taken from it: and God doeth it, that men should fear before him" (Ecclesiastes 3:14). "For I am the LORD, I change not; therefore ye sons of Jacob are not consumed" (Malachi 3:6). "And being fully persuaded that, what he had promised, he was also able to perform" (Romans 4:21). "Every good gift and every perfect gift is from above, and cometh down from the Father of lights, with whom is no variableness, neither shadow of turning" (James 1:17).

Returning to Pilate's inscription, we realize that the finger of God was behind it. In effect, that title on the cross was the execution of a divine command. It was the title decreed by God, although Pilate's hand unconsciously wrote it. Tell it out among the nations,

that the Lord is King! The curious irony is that Pilate was marked out to declare Christ's kingship. One expositor explains it in this way, "Amidst the conflicting passions of men, was proclaimed, in the chief tongues of mankind, from the cross itself and in circumstances which threw upon it a lurid yet grand light, the truth which drew the Magi to His manger, and will yet be owned by all the world!"

The finger of God is likewise behind all the Bible holds. Modernists may deny this and that part of the Word, but the whole is His revelation. What He has written He has written. He wrote the ten commandments, and they still hold good. "Ye shall not add unto the word which I command you, neither shall ye diminish aught from it, that ye may keep the commandments of the LORD your God which I command you" (Deuteronomy 4:2).

Can we not apply the willingness of God to fulfill any declaration of His, to specific promises of Scripture? For example, there is the promise of security: "And I give unto them eternal life; and they shall never perish, neither shall any man pluck them out of my hand" (John 10:28). Our name will never be erased from the Lamb's Book of Life. His gifts are without repentance. "For the gifts and calling of God are without repentance" (Romans 11:29). For our support and nurture we have the following: "Blessed be the LORD, that hath given rest unto his people Israel, according to all that he promised: there hath not failed one word of all his good promise, which he promised by the hand of Moses his servant" (I Kings 8:56). "He hath said, I will never leave thee nor forsake thee" (Hebrews 13:5). "God is not a man, that he should lie; neither the son of man, that he should repent: hath he said, and shall he not do it? or hath he spoken, and shall he not make it good?" (Numbers 23:19). Yes, what He has written He has written! As to our final redemption, the Lord will keep trust with His own, and return according to His Word. "Let not your heart be troubled: ye believe in God, believe also in me. In my Father's house are many mansions: if it were not so, I would have told you. I go to prepare a place for you. And if I go and prepare a place for you, I will come again, and receive you unto myself; that where I am, there ye may be also" (John 14:1-3). The night is dark! Daybreak is at hand! Christ's promise to deliver us from a groaning creation will not be broken.

C. *The Determined Allegiance of the Saint — What I have written I have written!*

Applying Pilate's answer to the Jewish request to alter the title he had placed over the cross to ourselves, we realize that it is imperative to write well, and then abide by what is written. Our common fault is we are too movable, oscillating, weak, shifty and undependable. We are not men and women of our word. We do not have the determination of Jephthah, who said: "I have opened my mouth unto the Lord, and I cannot go back" (Judges 11:35). A similar integrity is brought before us in Numbers 30:2; Esther 1:12; 4:16; Ecclesiastes 5:4, 5.

How we need more conscience in the fulfillment of our vows and covenants! Luther facing a hostile world cried, "Here I stand. I can do no other. God help me!" If you recently trusted Christ, writing your name to a "Decision card," may God preserve you from going back upon your signature. If you have taken upon yourself solemn baptismal vows do not keep back part of the price. Go out to live the baptized life! Surrender to no one but God. Endeavor so to live that you will not be ashamed of your record when it hails you in eternity. May grace be yours to write well, to be more reliable, dependable! The Lord would have us known and beloved by all, a living epistle.

D. *The Sad Confession of a Sinner — What I have written I have written!*

Life is full of tragic illustrations of this inscription. Here we have the sad confession of many a heart! We reap what we sow. "Be not deceived; God is not mocked: for whatsoever a man soweth, that shall he also reap. For he that soweth to his flesh shall of the flesh reap corruption; but he that soweth to the Spirit shall of the Spirit reap life everlasting" (Galatians 6:7, 8). David was graciously forgiven and therefore could write Psalm 32, but the fruit of his sin dogged his footsteps to the grave. Salvation does not always remove the effects of sin along with its guilt and penalty. Prodigal ways of parents in early life often bears its fruit in the godlessness of their offspring.

Here and now we reap what we sow. Sinners should not be elated if they are not presently suffering for their sin. God's accounting day is coming! "Sure, ah, sure, will the harvest be." Lost innocence can never be regained. The bloom rudely brushed from the flower can never be restored. Therefore, it is imperative to see how we live our days, seeing the stains of the soul are retained. That foul impressions abide, even the saved can testify with shame.

It is also true that hereafter we reap what we sow. There may be those who appear to forget what they have said and done wrong in the past, but while they may try to forget it, it is not forgotten elsewhere. Every trace remains with all the force and power of written evidence, which is the most damning of all. If a thing is in black and white it cannot be gainsaid. So, whether saint or sinner, let us never forget that a copy of the story we are writing is being taken down by God's recording angel above.

If we go on, heedless of our ways, the time is coming when we shall be horrified and distressed as we reread the story of our life at the Judgment Bar of God. Our sin, like Judah's, is written with the pen of iron and the point of a diamond. Yes, the day is coming when men must read the writing of a useless life and Christless character they are penning today. "Out of thine own mouth will I judge thee" (Luke 19:22).

Our only hope of deliverance from condemnation is to confess and repent of our sin, for all handwriting against us can be blotted out. Christ's nail-pierced hands can erase the past. "I have blotted out, as a thick cloud, thy transgressions, and, as a cloud, thy sins: return unto me; for I have redeemed thee" (Isaiah 44:22).

Cleansing us from the *guilt of sin,* and daily delivering us from the *power of sin,* Christ will overrule the *effect of sin.* Let us turn anew to the Saviour, then, that under the inspiration of the Holy Spirit we may write in the pages of life with the pen of faith and ink of love, a life story of which we shall never be ashamed to say, "*What I have written I have written!*"

How apt are the lines of Frank J. Exley in his book of poems published in 1942 —

The Book of the Year

I bring my Book of Days to Thee, O God,
  Marred with mistakes, its pages sadly soiled,
The record of the road that I have trod
  The story of the tasks at which I toiled.

I would not have it scanned by other eyes,
  None else could read what I have *meant* to be;
But what has meanest worth Thy love will prize,
  And what is worthless Thou wilt pitying see.

I thank Thee for the joys that Thou hast sent,
  For mercies new with every morning's light,
For gifts that fill my heart with glad content,
  For hopes that make my future pathway bright.

Nor would I thank Thee less for joys withheld,
  For cups of blessing that were cups of pain,
For those sweet sorrows that my heart compelled
  To seek its home and rest in Thee again.

So do I bring to Thee my Book of Days,
  Its every leaf a witness to Thy care;
Here is no day that does not speak Thy praise,
  No page but doth Thy boundless love declare.

Forgive the sins that soil this book of mine.
  Write not the record in Thy Book above,
And know — Thou only canst — my heart is Thine,
  For see, beneath the blots is writ my love.

For New Year's Day

For New Year's Day

One of the finest of the Wesley hymns which we always associate with the opening moments of the New Year — a hymn mingling warning and challenge to our hearts — reads,

> Come, let us anew
> Our journey pursue,
> Roll round with the year,
> And never stand still till the Master
> appear.
>
> His adorable will
> Let us gladly fulfil,
> And our talents improve,
> By the patience of hope, and the labour of love.
>
> O that each in the day
> Of His coming may say,
> "I have fought my way through
> I have finished the work Thou didst give me to do."

It was the late King George VI who made the following words of M. I. Haskins famous —

> "And I said to the man who stood at the gate of the year: 'Give me a light that I may tread safely into the unknown.'
>
> And he replied: 'Go out into the darkness and put your hand into the hand of God. That shall be to you better than light and safer than a known way.' "

MEDITATION FOR NEW YEAR'S DAY

THE SECRET OF A HAPPY NEW YEAR
Isaiah 41:10

In the goodness of God we stand at the portal of another year. The old year has rolled into eternity, and what a year of anguish and horror it proved to be! It may be that we would like to recall the vanished months in order to put a few wrong things right. Words were spoken we would like to unsay, acts were committed we have a desire to undo, but it is too late to make amends. The beginning of another year is here, and with it the assurance that the God of our years waits to make us victorious where we were defeated, strong where we were weak, hopeful where we were fearful, holy where we were sinful.

The Journal of John Wesley records conspicuous New Year resolves and prayers. It was New Year's Day, 1736, that found Wesley on board a ship bound for Georgia to engage in missionary work among the Moravians, and under this date we have the entry —

Oh, may the New Year bring a new heart and a new life to all those who seek the Lord God of their fathers.

On January 1, 1790, after fifty years of joyous service, Wesley wrote —

I am now an old man, decayed from head to foot. My eyes are dim; my right hand shakes much; my mouth is hot and dry every morning. I have a lingering fever almost every day; my motion is weak and slow. However, blessed be God. I can preach and write still.

Eighteen months later the old warrior laid down his sword crying —

"The best of all is God is with us." What a motto to have as day follows day in the year before us! If God is with and for us, who or what then can be against us?

In years gone by we have probably made new resolutions. We do not know what the untrodden way holds for us in surprises or sorrows, but, full of hope, we face the unknown future, believing that "So long Thy power hath blessed me, sure it still will lead me on." We do not see the distant scene. Realizing that the journey through the year will have to be taken a step at a time, we have determined to trust ourselves to our divine Guide, whose love and wisdom have already planned our

33

course. And, setting out as we are upon another stretch of earth's pilgrimage, it will be found helpful to hitch the wagon of our hopes to the star of a promise. Isaiah, for example, has a wonderful promise for the dark, critical days ahead. With hellish forces let loose upon the earth, and the prospect of a year of unprecedented woe and tribulation, we must have some inspiring message we can take to our hearts. Well, here is the prophet's promise which, if we will but appropriate it, will yield the secret of a holy, happy new year.

> Fear thou not; for I am with thee:
> Be not dismayed; for I am thy God:
> I will strengthen thee; yea, I will help thee;
> Yea, I will uphold thee with the right hand of my righteousness.
> (41:10).

As it is our custom to wish each other a prosperous new year, it is but fitting to remind ourselves that true prosperity will only reach us as day follows day, when, by the Spirit we understand what kind of a God we have as our Companion. If, in spite of the trials it holds, the new year is to be one of blessedness, we will have to learn how to rest in the joy of what God is. It is only as we know His name, that we can trust Him. For our encouragement, the Lord reveals Himself in a fourfold way in His exhortation through the prophet.

A. *His Prerogative.*

There are two "nots" we will have to guard against if we want a year of unbroken peace. "Fear thou *not* . . . be *not* dismayed." Fear and dismay! These are the enemies lurking within the shadows to rob us of trust and confidence. And, because of His poise, God possesses the sovereign right to command us to have a year without dread or discouragement. One of the blessed things about God is that He graciously supplies what He commands. It was this aspect of the divine character that led St. Augustine to pray, "Give what Thou commandest, then command what Thou wilt." God's appeal, therefore, is not merely negative. He waits to fortify our mind with His grace, so that we will not succumb to any gloom the year may hold.

Fear thou not! Fear is indeed something to fear. Fear and faith are never good companions. Fear is the child of doubt — faith is born of God. Fear ends in failure — faith leads to victory. To have, then, a year without fear, we must have a year of ever-increasing faith in Him who is able to do exceeding abundantly above all we could ask or think.

Be not dismayed! War breeds depression and we can see the hopelessness which earth's wars have given us. We find ourselves in a cheerless world. Multitudes have committed suicide rather than face the future as slaves ruled by a cruel despot. The enslaved nations are without song. From the margin of Isaiah 41:10 we have the suggestive reading, "Look not around thee." Men have sad hearts and faces because of what they see as they look around — and we frankly confess that the outlook is gloomy. "Change and decay in all around we see." Our eyes, however, must not be upon our environment.

Neither must we look back. If we do, past sins and failures will add to our dismay. Guilty of transgression though we were, we must not brood over our shortcomings. If they are under the blood of Jesus, then let them stay there.

To look within is likewise harmful to our faith. Introspection is apt to become morbid and depressing. Self-examination is apt to create unwarranted remorse in a child of God. It is true, as Plato has reminded us, that "the unexamined life is not worth having." But the only safe and profitable way is the divine examination of self.

No, the other way is to look up — not around, nor behind, nor within, but *up* to Him who is omnipotent. Look up — God reigns, and over unaccustomed paths He will lead us into deeper experiences of His love and power! Look up — for amid any storm that may rage He will be at hand to sustain with His peace! Look up — for our salvation is nearer than when we believed. We must *look up* and thus be ready to *go up.*

B. *His Presence.*

For the two "nots" there are also two "I am's." *I am with thee* — the consciousness of God's presence means a life without fear. *I am thy God* — the realization of God's power means a life without dismay. Many precious friendships are ours as we begin another year, but as time rolls by, one here and there will drop out of the journey. Life may become lonely as vacant chairs appear, but here is One who promises never to leave us. Living, loving hands will be forced to release their grasp of our hands. Christ, however, will never, never let go our hand. He declares that He will be with us, not merely near — within call if needed — but actually with us. In the dark hours that may befall us, He will be in the darkness saying, "O heart I made, a heart beats here," and the assurance of His tenderness and abiding companionship will inspire confidence and impart comfort.

As a very *present* help in trouble, He will preserve us from tormenting fears. The billows of grief may dash against our frail craft, but with Christ in the vessel we can smile at the storm.

C. *His Power.*

With our hand on the latch of the door of the new year, we can enter its days with boldness, knowing that God's infinite resources will be at our disposal. And such a promise of power is for the weakest of His saints. I am *thy* God — yes, *your* God! He is the God of Mary Smith or Tom Jones, just as he was the God of Jacob. "God," the primary name of Deity, is made up of *El,* meaning "the Strong One," and *Alah,* meaning to bind oneself by an oath, so implying faithfulness. Therefore, the God who declares that He will be with us is the Strong One who will carry out every promise on our behalf. He is mighty and faithful who promised. As needs arise, He will meet them. As enemies appear, He will vanquish them. As clouds gather, He will dispel them. May ours be a great faith in a great God!

D. *His Provision.*

It will be noticed that our New Year's promise contains three "I will's," and such a triplet of certainty ought to slay any fears we may have forever dead.

1. *The "I Will" of Strength.*

We shall not travel far into the new year without learning that the secret of strength is the consciousness of weakness. When we are weak, then we are strong. Our greatest victories will be won as the power of Christ covers our impotence. "When my weakness leaneth on His might, all is right." In a characteristic letter received from the late Dr. William R. Newell, the well-known Bible teacher, he requested me to pray that grace and strength would be his for some Chicago meetings. He was suffering much physical weakness at the time and he wrote, "I remember one day in the

Coliseum meetings in St. Louis in 1901, when after speaking on II Corinthians 12:9, 'My strength is made perfect in weakness,' I called for a time of prayer. One brother prayed, 'Lord, we'll furnish the weakness if you'll furnish the strength.' Now all I can provide at this time is weakness, but 'through your supplications' I shall, I hope, find strength." May each of us prove the Lord to be the strength of our life!

2. *The "I Will" of Sympathy.*

In His promise of help, God offers to take the heaviest end of our load and assist us in carrying it. As we are moved with sympathy if we see a child struggling beneath a burden too heavy for its little arms to carry, so the Lord offers Himself as our Helper. And the help we will need and receive will not be some thing but Some*one*. With boldness we will declare, "The Lord is my helper" (Hebrews 13:6). Surely it was this idea of God that the psalmist had when he wrote, "Thou art my help" (Psalm 70: 5). We can, therefore, greet the new year with courage, for no matter what loads may be ours, the heaviest among them will be light indeed for Him to whom nothing is too hard. He presents Himself, then, as a very present "help" in trouble, which actually means that He stands ready to undertake for us in tight places. In fact, the original of Psalm 46:1 implies that God runs out speedily to meet and help His troubled children.

3. *The "I Will of Support.*

What a threefold cord this promise holds! "I will strengthen thee — I will help thee — I will uphold thee with the right hand of my righteousness." Surely such a trinity ought to banish all fear and dismay! Strength — Help — Righteousness! What more could we ask for? If this promise does not produce a Happy New Year, then nothing will. Think of it! To be upheld by the hand that formed and upholds the world in its grasp — the hand that is full of righteousness in its dispensing of rewards and punishments! Why, here is power beyond our utmost thought, and yet at our disposal.

"You know the trysting place," James Gilmour said to his comrade, "the right hand side." In ancient courts, the pleader stood on the right hand, whether he pleaded for or against a person. The Bible presents the right hand as the place of power and the position of highest honor. Thus, the right hand upholding us suggests the support of omnipotence.

Compare this reference to God's right hand with another sweet promise. "The Lord thy God will hold thy right hand, saying unto thee, Fear not; I will help thee" (Isaiah 41:13). God's right hand is holding our right hand. We can go hand in hand with God! May this be our constant attitude in the new year, as its days run their course. Cling to the promise that Jesus will be with you *all the days* ahead (Matthew 28:20, RV, margin).

Upon the threshold of the year
  As one that keepeth tryst I wait;
The unknown way I shall not fear,
  If, close beside the op'ning gate,
One radiant form by faith I see
And Christ, my Lord, will go with me.

The sunshine shall be yet more bright
  With His dear presence by my side;
No gloomy vale shall me affright,
  Nor any ill my soul betide,
If, whether joy or sorrow be,
Through all the year He leadeth me.

So, at the threshold of the year,
  I wait that I may hear Him say —
"My presence shall be ever near,
  And strength be given for thy day,
For lo, through all the days," saith He,
"Thy Lord shall bear thee company."

For Valentine Day

For Valentine Day
Sweetheart Banquet Day

Chorus of Daughters

What is thy beloved more than an-
other beloved,
  O thou fairest among women?
What is thy beloved more than an-
other beloved,
  That thou dost so adjure us?

The Bride's Answer

My beloved is white and ruddy,
  The chiefest among ten thousand.
His head is as the most fine gold,
  His locks are bushy, and black as
  a raven.
His eyes are like doves beside the
  water brooks;
  Washed with milk, and fitly set.
His cheeks are as a bed of spices,
  As banks of sweet herbs.

His lips are as lilies, dropping liquid
  myrrh;
  His hands are as rings of gold set
  with beryl:
His body is as ivory work overlaid
  with sapphires;
  His legs are as pillars of marble, set
  upon sockets of fine gold:
His aspect is as Lebanon, excellent as
  the cedars;
  His mouth is most sweet: yea, he is
  altogether lovely.
This is my beloved, and this is my
  friend,
  O daughters of Jerusalem.

Song of Solomon 5:9-16
Moulton

MEDITATION FOR VALENTINE DAY
SWEETHEART BANQUET DAY

My Beloved Is Mine, And I Am His
Song of Solomon 5:9-16

Although commercialization has popularized St. Valentine Day to a tremendous extent, and turned it into a national event characterized by an outburst of sentimentalism among husbands and wives, parents and children, and sweethearts, it is to be questioned whether the countless numbers who send valentines know the origin of such a custom. The word "valentine" itself is supposed to be a corruption of *galatin*, a term meaning "gallant" or "a lover." Tradition associates the day with "The Feast of St. Valentine." This was held in commemoration of a Roman priest by the name of Valentine who was famous for the love and charity he manifested, but who was martyred around A.D. 270. Imprisoned under Emperor Claudius II for assisting those persecuted for their Christian faith, Valentine was thrown into prison and, while there, led a Roman officer, Astarius, and his wife and family to Christ. For this he was beaten with rods and beheaded and buried on the

Flaminian Way, February 14, A.D. 270. A church was built over his grave in honor of his sacrificial life and death.

Whether, however, this connection of the Saint and the Day has any historical basis, or is purely accidental, is hard to determine. It would seem that Valentine Day is more likely to be connected with the pagan Roman feast of *Lupercalia*, or "Lover's Festival." This festival was observed on February 15 when the priests of Luperci made a circuit of Palatine Hill, striking with goatskin thongs all women encountered, a rite believed to insure fertility and an easy delivery. Love tokens were likewise distributed among friends, and the first of the opposite sex seen that day was betrothed in a mock betrothal for a year.

Perhaps the most feasible explanation of Valentine Day is that it became connected with the spring season in general, particularly at the start of the third week of the second month when, as many fables have it, the birds choose their mates. Early allusions to the customs of the Day occur in the works of John Gower and John Lydgate, and in the Paston Letters. Shakespeare, in *A Midsummer Night's Dream,* alludes to the above association.

"Saint Valentine is past:
Begin those wood-birds but to couple now."

John Donne (1571-1631) in his *Ode* to two of royal birth being married on St. Valentine's Day, composed the couplet —

"Hail, Bishop Valentine, whose day this is
All the air is thy Diocese."

An ancient proverb reads —

"On Valentine Day will a good goose lay.
If she be a good goose, her dame well to pay.
She will lay two eggs before Valentine's Day."

The modern development of sending Valentine cards, then, has little relation to the saint of that name or to any incident in his life, but is a commercial expansion of the medieval custom which has become one of the most popular of special days. Nell Warren Outlaw, in *This Is the Day,* says of Valentine Day that, "it is the date when all hearts forget the calendar, turn back to the time of lad and lassie to speak their tender sentiment without restraint . . . Certainly there is no desire to rob this day of any of its delicate dreams and fancies. Regardless of age as years term it, one may continue young in heart and enjoy this opportunity to bespeak his regard for those beloved by means of the popular expressions of affection, so precious, at this season."

Although Valentine Day, or Sweetheart Day, as it has come to be called, is not dealt with as a religious day, yet it lends itself to an application which is Christian in content. Not only on February 14, but every day we should remember that, "I am my beloved's, and my beloved is mine" (Song of Solomon 6:3). All lovers of the Bible agree that in the ancient idyll, the Song of Solomon, our Lord Jesus Christ can be seen as the Lover of our soul, whose love is "better than wine" (Song of Solomon 1:2). As heartthrobs are only felt by the heart, the key to Solomon's love letter is our own heart. If we truly love Christ, we will love this Song, laden as it is with expressive similes of true love. Perhaps the most appealing section of this love song is that delineation of how the beautiful country girl, the Shulamite, yearns for her lover during his absence. She is asked the question —

"What is thy beloved more than another beloved,
O thou fairest among women?"

Out goes a valentine from her heart —

"My beloved is white and ruddy,
The chiefest among ten thousand."

His absence only made her heart grow more fond of her lover. So she proceeds to give a laudation of the one nearest and dearest to her, and how her heart thrills in the recital of all his virtues. Her language may seem to be somewhat extravagant but no words could ever express the love of Christ for His Bride. She expresses her love for Him as she confesses, "He is altogether lovely." The world may see no beauty in Him that it should desire Him, but for those who love Him He is beyond compare.

How applicable to Christ are the features the Bride uses to describe her Bridegroom! Let us select a few of them.

A. *The Purity of His Life* — "*My beloved is white.*"

Because Christ always pleased His

Heavenly Father, He could challenge His foes with, "Which of you convinceth me of sin?" (John 8:46). In all His ways and works He was "holy, harmless, undefiled, separate from sinners" (Hebrews 7:26). Even those who hated His witness declared His innocence.

B. *The Greatness of His Redemption — "My beloved is ruddy."*

> His blood so red
> For me was shed.

Does not the whiteness of His life set forth in vivid contrast the rich color of His sacrifice for a lost world? In his Calvary Doxology John extols what Peter calls "the precious blood of Christ" (I Peter 1:19; Revelation 1:5). And is not His ruby blood efficacious to save because of the sinlessness of the life He lived?

C. *The Infinity of His Wisdom.*

> "His head is as the most fine gold,
> His locks are bushy and black as
> a raven."

When Nebuchadnezzar was described as a "head of gold" (Daniel 2:38), supreme leadership was implied. How much more true is the simile of Christ, who is coming as the King of kings! *Head* represents wisdom and knowledge, and He came as the personification and perfection of heavenly wisdom. John speaks of His head and hair, "white like wool, as white as snow" (Revelation 1:14), and the adjectives Solomon and John employ remind us of the everlasting strength and vitality of our undecaying Lord into whose pure mind the thought of sin never entered.

D. *The Strength of His Salvation.*

> "His legs are as pillars of marble."

How expressive is this figure of speech in the Bride's valentine of her lover! "Pillars of Marble" suggest our Bridegroom's strength as "the strong Son of God" who bore the weight of the sin of the world. "Sockets of fine gold" can represent His perfect righteousness. Strength and righteousness are to characterize Christ's rule when He comes to reign.

E. *The Fragrance of His Words.*

> "His speech is most sweet . . .
> His lips are like lilies, dropping
> sweet smelling myrrh."

How true is the psalmist's commendation of Christ! — "Grace is poured into Thy lips." Never man spake like this Man! His beautiful and blessed words have wooed and won countless millions of hearts to Himself!

> Majestic sweetness sits enthroned
> Upon the Saviour's brow;
> His head with radiant glories crowned,
> His lips with grace o'erflow.
> — Samuel Stennett

Thus, on Valentine Day, as we find delight in selecting and sending affectionate sentiments to those we love, let us not forget Him from whom the blessing of true love flows. May we be found speaking well of Him who is "conspicuous above a myriad," and who is chief among ten thousand to our hearts. Unashamedly let us express to others that the One who became the Man of Sorrows is our Beloved and Friend, and tell Him anew in all sincerity —

"Thou knowest that I love Thee."

For St. Patrick's Day

For St. Patrick's Day

The traditional prayer of Patrick does not bear the mark of modern Roman Catholicism, but belongs to a purer form of Christianity that is closer to the Bible and to a personal experience of divine grace:

I bind myself today
The Power of God to guide me,
The Might of God to uphold me,
The Wisdom of God to teach me,
The Eye of God to watch over me,
The Ear of God to hear me,
The Word of God to give me speech,
The Hand of God to protect me,
The Way of God to prevent me,
The Shield of God to shelter me,
The Host of God to defend me.

Christ is with me, Christ is before me,
Christ behind me, Christ within me,
Christ beneath me, Christ above me,
Christ in the fort (that is, at home),
Christ in the chariot seat (traveling by
    land),
Christ in the poop (traveling by
    water).

I bind to myself today
The strong power of an invocation of
    the Trinity,
The faith of the Trinity in Unity,
The Creator of the elements.

Salvation is of the Lord,
Salvation is of the Lord,
Salvation is of Christ,
May Thy salvation, O Lord, be ever
    with us.

MEDITATION FOR ST. PATRICK'S DAY

THE SHAMROCK SAINT

Romans 8:35

It may come as a shock to many Irishmen that Patrick was probably a Scotsman. Legend and fancy are so mingled in the scanty historical records of the Irish saint that we can hardly disentangle them. We have no authentic statement of his birthplace or his race, except that he was not Irish. Some historians think he was born in Scotland, others say that he saw the light of day in England, and still others that he came from France. While written accounts of this "Apostle of Ireland" came late, and little is known of him for certain, they doubtless embody a stock of oral tradition.

Patrick was probably born in what is now known as Dumbarton, Scotland about A.D. 389. He, himself, left it on record that his father was both a deacon in the church and a councillor under the Roman government, and that his grandfather was a Presbyter — facts usually omitted by Roman Catholic writers since they clash with Rome's rule on cleric celibacy. At the age of

fifteen Patrick was carried off to Ireland after a raid on his home town, and for six years kept swine as a slave in Armagh. It was during these hard days that he experienced a great spiritual change and surrendered his life to God. He came to feel "the Spirit burning within him." After seven years in slavery he escaped and found his way back home, but he could not rest. In his dreams he seemed to hear the Irish calling him to return: "We pray thee to come and henceforth walk among us." His relatives begged Patrick not to return, but he was determined to go to Ireland as a missionary of the cross.

After preaching for some time, Patrick visited Gaul and Italy and studied under Germanus at Auxerre. When he was about sixty years of age, he returned to Ireland as a Bishop, and set out to preach the Gospel in the country where he had once been a slave. Tradition has it that he left the print of his foot on the solid rock of Ireland when he came to its shores to evangelize the pagan Irish. As the first Easter drew nigh Patrick determined to keep it in Tara, "which was the chief abode of idolatry and wizardry in Ireland." The Feast of Tara was accompanied by heathen practices which the missionary challenged. Leoghain, the overlord of the wizards, lost out to Patrick, and for thirty years opposed him, though in the end the fearless missionary baptized the ruler. He likewise led the daughters of Leoghain to Christ. It was after this encounter that he composed his hymn called *The Deer's Cry*, cited at the beginning of this article. He returned to Tara to preach saying, "I will go that I may manifest my readiness before the men of Ireland. It is not 'a candle under a vat' that I will make of myself."

Tradition also has it that Patrick wandered up and down Ireland preaching, building churches and working miracles. One legend credits him with having chased all the snakes out of Ireland. That he met with much opposition is evident by what the Ulster chief said of him — "This is the shaven head and the falsifier who is deceiving every one. Let us go and attack him, and see if God will help." Patrick's courage never failed him for he knew that God was ever near as his Helper. Described as "a lion in boldness, a serpent in cunning, a dove in gentleness and meekness, and a laborious servant to the Creator," Patrick was past ninety when he went to heaven, although some traditions declare him to have been one hundred and twenty when he died.

"Therefore Patrick sent forth his spirit, and he received communion and sacrifice from Bishop Tassach's hand, after gaining victories and triumph over the world and devil and vices. And he sent forth his spirit to the Lord for whom he had done ceaseless warfare on earth."

He had wished to die in his beloved Armagh, but an angel warned him that this must not be. Those who loved and revered him gave him a worthy funeral when he was "waked" for twelve nights. Fancifully, tradition says that — "A great host of heaven's angels came with a great light to attend him, and Ireland's elders heard the quiring of the angels on that night. The elders came for twelve nights with psalms and hymns."

On St. Patrick's Day, or Shamrock Day, Irishmen the world over keep his memory alive. As with other memorial days, commercialization surrounds March 17. Florists are busy before the day preparing sprigs of shamrock, and card manufacturers have cashed in on the occasion by putting out a variety of green cards. One before me reads, "Greetings on St. Patrick's Day" and inside is the meaningless jingle —

> Sure and lots of Irish luck
> Is bound to come your way,
> If you just get the special wish
> This brings to you today!
> Have a wonderful
> ST. PATRICK'S DAY

Although medieval biographers Romanized and canonized the saint, heaping legend upon legend upon his Irish ministry, it is doubtful whether he was a Roman Catholic. Schaff in his *History of the Christian Church* observes —

> Patrick never mentions Rome or the Pope; he never appeals to tradition and seems to recognize Scriptures (including the Apocrypha) as the one authority in matters of faith. In a hymn he wrote as a prayer for Divine help and protection when he was about to embark on the important and difficult work of preaching to the chief monarch, the principal doctrine or orthodox . . . but without the invocation of Mary, and the saints, such as we might expect from Patrick of tradition.

Describing his call to preach, Patrick

spoke of his commission as coming directly from God and not through the intervention of any ecclesiastical authority or episcopal consecration. In his endeavor to win the two daughters of Leoghain to Christ, Patrick affirmed that "Father, Son, and the Holy Spirit are not divided," and illustrated the truth by the three leaf shamrock twig in his hand. This is why the Shamrock became the symbol of Ireland. It is interesting to note that Pliny the Elder believed that no serpent would ever touch this plant.

As March 17 comes around each year, Christians can gladly honor the memory of Patrick the missionary because he honored the Word of God in a then heathen land, and because he was free from so many of the traditions and accretions of a later age that diluted and adulterated the truth he preached to the Irish before they were shackled by Rome. Accepting the Scriptures as his final authority, Patrick, a commendable saint, was nearer the Protestant Church than the Roman Church. He began his *Confession* —

"I, Patrick, a sinner, the rudest and the least of all the faithful, and the most contemptible of the multitude." On St. Patrick's Day we should pray that all the unsaved Irish might be brought to the simple, evangelical faith expressed by their patron saint, when he prayed —

"Salvation is of Christ;
May Thy salvation, O Lord, be ever with us."

The motto of The Order of St. Patrick is based upon Romans 8:35 — *Quis Separabit?* — Who shall separate? How reassuring it is to believe, as the Irish saint did, that no one and nothing can ever separate us from the love of God in Christ Jesus! While we may not have the widespread opportunity Patrick had, and leave behind us a trail of fame, we can be as true to the call of God in our generation as he was in his, knowing that our labor is not in vain in the Lord. The world knows little of its greatest saints, who live and labor in the light of eternity.

They have no place in storied page;
No rest in marble shrine;
They are past and gone with a perished age,
They died and "made no sign."
But work that shall find its wages yet,
And deeds that their God did not forget,
Done for their love Divine —
These were their mourners, and these shall be
The crowns of their immortality.
— Edwin Arnold

For Lenten Days

For Lenten Days

We beseech Thee, our most gracious God, preserve us from the cares of this life, lest we should be too much entangled therein; also from the many necessities of the body, lest we should be ensnared by pleasure; and from whatsoever is an obstacle to the soul, lest, being broken with troubles, we should be overthrown. Give us strength to resist, patience to endure, and constancy to persevere; for the sake of Jesus Christ our Lord and Saviour. Amen.

— Thomas à Kempis (1379)

"Lent consists in *doing something,* not merely *doing without something.*"

— Bishop Wilson

Come, Holy Comforter, a Saviour's
    love
Reveal, and fix our hearts on joys
    above;
Come, Holy Comforter, the flesh
    subdue,
And aid us, one with Christ, His will
    to do;
Hear, Holy Ghost, our supplicating
    cry,
Nor leave the grace Thou gav'st to
    droop and die.

— Henry Moule (1845)

MEDITATION FOR LENTEN DAYS

A Corn of Wheat
John 12:24

Although the period known as Lent is associated with self-denial, self-sacrifice, fastings and religious meditations, the word Lent itself does not suggest any of the customs which have gathered around its observance. From the ancient Saxon term, *Leneten,* it means "Spring," and originally represented the time of the year when the daylight increases in length. *Leneten* was a name identified with March — the month manifesting a drawing out of the days. Early in church history, the Lenten era became related with penance for sins, abstinence and self-discipline. "A lenten-faced fellow" meant one with a mournful and hungry look. The idea of giving up meat, or flesh, for forty days before Easter developed in the middle ages when most people in Europe belonged to the Roman Catholic Church. As each day came and people felt hungry, they would murmur and complain — "Why can't I have what I want to eat?" They were then taught to remember all Jesus had forfeited as

He suffered and prepared to die for them.

Strange though it may seem, a term nearer the religious significance of Lent is a word so opposite to its implications, namely, "carnival" which comes from two Latin words *carnis* meaning "flesh," and *vale,* the Latin word for "farewell." A carnivorous animal, like a lion or tiger, is one which eats flesh. Actually, then, *carnival* implies, "O flesh, farewell!" Carnivals are usually gay affairs and are often the means of raising money for local or national causes.

But when Roman Catholicism instituted a forty day fast before Easter to prepare the people for Good Friday, the feeling was, "Well, if we have to give up eating flesh and meat, and make our bodies suffer for six weeks, let us gorge ourselves before we begin, and really let ourselves go." And they did! On a day before the fast began they had a holiday, eating and drinking to the full, and called it "The Day of the Carnival" — the day of farewell to the flesh. But even in the middle

51

of Lent there were those who took a day off from their fasting and had a good feast to help them through the weeks of discipline. When the fast period was over the attitude was, "O flesh, welcome!" and the people over-indulged.

Lent, however, should not be a season of giving up something, but rather a taking on of something, or Someone. "Put ye on the Lord Jesus Christ" (Romans 13:14). Spiritual discipline and devotion form the most effective preparation for Easter, and not the surrender of material things. Sacrificial service, daily death to selfishness, the yearning for a deeper spiritual experience should be our aim not only during Lent but at all times. Is this not what Jesus meant when He spoke about a corn of wheat falling in the ground and dying (John 12:24)? This mystic word on self-crucifixion occurs in His last public discourse before His death, and was directed against the Greeks for their pride in self-gratification, self-preservation and self-culture. In the old Grecian world, the supreme aim was a good human life lived to the limit. Self-good and self-advancement were its motto. The gods of Olympus were represented as beings who lived only to enjoy themselves, and who, when they came to earth, came only on a pleasant adventure or selfish amusement with no care whatever for the sins and sorrows of the world.

When Jesus stood and called for self-renunciation to substitute for self-culture, self-sacrifice to supplant self-gratification, He reversed the whole outlook, thought and conduct of the Greeks and urged them to accept a concept of life and living diametrically opposed to the thought of centuries. Those Greeks who came to see Jesus, came to see the remarkable miracle-worker of whom they had heard. They were not interested in Him as the Man of Sorrows, as the One who had been so rich but became poor to enrich a bankrupt world. Thus, in effect, He said to them, "If you want to see Me, it is as One in the process of dying." Yet somehow the sorrowful heart of Jesus was encouraged, for in those seeking Greeks He foresaw the advent of a great multitude of redeemed souls glorifying Him for being willing to be lifted upon a cross to die for their salvation.

The burden of our Lord's message to His own was that the only way both He and they could bring blessing to others was by the way of the grave in which selfish interests were buried. Voices cry "Feast," "Enjoy," "Each for self," but Christ calls us to renounce self and find true joy in sacrifice; that by dying we live, giving we get, losing our life we find it; that gain comes from loss, victory through suffering, life out of death; that self-preservation results in isolation from the needs of the world; that only from buried seed can there come a harvest. There are two ways of looking at the cross —

First, as the beginning of our Christian life, and as the basis of all hope. "Simply to Thy Cross I cling," and we are thrice blessed if we have been to the cross for its cleansing and pardon.

Second, as the example of our lives. If we would be Christ's true disciples we must take up the cross and follow Him. This is the aspect He emphasizes here in the simile of the corn of wheat dying in order to produce fruit. Paul learned how to "die daily," to be crucified not only to what was sinful, but also to desires and habits, innocent and harmless in themselves but a hindrance to spiritual progress. The apostle knew that he could not bless others unless he entered Gethsemane and its shadows, and climbed Golgotha with its shame and reproach. The sacrificial life and labors of Paul illustrate that we cannot save souls and self at the same time, so he was content to become a shattered vessel in order to fill the world with the fragrant odor of the Gospel.

A cross and a grave might be an offense to the unspiritual, but to those who are dead with Christ, co-crucifixion with Him results in glorification. It is interesting to note how suffering and glory are united. Dying to self and living unto God mean the liberation of power in service, and a fruitfulness glorifying to Him. There is a twofold observation we must make before passing on to consider Christ's figure of speech more specifically.

First, the surrender of self is never easy or pleasant. Death is never alluring to the flesh. Falling into the ground and dying is beneficial in the end. We must be prepared to erect our altars if we yield to God in sacrifice those habits and associations alien to His supreme will. We may find it hard going on the road of obedience as we forego, for His sake, coveted friendships, and are called to leave a quiet walk in life with its contentment for a less congenial one, or to forsake a good position in the world for service in some dark spot in distant parts. If the knife is sharp, if the fire burns, and if the cup is bitter, we must be of good comfort, for Christ's own cross budded with a wonderful fertility. We must accept cheerfully, not tearfully, the slaying of the self-life, if we would be crowned with power. An ancient, beautiful custom was to hollow out a cross and fill it with flowers which fell out and spread their perfume as the cross was carried.

Second, self-sacrifice solves many problems. There is nothing more beautiful in the world than self-sacrifice. How ugly selfishness and grasping greed are! A monster of the deep is known as the "Devil Fish" because it is made up of tentacles grasping everything within reach. It has no hands to give. There are far too many devil fishes in our world with two hands grasping all and giving nothing, and they are as equally ugly and repulsive as the ocean's "Devil Fish." The magnetism of the cross is appealing for there we see Christ dying to self, as well as dying for sin. Think of how the spirit of Calvary between employer and employees would solve industrial problems. If master and men were self-sacrificial, there would be no glaring inequalities between capital and labor! Then, if we ministered to each other in our homes in the spirit of the crucified Lord, each dying to self-interest, domestic strife and unhappiness would cease. The same principle can be applied to church members who, if only they lived near the heart of the cross, would not be guilty of those frictions, jealousies, criticisms and divisions all too common today. If, as one has expressed it, "the Church was born crucified," she is fruitless in a world of need because she has not remained crucified.

A. *The Life of Self Is Death.*

Now that the season of Lent is upon us again, let us follow Jesus as He takes us out to the fields for a pattern of highest consecration, for under the simile of the corn of wheat falling into the ground and dying, He teaches us that the self-life is death. Wheat is our staple food and a fitting metaphor of all Christ is as the Bread of Life. But before wheat can feed hungry men it must be bruised, broken and buried. In the miracle of feeding the thousands, the loaves had to be broken. Every true believer is a separate grain of wheat, and there is life within the seed able to multiply itself. But the piercing word of Jesus is, "Except it die, it abideth alone!" (John 12:24). Its death is its life. Its burial is its resurrection. Self-sacrifice is the law of self-preservation. There are three general ways of using wheat.

1. *We can store it up.*

If wheat is kept in a granary it will retain its form but never multiply itself. It "abides alone," or has no increase. True, it retains inherent vitality, but germs of life are encased, taken care of, kept intact, unbroken, and neither receives or gives. The wheat is not without substance, form and comeliness, but stored it gives nothing of itself to the outside world where millions need food. It has within it the germ of a larger life but it must first die, or be willing to part with its neat compact little form and go forward to burial. By saving its life, it loses it. The latent germ of life needs the fructifying influences of the soil, the penetrating sunbeams, the warm rain from heaven, decay and death out of which will spring life, beauty and fertility. Can it be that our latent powers are dormant because they are kept from death? What divine possibilities are stored up in our lives! Talents and gifts remain isolated in a granary, or we ourselves are too self-encased in our own wishes, desires, preferences and affections to be of any benefit to God or man. A harvest comes only as the wheat is taken from the granary and buried in a grave.

2. *We can grind it in a mill and eat it.*

Once wheat is ground by the miller it is then ready to be consumed in the various forms. How we fail of the divine purpose if our life is regulated by the principles and preferences of the flesh or our own self-life and not by the wish and will of God! If life is used for present gratification and security of the greatest self-enjoyment then we save or eat our own life. If life is employed to satisfy self then the life of self is death, seeing we preserve or consume it for our own ends. Thus spent, life becomes lost or barren. It may not be one of vicious indulgences and wild extravagances, but a life far too common to all of us, namely one of self-seeking, self-planning, and proud, indulgent scheming. As the couplet reminds us, if we

Live for self, we live in vain.
Live for Christ, we live again.

3. *We can sow or bury it.*

All seed is alone until it dies. It has no living union with living things. But the day of its death is the day of its birth into a fuller, richer life, and the law of the seed is the law of human life. Your life and mine form the seed of God which He seeks to bury in the fertile soil of other hearts. Dying, then, as the seed, and buried, means life with God, and not self as its center. Selfishness is dethroned as the ruling principle of life. The seed, of course, does not die in an absolute sense. It is not annihilated nor does it cease to exist, but decaying sheds its outward husk and in so doing frees its imprisoned life. At His death Christ did not perish, but through the grave came to a more glorious life. At our death, we too, if we die in Christ, reach a fuller, completer life. Similarly, the death of self brings abounding fertility.

As the seed surrenders itself to death, the forces of nature seize upon and destroy its original shapeliness, and through death transforms it into greater fruitfulness and beauty. In like manner, it is only as we submit to the death of all associations of the self-life, that dormant possibilities and capabilities are quickened and we come to experience that self-sacrifice releases a life of power and joy, just as the death of winter precedes the colors of spring and the fruits of summer.

B. *The Death of Self Is Life.*

Although it may sound paradoxical, the corn of wheat, if isolated, is alone, or apparently dead because it has not died. Death is essential to life because by mortification a new life is begotten. Thus, as soon as the seed begins to die, it begins to live. How true this is in the whole realm of nature! Life is surrendered in order to quicken fuller life in other forms.

> Life everywhere replaces death,
>   In earth and sea and sky;
> And that the rose may breathe its
>   breath,
>   Some living thing must die.

1. *This is true of the seed.*

After the seed has been buried in the soil the external wrapping falls off and it becomes the prey of decay and decomposition. If you dig up a field of wheat seed a week after its burial you would not get a penny for a bushel of it, for in its rotting nature it is worthless. But failure is necessary in order to succeed. If you put a corn of wheat in a drawer and leave it for a year it will still be there unchanged. But sow it in a flower pot and how quickly it will multiply itself. Deposit grains in the ground and its life within hastens death. Growth comes through the process of mortification, which is also the principle of Christian growth.

2. *This is true of Christ.*

Was He not the corn of wheat who, at Calvary, fell into the ground and died? Is it not somewhat suggestive that the Master's mystic word was uttered when the world was going after Him? His miraculous works and marvelous words brought Him much popularity, so much so that it seemed as if His Kingdom had come with Jews and Gentiles ready to carry Him to the highest pinnacle. But He knew that sovereignty could come only from sacrifice — that the way to a throne was from a tree — that His one death would result in multiplying Himself a million-fold. Thus, the principle He enunciated was that loss meant increase — that by dying as the Christ, He would produce *Christ*ians. What is a born-again Christian but Christ in a new form, His body, His dwelling place. In the consecrated lives of His own He sees His seed and prolongs His days.

Think of the rich harvest He has already gathered as the outcome of the death of the cross! Pentecost, with its 3,000 souls added to Him, was the beginning of the fruit of death. Finally, in heaven, He will have a great multitude of redeemed saints which no man can number. Then think of the deeds of heroism and the graces of self-denial to which the cross has given rise, of the ever-increasing role of saved souls all because of the death He dared to die. Why, every moment of every day He sees of the travail of His soul and is satisfied. As the seed of the woman He died, and through death and resurrection has reproduced Himself in countless numbers through the ages.

3. *This is true of those who have influenced the world.*

In its dark, damp home, the seed robes itself with new life, and out of the ruins of what is sown takes on a new and beautiful garment, charming to behold both by God and the great world of nature. The law of the seed is the law of every moral and spiritual reform and personal transformation. Men must die to their own wishes and ways in order that life may come to others. As the seed produces a harvest in its own likeness, the same principle operates in the lives of those who serve the world. William Booth died to self-respect, honor and ease when he was willing to be pelted with eggs as he preached in marketplaces. What a harvest of Salvationists has been gathered, however, as the result of the General's willingness to die to self. Mary Slessor, the Dundee mill-girl was a frail, single corn of wheat who died to all self-comforts when she buried herself in Africa. Through the ages the blood of martyrs has been the seed of the Church. "Fear not, Brother Ridley," said Latimer on their way to be burned at the stake, "we shall this day light a candle in England which will never be put out." Out of their cruel death came a mighty spiritual reformation.

4. *This is true of ourselves.*

Often a mother faces near death that a child might be born. Parents are willing to die to many legitimate possessions and pleasures in order to give their children opportunities of education and advancement in the world. How majestic is the cross with its exhibition of the self-sacrificing of love! Lifted up in agony and shame, Christ now draws all men unto Himself. Is it not also true that the measure of our drawing power in a world of sin corresponds to the measure of our self-emptiness? When with Paul we can say, "I live; yet not I, but Christ liveth in me" (Galatians 2:20), then possessed by and for Him we experience what it is to function as fruitful branches of the vine. Is this not the blessed truth George Matheson has taught us to sing in the following lines?

> O Cross that liftest up my head,
>   I dare not ask to fly from Thee;
> I lay in dust life's glory dead,
> And from the ground there blossoms
>   red
> Life that shall endless be.

This, then, is the true spiritual significance of Lent — the decision to die to self that we might be a blessing to others.

For Palm Sunday

For Palm Sunday

Ride on! ride on in majesty!
Hark! all the tribes hosanna cry;
O Saviour meek, pursue Thy road
With palms and scattered garments
    strowed.

Ride on! ride on in majesty!
The winged armies of the sky
Look down with sad and wondering
    eyes
To see the approaching sacrifice.

Ride on! Ride on in majesty!
The last and fiercest strife is nigh;
The Father on his sapphire throne
Expects his own anointed Son.

Ride on! ride on in majesty!
In lowly pomp ride on to die;
Bow thy meek head to mortal pain,
Then take, O God, Thy power and
    reign.

          — Henry Hart Milman

"As on this day we keep the special memory of our Redeemer's entry into the city, so grant, O Lord that now and ever He may triumph on our hearts. Let the King of grace and glory enter in, and let us lay ourselves and all we are in full and joyful homage before Him; through the same Jesus Christ our Lord. Amen."
— Bishop Handley C. G. Moule (1841)

MEDITATION FOR PALM SUNDAY

PALMS AND WILLOWS
Mark 11:1-11

The week of the cross, known as "Passion Week," which began with Palm Sunday and ended with the resurrection on the following Sunday, was a period filled with anguish and heartache for the Saviour. What a week of pathos and suffering it was! Christ's entry into Jerusalem amid the plaudits of men did not produce any undue feeling of exaltation. He knew that the "Hosannas" of one day would change into "Crucify him!" almost the next.

In some church circles today palms, as the symbol of victory, triumph, conquest, are used when Palm Sunday comes around. One wonders, however, whether all who carry their palm branches to the church of their choice realize their true significance. A suitable meditation for such a day can be found in the instruction given the Israelites concerning the observance of the Feast of Tabernacles. Upon the first day of this feast the people had to bring the boughs and branches of certain trees before the Lord, and rejoice in His presence. Two parts of the tree world are specifically mentioned, namely, palms and willows of the brook (Leviticus 23:40), and are symbolic of opposite experiences confronting us as we journey through life.

A. *The Distinctive Meaning of Each.*

The palm, Biblical symbol of rejoicing, was once found in all lands, and in ancient times furnished many of the necessities of life. It has been estimated that over 800 uses have been ascribed to this renowned tree. Gifts of the palm tree are still ours. It has been called "The Prince of Vegetation," "King Among the Grasses." Victors are given a palm leaf as a reward.

The royal palm, growing majestically upright toward the sun, has become the emblem of gladness, renown, life — in its best colors. All that is brightest in life can be likened unto the palm tree. This is why we speak of our good days, or our palmy days. When the psalmist came to describe the prospects of the righteous, he said they flourished as the palm tree (Psalm 92:12).

59

The willow, on the other hand, symbolizes sorrow, humiliation, captivity and death. It is as though God said to the willow, "Stand by the water courses and weep." We speak of it as "the weeping willow tree," seeing it is the reverse of all that the palm suggests. Yet every year when the feast came around, the people had to bring the palms and willows together and rejoice before the Lord.

B. *The Close Association of Both.*

The palm and the willow were brought together because they grow together in human life and experience. No matter who or what we are, life is a mixture of all that these trees symbolize. Have you ever noticed the sign in a florist's shop, "wreaths and bouquets made up"? What striking contrasts — what extremes! Bouquets speak of the union of hearts, of the happy, singing company gathered for a wedding. Wreathes, on the other hand, are what we carry to the grave. They represent the separation of hearts, the grief-stricken multitudes. We go through life with a bouquet in one hand and a wreath in the other. There are times when the two are not so very far apart. Church bells are often rung for both marriages and funerals.

Doubtless all of us have felt the velvet touch of the palm. We have had our days of success and sunshine, of victory and blessing. We have had days when all our dreams were realized and our difficulties conquered, and our lives were radiant with good things from above. But we have also experienced the sting of the thorn, the droop of the willow. Days of sickness, sorrow, separation and loss have been ours. Isaiah speaks of those who carried their treasures to the brook of willows (Isaiah 15:7), and this is a pathetic journey which all of us must

take sooner or later. Willows are our common lot. There are no empty houses alongside the brook where the willows grow. Our pilgrim life is a remarkable combination of palms growing in the sun and willows drooping alongside the brook. In the Providence of God our smiles and sighs, our pleasures and pains, our triumphs and tears are intermingled. All our joy is touched with pain. Life is something like the organist who contrived a somewhat unique overture. It was a mixture of the "Hallelujah Chorus" and the "Dead March" from *Saul.*

All writers and poets and singers touching the heart of man are those who see vividly this dual aspect of life and are able to portray it accordingly. And the Bible is so rare, precious and fascinating, seeing it depicts our lot as being a combination of delight and darkness, glory and gloom.

C. *The Grateful Offering of Both.*

Upon the first day of the feast, the Jews had to bring the palms and willows together and rejoice before the Lord for seven days. Both had to be offered with grateful praise. Such joy was not merely natural, worked up or superficial. It had to be deeply spiritual — "before the Lord."

1. *Grateful for Palms!*

One might be tempted to say that this is natural and easy, but, this is the very time some people forget God. Often the good things of life are received in the spirit of self-praise and vanity. The palm three appears to be home grown. But what has thou that thou didst not receive? Jeshurun waxed fat, yes, but he kicked and forsook the rock of his salvation (Deuteronomy 32:15). If prosperity reaches us in any realm may grace be ours to say, "O soul of mine, never forget that the palm tree growing in the garden of life was planted by the hand divine!"

2. *Grateful for Willows!*

Do we not find it hard and irksome to praise God for drooping willows? It does not come easy to rejoice over the ministry of pain and loss. Yet we triumph in life when we can bless God for the willows as well as the palms. We must never despise the willows as being unworthy of thanks. Often the noblest life is the product of sanctified tribulation. We would not be the men and women of character we are, had it not been for the dark and difficult hours of the past.

The greatest of all gardeners makes no mistake when He permits willows to grow in your garden and mine. He created both in the natural realm, and can overrule their appearance in the realm of experience. Not only this, but He knows how to transform weeping willows into beneficial palms. Job proved this. He had palms in abundance, but overnight they became willows. Although the patriarch found himself stripped bare, he did not moan. "What? shall we receive good (palms) at the hand of God, and shall we not receive evil (willows)? . . . Though he slay me, yet shall I trust him" (Job 2:10; 13:15). What was the result of Job's acceptance of his willows as well as his palms? Why, he lived to see the day when all his willows were changed into palms, for God gave His honored servant twice as much as he had at the beginning. It was thus with George Matheson, the blind Scottish preacher and poet, who, as he mused upon the dual aspect of life which we are considering, could pray, "My God, I have never thanked Thee for my thorns. I have thanked Thee a thousand times for my roses, but not for my thorns. I have been looking forward to a world where I shall get compensation for my cross, but I have never thought of my cross as itself a present glory. Teach me the glory of my cross: teach me the value of my thorn. Show me that I have climbed to Thee by the path of pain. Show me that my tears have made my rainbow."

If we bring our palms before the Lord, that is, the good things of life He makes possible, and in holy gratitude praise Him for His bounty, then He will make them richer gifts still. If we bring our willows — the dark, inexplicable experiences of life — before the Lord and bless Him for His unerring love and wisdom, then He whom Mary mistook to be the Gardener will transform the willows into the palms of peace.

On this Palm Sunday we are reminded of the fact that the palms and willows formed the earthly lot of our glorious Lord. He knows all about the gladness and the gloom alternating within the human heart. He was anointed with the oil of gladness more than His fellowmen, yet at the same time He was the Man of Sorrows, acquainted with our grief. As He entered Jerusalem, the people carpeted His way with palm leaves and sang His praises. Christ, however, was not unduly exalted. He was on His way to Calvary, and He knew that those giving Him palms one day would give Him willows almost the next. His Good Friday was not far away from His Palm Sunday.

If, presently, we have our palms, let us not be overelated, but walk humbly before God. We may find the willows at the next bend of the avenue, and if we are not to droop when they appear, we must accept all the good things with gratitude to Him from whom all blessings flow. If the willows are ours, let us not murmur and complain as if God had made a mistake in the ordering of our life. The Jews of old had to praise God over the willows, as well as over the palms. Jesus could take the cup, the bitter cup, and give thanks. And we triumph in life when, with the Apostle Paul, we can give thanks in everything. God can make us fruitful even in the land of our affliction.

Praise God, our faces are toward sunrise, even toward the garden of God where the roses never fade! There are no willows in heaven. When John beheld the redeemed in glory, they had palms in their hands. How suggestive! Here we have a palm in one hand and willow in the other. But once in heaven, palms will fill both hands. Willows will have vanished, for sickness, sorrow, separation and sin can never enter the realms above, to mar the eternal happiness of the redeemed. We are still among the shadows of earth, however, and until the last burden has been borne, the last battle fought, the last tear shed, we must learn how to bring our joys and sorrows, our triumphs and tears, our palms and willows before the Lord. We must do this with praise, however, knowing that He has the power to cause all things, whether palms or willows, to work together for good, if we but love Him and are called according to His purpose.

For Good Friday

For Good Friday

The head that once was crowned with
   thorns
  Is crowned with glory now;
A royal diadem adorns
  The mighty Victor's brow.
                   — T. Kelly

Is there diadem, as monarch,
  That his brow adorns?
"Yea, a crown, in very surety,
  But of thorns!"
              — Stephen the Sabaite

See, from His head, His hands, His
   feet,
  Sorrow and love flow mingled
   down;
Did e'er such love and sorrow meet,
  Or thorns compose so rich a crown?
               — Isaac Watts

Thorny was the crown that He wore,
  And the Cross His body o'ercame;
Grievous were the sorrows He bore,
  But He suffered not thus in vain.
          — Sankey's Sacred Songs

Duty is a path of pain and peril,
  Roses grow on bushes thick with
   thorns;
A mother wears a crown of ancient
   travail;
  Calvary's Cross a suffering Christ
   adorns.
           — William L. Stidger
              in *Motherhood*

MEDITATION FOR GOOD FRIDAY

A Crown of Thorns
Matthew 27:29

It was Matthew Arnold who wrote of the blessed Redeemer as —

> That gracious Child, that thorn-crowned Man,
> He lived while He believed.

The mock crowning was only one of the many indignities endured by Jesus throughout the last days before His death. The soldiers who plaited that false crown meant it to be a circlet of torture to pierce deep into His lovely brow until from His head "sorrow and love flowed mingled down." Already He had endured much scourging, then, with the binding of His hands, He was not able to ease the pain of His head by a softening touch. How it would have helped if only He could have lifted that thorny crown for a minute to relieve the smart, and wipe His bleeding brow! But, no, unrelieved anguish was His until He drained His bitter cup of its dregs. How full of spiritual import for our reverent, adoring hearts is the willingness of Jesus to endure that crown of thorns, despise the shame of it, and for the joy set before Him bear all the indignities of the cross alone!

A. *His Condescension.*

To wear such an ignoble crown Jesus willingly laid aside His crown of past glory and divine majesty. Being rich, for our sakes He became poor. Think of the honor He received from the retinue of heaven, then compare it with the shame, ignominy and rejection He suffered for our sakes! He left a world of glory for one of meanness — one of bliss for one of misery — one of purity for one of crime, life and death. Does not the cross magnify His marvelous condescension of love?

He who will yet be seen as the Prince of the kings of earth was treated as a criminal, as the offscouring of earth.

He who created all things, lived and died poor, and was sold for the price of a basest slave.

He who came to set the prisoner free, found Himself bound as a felon and nailed to a tree.

He who had borne the crown of universal dominion, and had experienced the royalties of heaven, was diademed with a spiky cross of contempt and made to endure the ignominies of men.

He who was the Source of the fountain of bliss, was forced to die in anguish of thirst.

> Is there diadem, as monarch
>   That His brow adorns?
> Yea, a crown in very surety
>   But of thorns.

Have we discovered, as Paul did, that identification with Christ means a cluster of thorns? A thorn in the flesh implies something intensely galling in the realms of the natural. What the apostle's thorn in the flesh was we are not told. Therefore it can stand for everybody's thorn, or any thorn, so that the countering revelation of comfort may cover *all* thorns. Paul gathers together a whole crop of thorns which he willingly suffered for Christ's sake. "Therefore," he says, "I take pleasure in

"infirmities" — faltering exhaustions, physical failure — "in *reproaches"* — slights, insults, rejection, losses — "in *necessities"* — the hard drive of need, of poverty — "in *persecutions"* — unmerited scorn, censure, or open hate — "in *distresses"* — things that hurt the spirit, and wound the heart — all "for Christ's sake" (II Corinthians 12:10). What a crown of thorns the apostle had! It is doubtful if there is a saint today who is not somewhere in the above listing. Through Paul and his undiscovered thorn, the responding oracle of God covers all cases and embraces all time. The reason for his thorn is stated, "that I should not be exalted above measure" (II Corinthians 12:7). The apostle had had a most remarkable spiritual experience and "to save him from falling he was impaled

upon a stake." Amid his trial, he proved the sufficiency of divine grace.

B. *His Exaltation.*

Because of Christ's willingness to wear the crown of mockery a greater luster has been added to the crown of glory adorning His brow. The head once "crowned with thorns, is crowned with glory now." It is not the weight of gold and costly jewels composing a crown that are the measure of its worth, but the character of its wearer. Judged thus, what value and majesty are attached to the rude crown on the brow of Him who was the purest of the pure. Every thorn or spike in that cruel crown was a jewel inwrought with that of His divine honor. Although it represented the scorn of men, He transformed it into the sign of divine regal power. Having endured the death of the cross, He is now highly exalted. Treated as a felon, He yet died as a king, withal in disguise. An instructive writer has suggested a mournful list of honors which the blinded people of Israel awarded their long-expected Messiah.

They gave Him a procession of honor — Roman legionaries, Jewish priests, a jeering multitude — as He carried His cross to Calvary. The only paean of praise He received was the cruel taunts of those who thirsted for His blood. What a hollow triumph for Him who came to overthrow man's dark foe!

They presented Him with the wine of honor, but instead of it being a golden cup overflowing with generous wine, they offered him — seeing they treated Him as a criminal — a stupefying death-drug. But He refused it that He might taste death for every man. When He cried, "I thirst," His crucifiers thrust a sponge into His mouth having a mixture of vinegar and gall on it. What wretched, detestable inhospitality for the King's Son!

They provided Him with a guard of honor, but what kind of a bodyguard did He have? Avaricious soldiers who gambled for His seamless robe. Previously adored in heaven by a vast angelic host, He now has a quaternion of brutal gamblers.

They raised Him to a throne of honor — the bloody tree, the only place where rebel creatures place the Creator. How evident it is that His cross is the fullest expression of the world's estimation of Him. At Calvary's cross we have God's best, and man's worst.

They bestowed upon Him a title of honor — King of the Jews. When, however, the religious leaders preferred Barabbas to Jesus they actually counted Him as the king of thieves. Placing Him between two thieves, they gave Him the place of highest shame. What "scoffing rude" He endured when in our place He stood! May we ever give Him a true coronation!

C. *His Redemption.*

The marvel of His grace is that He allowed that crown of thorns to pierce His manly brow, in order that we might have a crown without thorns. Several crowns are offered the saints, but not one of them is thorn-studded. The blood He shed was the price of our salvation, the inspiration of our pilgrim life and the foundation of future bliss. He was crowned with mockery in death that we might be crowned with life everlasting, and when we reach heaven His nailmarks will have our ceaseless praise. Thorns and briars were the first product of the Fall, but Jesus was manifested to destroy the works of the devil and so those thorns were woven into the crown He bore. He took our curse and made it His own.

His cruel thorns, His shameful cross
  Procure us heavenly crowns.
Our highest gain springs from His love,
  Our healing from His wounds.

Joseph Plunkett, the renowned Irish Republican who died in 1916, left us an exquisite poem in which he related the Saviour whom he dearly loved, to His creative works and to human experience. It reads —

I see His blood upon the rose,
And in the stars the glory of His eyes.
His body gleams amid eternal snows,
His tears fall from the skies.
I see His face in every flower,
The thunder and the singing of the birds
Are but His voice — and carven by His power
Rocks are His written words.
All pathways by His feet are worn,
His strong heart stirs the everlasting sea,
His crown of thorns is twined with every thorn,
His cross is every tree.

D. *His Sovereignty.*

What undying power Christ gained over the souls of men by wearing the crown of thorns so silently and bravely! Blood-stained, He was still the regal One and made His cross, His throne. Sovereignty became His because of His scars. His murderers thought they were ending His claim as King, but as the Lamb that was slain He will yet reign supreme over all. When they placed the reed in His hand, they flouted His declared authority, and nailing His hands to a gibbet indicated, thereby, that their power was ended. Blind fools, they only added to the miracles of those pierced hands! Those who clamored for His death felt that when they stabbed His heart they had stopped the flow of its love, but they only multiplied the richness of its flow. Making sure He would remain dead, His crucifiers sealed His tomb, but He tore the bars away and rose a Victor o'er the dark domain.

Does not the conquering Nazarene conquer us by His wounds, and rule our hearts by His cross? Do not His tears, anguish and sufferings cause Him to take deep root in our lives and result in Him seeing of the travail of His soul in our full surrender to His claims? Certainly His earthly life with its gracious miracles and winsome words charm and enthral us, but "love so amazing, so divine" as witnessed in His outpoured blood conquers us completely. May we be preserved from giving Him any more thorns!

> With thorns His temples gor'd and gash'd
> Send streams of blood from every part,
> His back's with knotted scourges lash'd
> But sharper scourges tears His heart.

Are we not warned against grieving His tender Spirit? The word Paul used for "grieve" is a Gethsemane one and is equivalent to the phrase, "He began to be sorrowful." What are the thorns we are guilty of giving Him? Among the cluster we have —

— indifference to His sufferings, and the absence of wonder concerning Calvary. We fail to understand what it meant for Him, the Holy One, to bear away our sin.

— unbelief in the marvelous efficacy of His shed blood. It is nothing to the multitudes as they pass by His cross, that the One thereon died in their room and stead.

— unreality of professed belief. Are we not in danger of calling Him Lord, yet not doing the things He says? We admire His life, but shun identification with Him in His cross.

— greed of worldly gain and pleasure.

Christ died naked and was buried in another man's grave. But can we say that the lusts and affections of our flesh are crucified?

— neglect of the salvation of others for whom He died. If we have been drawn by His cross and have entered into fellowship with His sufferings, how can we be silent as to all the Saviour means to us. If a friend had rescued me from drowning would it not be mean and ungrateful of me not to sing His praises? "Let the redeemed of the Lord say so." Have we not need to pray that we may be preserved from adding to His sorrows, ever giving Him roses instead of thorns?

THE WONDERFUL CROSS

When I survey the wondrous cross, On which the Prince of glory died, My richest gain I count but loss, And pour contempt on all my pride. Forbid it, Lord, that I should boast, Save in the death of Christ, my God; All the vain things that charm me most, I sacrifice them to His blood. See, from His head, His hands, His feet, Sorrow and love flow mingled down; Did e'er such love and sorrow meet, Or thorns compose so rich a crown? Were the whole realm of nature mine, That were a present far too small; Love so amazing, so divine, Demands my soul, my life, my all.   Amen.

For Easter Day

For Easter Day

Yet Love will dream, and Faith will
    trust,
(Since He who knows our need is
    just:)
That somehow, somewhere meet we
    must.
Alas for him who never sees
The stars shine through his cypress
    trees!
Who hopeless lays his dead away,
Nor looks to see the breaking of the
    day
Across the mournful marbles play;
Who hath not learned in hours of
    faith
This truth to flesh and sense unknown;
That life is ever lord of death,
And Love can never lose its own.
             — John Greenleaf Whittier

O God, who for our redemption
didst give Thine only begotten Son
to the death of the cross, and by His
glorious resurrection hast delivered
us from the power of the enemy, grant
us to die daily to sin, that we may
evermore live with Him, to the joy of
His resurrection; through the same
Jesus Christ our Lord. Amen.
             — St. Gregory (590)

MEDITATION FOR EASTER DAY

MY REDEEMER LIVETH
Job 19:25-27

At this glad season of the year we naturally turn to the gospel narratives for evidences and expressions of the Easter message. And, truly, one cannot follow Matthew, Mark, Luke and John without realizing how each writer produces positive proof of Christ's glorious victory over death and the grave. Each gospel ends with our Lord's triumphant mastery over the king of terrors. Tearing away the bars of the tomb, He emerged as the Lord of life.

However, let us dip into the Old Testament and discover whether we can light upon any saint who, by the aid of the telescope of revelation, saw Christ as the mighty Victor. Even a casual reading of Old Testament Scriptures reveals that Easter is everywhere in promise. Listen to Job's astounding declaration:

> For I know that my Redeemer liveth,
> And that He shall stand at the latter
>   day upon the earth:
> And though after my skin worms de-
>   stroy this body,
> Yet in my flesh shall I see God;

> Whom I shall see for myself,
> And mine eyes shall behold, and not
>   another;
> Though my reins be consumed within
>   me. (Job 19:25-27)

The chapter out of which the above paragraph is taken contains Job's answer to Bildad's second speech and registers Job's protests against the unkindness of so-called friends who only added to his torture by their reproaches. At first we see Job recounting his woes, but then he proceeds to avow his lofty faith as a truly prophetic soul. He had a heavenly Redeemer, a Vindicator of righteousness, seeking the right-doing of men. And, as in all Easter passages, we can detect the unmistakable tone of exultation and triumph in Job's bright, passing glimpse of his living Redeemer.

Various efforts have been made to explain away the somewhat mysterious import of the verses. We readily concede that perhaps the Holy Spirit intended in Job's words more than Job himself fully understood, but it is clearly evident that the language he uses covers two advents of Christ. Job's

71

friends urge him to set his hopes upon a return to temporal prosperity, to health, wealth and friends. Job, however, longs for God and His salvation. Upheld by Spirit-given hope, the patriarch speaks of a vindication in a future life.

Also, Job's declaration of the Redeemer he knew is all the more striking if, as some scholars affirm, Job was the first book of the Bible to be written. Dr. C. I. Scofield affirms that Job was certainly written before the giving of the law. Job, then, was probably the first herald of Easter.

In spite of the tragedy overtaking Job, he possessed a clear and steadfast recognition and assurance of a coming Deliverer. Thus he flings out a bold challenge to all ages: "I know that my Redeemer liveth." "Perhaps," "possibly," or "maybe," were not words in Job's vocabulary when it came to faith. He had a deep-rooted conviction. Although he lived years before Christ, yet he knew that, as the Redeemer, Christ would come.

At this point the word "know" claims our attention. To know anything is to be confident of its existence. But how did Job know that His Redeemer was alive and that ultimately he would see Him? From where did this certainty come? If Job wrote his book before Genesis, then he had no previous promises of a coming Redeemer to beget his assurance. If, on the other hand, Job was a contemporary of Moses, and had a knowledge of some of the prophecies in the Pentateuch of a coming Deliverer, like Genesis 3:15, would what Job had learned from Moses have been sufficient to create such a glorious certainty as the declaration before us contains?

Knowledge such as Job speaks of is not a mere mental comprehension founded upon specific statements. As used by Job, the word "know" implies an inner knowledge, an inborn conviction. Such a knowledge regarding the reality and redemption of Christ can never be acquired merely by accepting definite statements of Scripture, but only by the Holy Spirit burning into our consciousness what such inspired statements actually mean for our own heart and life. There is nothing more tragic than to rest upon a superficial head-knowledge of the finished work of Jesus, and yet not to experience that heart-knowledge so essential to eternal security.

Just when this unshakable certainty gripped the heart and mind of Job we are not told. Whether the truth of a living, loving Redeemer came as a flash or as a process in Job's experience is unrecorded. He knew, and that was sufficient for time and eternity. And Job gathered strength and consolation from such an assurance in the darkest hours of his life.

When the Old Age Pensions Act was introduced in Britain several years ago, hundreds of elderly people had no birth certificates to produce, proving that they were eligible for a pension. They did not know when they were born and how old they were, but they knew they were alive and aged. Thus it is in the spiritual realm. There are many saints who cannot name any time and place of their new birth, but who share the same happy assurance of those who know just when it happened. We think of many dear children of godly parents who, because of their contact with spiritual influences, gradually surrendered to the Saviour as a bud opens to the morning sun.

The question each of us must be assured of at this Easter-tide is whether the Redeemer, whose death and resurrection we commemorate, has delivered us from the guilt and penalty of sin. Can we say with Job, "I know that my Redeemer liveth"?

> I know, I know that Jesus liveth,
> And on the earth again shall stand;
> I know, I know that life He giveth,
> That grace and pow'r are in His hand.
> — Jesse Pounds

Just what did Job mean when he affirmed that he knew that his Redeemer lived? Did he understand what we do, as in the full blaze of Calvary, we use this term? Some expositors explain the word "Redeemer" by saying that Job expected one of his relatives to arise after his death as the avenger of his blood, and to exact retribution for it. Job's hope of a beatific vision, however, contradicts such an interpretation.

Already Job had expressed his desire for a "Daysman" between himself and God, who could be no other than a divine personage (9:32-35). He also declares his conviction that he had his "witness in heaven" (16:19). Job longs to have an "advocate to plead his cause" (16:21). He calls upon God to be "surety for him" (17:3). Thus, having already acknowledged God as his Judge, Umpire, Advocate, Witness and Surety, Job is not taking a long step in the acknowledgment of God as his "Redeemer."

The word he uses for "Redeemer" is of intense significance and is invested with virtue. In the original it is *Goel* or *Gaal*, that is, "kinsman-redeemer," a term meaning one who has the right and duty to vindicate someone of near kin who has suffered wrong. It is a technical expression for the avenger of blood. The Old Testament *Gaal* was one who bought back a forfeited inheritance, redeemed a slave, avenged the slain, or one perpetuating a family name and heirship among the families and estates of Israel.

Personally, we have no hesitation in affirming that Job's "Redeemer" is likewise ours, for the language he uses suggests the divine *Gaal*. "My Redeemer . . . is my God." Dr. Scofield reminds us that the Old Testament "kinsman-redeemer" is a beautiful type of Christ in the following ways:

1. The kinsman redemption was of *persons,* and an inheritance (Leviticus 25:25,48; Galatians 4:5; Ephesians 1: 7, 11, 14).

2. The redeemer must be a kinsman (Leviticus 25:48, 49; Ruth 3:12, 13; Galatians 4:4; Hebrews 4:14, 15).

3. The redeemer must be able to redeem (Ruth 4:4-6; Jericho 50:34; John 10:11, 18).

4. The Redemption is effected by the *Gaal* paying the just demand in full (Leviticus 25:27; Galatians 3:13; I Peter 1:18, 19).

Going on to explain the New Testament doctrine of redemption Dr. Scofield says that there are three words translated "redemption." One word means "to purchase in the market," in which there is the thought of a slave-market. Another word implies "to buy out of a market." And yet another word suggests "to loose" or "to set free by paying a price."

That Christ is our *Gaal* is the truth we emphasize as Easter comes around. Our heavenly inheritance was mortgaged by sin, and we were utterly unable to redeem it. Christ, as our near of kin, was able to pay the debt, satisfy God's justice for sin, remove our mortgage and provide a new settlement of our inheritance. Ruth, the Moabitish woman, as the widow of Mahlon, was involved with her first husband in his losses and liabilities, but when she became the wife of Boaz, the redeemer of her estate and the lord of the harvest, she and her inheritance were redeemed, and she became the sharer of his wealth and social standing. In Christ, we who in Adam were condemned and alienated, are justified and reconciled.

From another angle we were slaves of Satan and justly doomed to eternal woe, having no kinsman to vindicate our cause and interpose for us by power or price. We were sold under sin.

Easter, however, reminds us of the catchless grace of Christ our Redeemer who, veiling His deity in a real human body that He might sympathize, suffer with and save His enemies, paid a terrible price to redeem them from their curse. "He gave himself a ransom for all" (I Timothy 2:6). By His own blood He redeemed us from sin and the grave, and by His power He conquered our murderer. Hallelujah, what a Saviour!

The story is told of a Russian officer whose accounts could not be made to balance, and who feared that the merciless despotism of the empire would allow no room for leniency in dealing with him. While hopelessly poring over his "balance sheet" and in despair of ever making up his deficiency it is said that he wrote, half inadvertently, in the page before him: "Who can make good this deficit?" and fell asleep at his table. The Czar, passing by, saw the sleeping officer, glanced curiously at the page and, taking up the pen, wrote underneath, "I, even I, Alexander." And who is there sufficiently able to pay our debt to a broken law? There is One who died and rose again, who from the cross of Calvary, the tomb in the garden, and the throne in heaven, answers, "I, even I, the Lord Jesus."

The late Lady Kinnaird used to tell the following touching incident concerning the then Prince of Wales, now the Duke of Windsor. Invited to visit a special hospital on the outskirts of London, where three dozen of the worst wounded men of World War I were being cared for, he at once agreed to pay a visit. Arriving there, he was shown over the principal ward. He shook hands with some, spoke kind words to many and sympathized with them all. Then, looking around, he said: "I thought there were thirty-six. I have seen only thirty." It was explained that six of the very worst cases were in a special side ward not usually visited. "I must see them," he said. Guided by the doctor, he saw the men, bruised, maimed, helpless wrecks. "But there are only five," the Prince exclaimed. "Where is the other?" It was again explained that one poor man was so badly maimed that he was kept in a room alone, and it would be wiser not to see him. "I must see him too," he said. Taken into the room he saw a sight which touched his heart and transfixed his feet. There lay all that was left of a brave soldier. He was blind, deaf, legless, armless and disfigured almost beyond recognition as a human being. Standing silent a moment, touched beyond measure, he stooped down, kissed the brow of the veteran, and with broken voice exclaimed, "Broken for me!" And that princely kiss will always retain its fragrance. But the Redeemer is a nobler Prince by far, and He it is who was "wounded for me." It is by His stripes that I am healed.

One of the amazing aspects of Job's Easter evangel is that he knew that his Redeemer was alive. "I know that my Redeemer *liveth*." Liveth! This word in the present tense implies a continuous existence. As the Eternal One, the Redeemer must have been alive *in*, as well as *before*, Job's day. It is also evident that Job used the term "liveth" in opposition to himself. He dies — his *Gaal* lives!

Because of the ravages of a skin disease, Job anticipates the utter destruction of his bodily frame, but his Redeemer is deathless. Having been made by the living God, Job needs a living Redeemer, One who will be able to undertake for him as he disappears amid the shadows of the tomb.

The biographer of Dr. Dale of Birmingham, England, tells of an experience the eminent theologian had one Easter. A day or two before Good Friday, Dr. Dale was in his study preparing two or three Easter messages. Coming to the truth of the empty tomb, it dawned upon him, with a new consciousness, that Christ was actually alive. Jumping up from his study chair, he paced the floor, shouting, "He lives! He lives!" And as Easter Sunday came around, he preached unforgettable messages.

Yes, He lives! In the revelation of Himself to John, did He not say, "I am he that liveth!" (Revelation 1:18). And the Gospel of Easter is that, although the Redeemer died, He is alive forevermore, and waits to make every sinner the recipient of His risen life. "Because I live, ye shall live also" (John 14:19).

Because He lives, He can intercede for us and save us with an uttermost salvation. The question, however, each of us must answer is "Does the living Redeemer live *in* me, as well as *for* me?" Paul could humbly confess "Christ liveth in me" (Galatians 2:20). Is it thus with ourselves? Do we bow before a living Lord? Do we love and serve a risen Saviour?

Is this not the truth to fling into the face of a war-scarred, blood-saturated world — *He lives?* Amid the slaughter

of millions, the crumbling of empires and the decay of proud civilizations, Christ lives, and will yet return to take over the disordered condition of international life.

The personal pronouns of Scripture form a fascinating study. Here are two of them: "I" and "my." Phrases like, "I know," "My Redeemer," "I shall see for myself," speak of Job's unshakable faith. What others did not know, he *knew*. Had Job known the hymn of assurance we often sing, he, too, would have echoed forth the lines —

Blessed assurance, JESUS IS MINE,
Oh, what a foretaste of glory divine.

There were many things Job did not know. Suddenly stripped of all his possessions, and crushed by sorrow and disease, Job did not know the reason for all his anguish. He could not read the meaning of his tears, but he knew that his Redeemer was alive for evermore and that one day, out of the windows of his body, he would see Him who was so real to faith.

Have we this joy of a personal assurance? Separating ourselves from the multitude around us, can we say, "I know that my Redeemer liveth"? While countless myriads are trusting the Saviour, can you look up into His face and confess, "Thou art my Redeemer"?

A personal faith requires appropriation. If the Christ of Easter is not our personal Saviour, He can become so only by the exercise of a personal faith. And so again the question you must answer is, "Does my profession of religion resound with the ring of a personal conviction? Is all heaven thrilled with the music of my personal testimony to the redeeming grace of the Saviour?"

As Job uttered the words before us, he had a diseased body and was wasted to a skeleton, but he knew that, in a glorified body, he would serve God. Afflictions clouded his faith, but a certain resurrection provided a solution of his trials. As war drums continue to beat, and as the earth is more than ever a vale of tears, let us be encour-

aged by the same hope. Beloved, our redemption draweth nigh!

> Jesus, Thou Prince of Life,
>   Thy chosen cannot die!
> Like Thee they conquer in the strife
>   To reign with Thee on high.
>
> — A. H. C. Malan

For April Fool's Day

For April Fool's Day

A fool's vexation is presently known:
But a prudent man concealeth shame.

He that uttereth truth sheweth forth
  righteousness:
But a false witness deceit.

There is that speaketh rashly like the
  piercings of a sword:
But the tongue of the wise is health.

The lips of truth shall be established
  for ever.
But a lying tongue is but for a
  moment.

Deceit is in the heart of them that de-
vise evil:
But to the counsellors of peace is joy.

Lying lips are an abomination to the
  Lord:
But they that deal truly are his delight.

A prudent man concealeth knowledge:
But the heart of fools proclaimeth
  foolishness.

The hand of the diligent shall bear
  rule:
But the slothful shall be put under
  taskwork.

Heaviness in the heart of a man
  maketh it stoop:
But a good word maketh it glad.

The righteous is a guide to his
  neighbour:
But the way of the wicked causeth
  them to err.

The slothful man roasteth not that
  which he took in hunting:
But the precious substance of men is
  to the diligent

In the way of righteousness is life;
And in the pathway thereof there is
  no death.

Proverbs 12:16-28
Moulton

MEDITATION FOR APRIL FOOL'S DAY

Fools and Their Folly
Proverbs 12:16-28

While we know that an April Fool is one sent upon a useless errand on the first of April, the exact origin of such a custom is hard to trace. In Scotland this kind of fool is known as a *gowk*, meaning "a cuckoo" or "a fool." The French — *un poisson d'Avril* or April-fish, or an April fool's errand or hoax implies a similar thought. In Hindustan pranks and tricks are played at the Huti Festival on March 31st. There is a superstition that April Fool's Day is related to the mockery trial of our Redeemer. More probably it is a relic of the Roman *Cerealia* held at the beginning of April. The tale is that Proserpina was sitting in the Elysian meadows and had just filled her lap with daffodils, when Pluto carried her off to the lower world. Her mother, Ceres, heard the echo of her screams, and went in search of "the voice." But her search was a fool's errand, it was hunting the gowk, or looking for "the echo of a scream."

The custom of making fools of each other on the first of April usually consists in innocent and harmless pranks. Those who indulge in this should shun any kind of hoax injurious in effect. A further explanation of April Fool's Day is that springtime is especially fruitful in fun play.

> When beans are in flower
> Fools are in full strength.

In his *The Old Bachelor*, William Congreve (1670-1729) refers to him as "one of love's April fools."

That the Bible has much to say about fools and their folly is evident from its some 200 references to them. In the course of time words change their meaning and we often think of a "fool" as a person who is mentally deficient. But in Scripture the term is used of the intelligent and cultured, and generally implies self-sufficiency, self-centeredness or arrogance. It is said that Henry IV remarked of James I of England that he was "the wisest fool in Christendom." Sinners and their sin are presented in unflattering light as fools and their folly. Herbert Spencer gave us the phrase, "The ultimate result of shielding men from the effects of folly, is to fill the world with fools." God's Word never shields men from the nature and effect of their folly. Multitudes, however, are fools for not giving heed to the Bible's exposure of their foolish ways. Byron in *English Bards and Scotch Reviewers* wrote —

I'll publish, right or wrong:
Fools are my theme, let satire be my song.

Fools, then, are our theme, and glancing over what Scripture has to say about them we note their marks and types.

A. *The Traits of a Fool.*

That Scripture is the biography of human nature — good and bad — is evident from its several descriptions of fools. In unmistakable language it delineates the traits of a fool:

1. *Conceit* — "The way of a fool is right in his own eyes" (Proverbs 12:15).

What a classic illustration of this particular trait of foolishness we have in King Saul who was forced to confess to David whom he tried to destroy, "I have played the fool, and have erred exceedingly" (I Samuel 26:21). The fool Solomon speaks of was right in his own eyes, but in no one else's eyes. He is also a person to whom there is a way that seemeth right but which ends in death (Proverbs 14:12). When Israel had no king to govern, "every man did that which was right in his own eyes" (Judges 21:25). Our constant desire, if we would be wise, is to do that which is right in the eyes of the Lord.

2. *Mockery* — "Fools make a mock at sin" (Proverbs 14:9).

A similar description is found in a previous chapter, "It is as sport to a fool to do mischief" (Proverbs 10:23). This was the attitude of Nero as he fiddled while Rome burned. How unwise it is to belittle sin and act ignorant of its dire consequences for both here and hereafter. For those who mock at sin there is the solemn divine warning, "I will mock when your fear cometh" (Proverbs 1:26). Sinners may laugh at sin but God will have the last laugh. "I also will laugh at your calamity" (Proverbs 1:26).

3. *Folly* — "The foolishness of fools is folly" (Proverbs 14:24).

The ways, talk and pleasure correspond to their nature. "The mouth of fools feedeth on foolishness" (Proverbs 15:14). What they are in character is manifest in speech and conduct. One cannot expect fools of this sort to be wise in words and actions. No fountain can yield both salt water and fresh (James 3:11, 12). As a man is in heart, so is he. *Nabal* means a "fool," and as his wife confessed to David, "folly was with him" or in other words, "He's a fool by name, and a fool by nature."

4. *Aimlessness* — "The eyes of a fool are in the ends of the earth" (Proverbs 17:24).

Isaiah reminds us that "the wicked are like the troubled sea, when it cannot rest" (57:20, 21). They are destitute of peace and of any definite purpose in life. They roam in thought and deed, strangers to the consecrated concentration of the Apostle Paul who can say, "This one thing I do." Jude speaks of those who are "wandering stars, to whom is reserved the blackness of darkness for ever" (Jude 13). How wise it is to abide in Christ!

5. *Strife* — "A fool's lips enter into contention, and his mouth calleth for strokes. A fool's mouth is his destruction, and his lips are the snare of his soul" (Proverbs 18: 6, 7).

The pot is always boiling when fools are around. What strife and trouble they cause when they open their mouths! Not knowing how to set a watch upon their lips, their unguarded speech results in their destruction.

6. *Self-trust* — "He that trusteth in his own heart is a fool" (Proverbs 28:26).

Of course he's a fool because his unregenerate heart is desperately wicked and trusting in it becomes like it. Christ had no justification for the Pharisees who trusted in themselves that they were righteous, but He had an abundance of it for the tax-gatherer who, conscious of his nothingness could only cry, "God be merciful to me a sinner." We reveal true wisdom when we trust in the Lord with all our heart, and lean not on any fancied righteousness of our own.

7. *Ignorance* — "The fool walketh in darkness" (Ecclesiastes 2:14).

Blinded by the god of this world, what else can the sinner do but walk in darkness, that is, in ignorance of all God has so freely provided for his soul? The tragedy is that this state of spiritual darkness is loved because of the love of sin (John 3:19). To die in such darkness, rejecting Him who came as the Light of the world, means the blackness of darkness for ever. How blessed we are if we are found walking in the light, as He is in the light!

8. *Indolence* — "The fool foldeth his hands together, and eateth his own flesh" (Ecclesiastes 4:5).

Strength and substance are spent on self. Such a fool lives only for self-gratification, having no aspiration to live for God and for the benefit of humanity. God opens His hands, and satisfies the desire of all his living. Satan and sinners are too self-centered to have open hands, bearing blessing to the needy.

9. *Pleasure* — "The heart of fools is in the house of mirth" (Ecclesiastes 7:4).

Such people lack solemnity of purpose, and their mirth is short-lived, "For as the crackling of thorns under a pot, so is the laughter of fools" (7:6). Was it not this empty, passing pleasure which Robert Burns, who knew much about "the house of mirth" had in mind when he wrote? —

> For pleasures are like poppies spread
> You seize the flower, the bloom is
>   sped.
> Or like the snowflake on the river
> A moment white, then melt for ever.

10. *Confusion* — "A wise man's heart is at his right hand; but a fool's heart at his left" (Ecclesiastes 10:2).

The word "heart," here, is not to be taken as our physical heart, but one's purpose or desires and inclinations in life. "At his right hand" means, toward the right hand, and implies that the inner impulse of the wise man leads him to go to the right hand — the position of power — and walk the right way. Ellicott comments that, "the thought here is the same as in Ecclesiastes 2:15, namely, that though the actual results of wisdom are often disappointing, the superiority of wisdom over folly is undeniable." Solomon says, "Wisdom excelleth folly, as far as light excelleth darkness" (Ecclesiastes 2:13). The right hand is more often used than the left hand, and is more apt to be quick. Thus, a wise man uses his thoughts more promptly and profitably. The action and direction of a fool are muddled and confused.

Going to the left, the fool in his self-conceit, attributes folly to everyone else. "He saith to every one that he is a fool" (Ecclesiastes 10:3). What a self-betrayal of folly such an attitude is! "A fool layeth open his folly" (Proverbs 13:16). Fools have a manifest contempt for anyone different than themselves.

    11. *Talkativeness* — "A fool also is full of words" (Ecclesiastes 10:14).

Such a person is a "babbler," or, as the margin expresses it, "the master of language" (10:11). His lips swallow him up (10:12), and are full of empty words (10:14, see 5:3). Like a balloon, he is full of wind. "Excellent speech becometh not a fool" (Proverbs 17:7). How aptly John Bunyan describes such a fool in his character, *Talkative*, who was "a tall man, and more comely at a distance than at hand." *Faithful* joined him and, attracted by his talk and extreme fluency in conversation, asked *Talkative*, "What is one thing upon which we shall at this time found our discourse?" Then with an unexpected volley, true to his character, he replied that he could talk on all subjects —

> I will talk of things heavenly, or things earthly; things moral, or things evangelical; things sacred, or things profane; things past, or things to come; things foreign, or things at home; things more essential, or things more circumstantial; provided that all be done to our profit.

But such a man, full of talk, is only an empty breath and hollow sound. How apt is the question of Zophar to the talkative fool, "Should a man full of talk be justified?" (Job 11:2). No, talk is one thing, even though one may "speak with the tongues of men and of angels," but sanctifying grace and love are another matter altogether. If the meditations of our heart are heavenward, then the words of our mouth will be fitting and fruitful.

    12. *Deliberate Loss*—"The preaching of the cross is to them that per-

ish foolishness" (I Corinthians 1:18).

It could also be expressed as "nonsense to those involved in this dying world." Is it not the height of folly to reject the only remedy for sin, and the only avenue of escape from eternal doom? "The thought of foolishness is sin" (Proverbs 24:9), and self-pride, unwilling to acknowledge sinnership, is indeed a manifestation of sinful foolishness. Perishing sinners may not think of their rejection of the cross as foolishness, and declare "the prophet a fool, and the spiritual man mad" (Hosea 9:7), but what a terrible awakening will be theirs in hell. The same lack of spiritual perception is indicated by Paul when he wrote of the natural man as treating the things of the Spirit of God as foolishness (I Corinthians 2:14). How can a blind man behold the beauty of the sky? To see, he must have sight.

B. *The Types of a Fool*

As a noun, "fool" carries various meanings in Scripture in which many fools are described in no uncertain terms. Let us see if we can distinguish some of these mental oddities.

    1. *Atheistic Fool* — "The fool hath said in his heart, There is no God" (Psalm 14:1).

Doubtless we are all familiar with the lines of John Milton in his *Paradise Regained* —

> Just as the ways of God
> And justifiable to men;
> Unless there be who think not God at all.
> Of such doctrine never was there school,
> But the heart of the fool,
> And no man therein doctor but himself.

In these apostate days we have an ever increasing number "who think not God at all." Why, there are some religious leaders teaching the world that God is dead! What a company of fools they are! The word for "fool" which the psalmist uses means "an empty person," and how empty the life is when God is not recognized as Creator, Redeemer and Governor. The Hebrew *nabal* is from a root meaning — "to wither." Then the two words, *There is,* are in italics meaning that they are not in the original but were added to give fuller sense to the passage. So we can read it, "The fool hath said in his heart — No God," that is "No God for me." This does not imply the speculative atheism at the heart of Communism but a practical atheism or the denial of the moral government of God. This is why the fool and the wicked are often synonymous in Scripture. "Let us break their bands asunder, and cast away their cords from us" (Psalm 2:3).

2. *Blind Fool* — "Ye fools and blind," or "blind fools" (Matthew 23: 17, 19).

Here we have a different word for "fool." This word signifies "a rebel" which fittingly describes those religious rebels, the Pharisees whom Christ condemned. We have a saying that "none are so blind as those who will not see," and the foes of Christ were guilty of wilfull blindness and became blind leaders of the blind. They thought they saw the need of others but were blind to the fact that there was a profession without possession. Their faith was in their own fancied self-righteousness and not in a divinely provided righteousness (Luke 18:11), and led them to demand the crucifixion of Christ, who came as the righteous One.

3. *Sleeping Fool* — "Five were foolish" (Matthew 25:2).

What must not be forgotten is the fact that in this parable which Jesus told, *all* of the ten virgins slept. The difference was that the five wise virgins had oil in their lamps and were ready to welcome the bride and bridegroom when the invitation was given to attend the marriage feast. Fool, as employed here, carries the idea of being dull or slow, and the other five virgins were foolish in that they failed to prepare sufficiently for their lamps. When they realized their dilemma they urged their fully-prepared companions to give them of their oil, but no believer can communicate the grace he has received to another. Personal appropriation alone can make us the recipients of the oil of the Spirit.

4. *Heedless Fool* — "Thou fool, this night thy soul shall be required of thee" (Luke 12:20).

This rich fool of whom Jesus spoke was likely a man of whom everyone said, as they saw his bursting barns and accumulated wealth, "He's no fool." But the Master exposed his folly and declared that in hoarding his gains he was a fool to himself. He was a fool for loving his life and his gains so he lost them. Think of the blessings of those whose burdens could have been lifted if only he had been generous! How they would have been gladdened and enriched! But his was a shriveled soul. "Fool" in the narrative means "heedless," which was the folly of this rich fool whose sin consisted not in being prosperous but in excluding God from his gains. "What hast thou that thou didst not receive?"

5. *Christian Fool* — "O foolish Galatians . . . Are ye so foolish?" (Galatians 3:1, 3).

Make no mistake about it, those Galatians were Christians, but they were guilty of permitting themselves to be sidetracked by legalizers — the Judaizing missionaries from Palestine. The word Paul used for "foolish" indicates "thoughtlessness," and being fickle-minded the Galatians were easily bewitched to countenance a mixture of grace and works. Regenerated by the Spirit, they now tried to reach spiritual perfection by fleshly methods. But Christians are saved — and kept saved — by the grace and power of God alone.

6. *Christ's Fool* — "We are fools for Christ's sake" (I Corinthians 4:10).

, Are we among the numbers who, for His sake, are labeled "foolish"? William J. May, famous Methodist preacher tells of a Salvation Army officer friend of his who was wont to parade the streets wearing an embroidered jersey, which had on the front the words, "A fool for Christ's sake," and on the back, "Whose fool are you?" Are you glad that on this April Fool's Day you are among the number willing to be numbered among Christ's fools? Solomon would have us "forsake the foolish, and live; and go in the way of understanding" (Proverbs 9:6), but the paradox Paul uses implies that we are foolish and wise at the same time. "Fools for Christ, but ye are wise in Christ." Does He not choose foolish things to confound the wise, and are we not exhorted to become as fools that we may be wise (I Corinthians 1:27; 3:18)? The devil's fools are utterly foolish or destitute of true wisdom, and only God's mercy can save them from their mental blindness (Psalm 69:5; Titus 3:3). "The fear of the Lord is the beginning of wisdom: and the knowledge of the holy is understanding" (Proverbs 9:10). Disciples though we are, may we never be counted by Christ as being among those "fools, slow of heart to believe all that the prophets have spoken" (Luke 24:25).

For Ascension Day

For Ascension Day

O God, who hast inspired Thy Church to celebrate this day in memory of our Saviour's Ascension, when, having finished on earth the great work of our redemption, He carried up His glorified humanity above the clouds to its eternal rest, grant, we humbly beseech Thee, that, taking our eyes from the verities here below, we may stand continually looking after Him into heaven; and, heartily expecting His appearance thence again at His Coming, may be always ready to obey His call, and meet Him in the clouds, and follow Him into those blissful mansions when He went to prepare for us at Thy right hand for evermore; through the same, our Lord Jesus Christ, who with Thee and the Holy Spirit liveth and reigneth ever one God, world without end. Amen.

— Bishop George Hickes (1642)

MEDITATION FOR ASCENSION DAY

THE RAPTURE OF THE REDEEMER
Luke 24:50, 51

The ascension of the risen Lord was the event when He departed visibly from His disciples into the immediate presence of God the Father, and constituted His crowning miracle as the sent One of God. Some ten appearances of the risen Christ are recorded in the gospels, five of which are associated with the day of His resurrection. Of the ten appearances Luke cites three, namely,

1. That to the disciples on the road to Emmaus (24:13-33)
2. That to the ten apostles and others (24:36-49)
3. That on the occasion of the ascension (24:50, 51; Acts 1:9, 10).

Among other ascensions to heaven we have the translation of Enoch and of Elijah, neither of whom died, and of the saints at the return of Christ who will be made up of the dead raised and the living changed. These ascensions, along with that of Christ's, provide an evidence of immortality and are the foundation of our title to it.

The ascension of Christ as an article of faith in our Christian Creed proves the certainty of the future life and of our reunion with departed saints in the unimaginable happiness of Christ's presence above.

The departure of Christ from His disciples and friends and from His personal earthly ministry represented the culmination of His life of action which began in Bethlehem when He wrapped Himself with the garment of our humanity. Entering a troubled world at a precious moment of human history, He left it on a day always to be remembered. Although Paul tells us of the hundreds who saw the risen Lord (I Corinthians 15:5-7), no one actually saw Him rise again from the dead. There were, however, many who witnessed His ascension to heaven. We also have the record of those who saw Him *after* His departure, as the exalted One. Stephen, at his martyrdom, saw Him as such (Acts 7:55, 56), so did Paul on the Damascus Road (Acts 9), and when he was caught up into paradise (II Corinthians 12:1-4). John likewise saw Jesus as the throned One, as his Book of Revelation clearly proves (1:10-20). The absorbing theme of the ascension can be summarized in the following threefold way — Its Foregleams, Its Facts, Its Fruits.

A. *Foregleams of the Ascension.*

The resurrection and the ascension of Christ are inseparable, the one event being the complement of the other. Both were proclaimed together by the prophets, our Lord, and His apostles. Both Enoch and Elijah, who were translated without tasting death, prefigured the ascension of Christ, the difference being that He died and rose again and then was translated. David has given foregleams of His exaltation —

> Thou hast ascended on high, thou hast led captivity captive; thou hast received gifts for men; yea, for the rebellious also, that the Lord God might dwell among them (Psalm 68:18, see Ephesians 4:8).
> The Lord said unto my Lord, Sit thou at my right hand, until I make thine enemies thy footstool (Psalm 110:1, 2, see Isaiah 9:7; I Corinthians 15:25).

During His public ministry, Christ foretold His resurrection, ascension and exaltation. He steadfastly set His face to meet these events. Several times He spoke about returning to His Father — "Ye shall see the Son of man ascend up where he was before" (John 6:62); "Rejoice, because . . . I go unto the Father" (John 14:28); "Now I go my way to him that sent me" (John 16:5); "I ascend unto my Father, and your Father: and to my God, and your God" (John 20:17).

B. *Facts of the Ascension.*

First of all, the apostles taught the resurrection, ascension and exaltation of Christ as vital facts of the faith delivered once and for all to the saints. Both Peter and Paul unite in declaring that He was received by heaven there to continue His ministry in a different form. Key passages to consider are Acts 2:32-34; 3:15-21; 5:30, 31; I Peter 3:21, 22. Paul's explicit references to the triad of such truth can be found in Romans 8:34; Ephesians 1:20, 21; 2:6; 4:8; Colossians 3:1; I Timothy 3:16; Hebrews 1:3; 4:14; 8:1; 9:24; 10:12; 12:2).

The aspect of our meditation worthy of note at this point, however, pertain to facts related to Christ's ascension as it happened. Comparing the narratives recording this event (Luke 24:49-53; Acts 1:1-11), we know that it took place —

1. *After forty days* (Acts 1:3).

As the ascension was an integral part of God's redemptive plan there was nothing mysterious associated with Christ's prophesied disappearance at the end of the forty days He tarried on the earth after His resurrection. A like period appears several times in the Bible. Moses was on the mount with God forty days, preparing for the deliverance of the Law. Elijah was in the desert forty days before he came forth for his dynamic work in Israel. Jesus Himself spent forty days in the wilderness at the beginning of His public ministry. Can it be that those forty resurrection days were a preface to the glorious ministry He was to exercise in heaven — a ministry He was to continue forevermore?

2. *He led them out* (Luke 24:50).

As soon as the period of probation was ended and the closing counsels and commissions had been given, Jesus led the little band through the streets of Jerusalem, and over Kedron, and past the shadows of Gethsemane. What silence must have reigned! Their hearts were too full of memories as they passed out to the upland ground near Bethany. As the Guide, Jesus led His own to a quiet and lonely spot for their farewell glimpse of Him, teaching them, thereby, a parting lesson of humility.

Jesus led His disciples out as far as Bethany — His beloved Bethany, the place of hallowed memories, the abode of Martha, Mary and Lazarus whom He loved. Bethany signifies "The House of Sorrow," and those who go to heaven ascend there from the house of sufferings and sorrow here below. Bethany is adjacent to the Mount of Olives which is also conspicuous in our Lord's life. It was from here He began His triumphant entry into Jerusalem, and in the same garden His agonizing suffering was endured. This historic mount also witnessed His extreme loneliness. At night, when others went to their rooms, Jesus went to the Mount of Olives where, with the darkness of the night to cover Him as a blanket, He spent the lonely hours in communion with His Father. But the mount associated with His *solitude* will witness His *sovereignty,* for when He returns to reign as the universal King, His feet are to stand upon the Mount of Olives (Zechariah 14:4). His reproach was rolled away by His glorious ascension from this mount, which was a forecast of His descension at His coming again, as the two men from heaven declared (Acts 1: 10, 11).

The first chapter of Christianity began with the advent of Christ into our humanity when He was seen, heard and touched. This chapter closed with His death and resurrection. The second chapter of Christianity began with the ascension of Christ to heaven. No longer was He to be seen in the flesh, yet He was to be active and vital in the world and in the hearts of His own. This chapter is still open, and will remain so for He ever liveth at the right hand of God — a statement describing His power and authority.

3. *He lifted up His hands, and blessed them.*

As he was in the act of pronouncing His benediction upon His own, He was taken from them. Thus He ascended with uplifted hands — a representation of the perpetual ministry of intercession He was about to exercise. All the while the hands of Moses were upraised on the mount, Israel prevailed over her enemies below, and Christ's Church cannot fail because behind her is the ceaseless prayers of her Head in heaven. His last word and act, then, assured the small band which He had to leave of His favor, and of His protection and guidance amid all that the future held for them. Leaving His own, He left a blessing behind Him which confirmed them in the belief that having loved them, He would love them to the end. Matthew Henry has the suggestive comment on Christ's parting blessing — "To intimate that His being parted from them did not put an end to His blessing them. He *began* to bless them on earth, but He went to heaven to *go on* with it."

4. *He was parted from them, and carried up into heaven.*

His ascension is described as being "received up into heaven" — "carried up into heaven" — "received up into glory" (Mark 16:19; I Timothy 3:16). The day comes when those who love us, instruct us, pray for us are parted from us, and we know them after the flesh no more. Christ went up for He knew the way, having come from heaven at His incarnation, and He required no chariot of fire, nor horses of fire at His ascension as Elijah had at his translation.

5. *A cloud received Him out of their sight.*

Clouds became His chariot as He was carried away. Bright clouds enveloped Him in His transfiguration which was a rehearsal of His ascension. Had He wished, He could have ascended then (Matthew 17:5), for He was perfect in creation, perfect in probation, and was now ready to be perfected in glory. But for the joy of having myriads share His glory, He came down from the Mount of Transfiguration and went to Mount Calvary.

Through the media of clouds a communication is kept up between the upper and lower worlds; in them the vapors are sent up from earth, and the dews sent down from heaven. It was symbolic, then, that Christ should ascend in a cloud for was He not the Mediator between God and man, by whom God's mercies come down upon us and our prayers come up to Him. It is somewhat remarkable that when His return is mentioned, it is uniformly said that He will come back *in the clouds* (Daniel 7:13; Matthew 24:30; 26:64; Mark 13:26; I Thessalonians 4:17; Revelation 1:7). As clouds are emblematic of sublimity and grandeur (Deuteronomy 4:11; II Samuel 22:12; Psalms 97:2; 104:3), these are associated with the splendor of His translation.

6. *While they beheld . . . out of their sight.*

The time and manner of the ascension was divinely planned so that Jesus would ascend during the bright day and not at night. It was not to be secretly, but openly, so that the apostles could testify to what they had both heard and seen. And seeing Him vanish they knew that God had approved of all His Son had accomplished. Furthermore, watching Him ascend to heaven, they knew where He was. When He was beyond their sight, the disciples continued to look steadfastly toward heaven with a hope, perhaps, that He would come back to them in bodily form. But any curiosity was checked by the question, "Why stand ye gazing?" One day they would follow Him where He had gone.

7. *They worshiped Him.*

Although no longer seen, Jesus continued to receive homage from His own. He had blessed them — now they bless and magnify Him. The cloud that had received Him out of their sight did not put them or their services out of His sight. They offered their worship to an absent Saviour, and this first religious homage He received after leaving the world teaches us that although He is unseen by bodily eyes, He can be worshiped by us.

> What though Thy form we cannot see,
> We know and feel that Thou art near.

8. *They returned to Jerusalem with great joy.*

When Christ told His own that He was about to leave them, sorrow first filled their hearts, but now they are filled with joy. They overflowed with happiness at the assurance of redemption. Their Saviour who had died, and had conquered death, had ascended to God, and a joy unspeakable and full of glory was theirs. Further, ringing in their ears was His last promise that power would be theirs to tell the world all they witnessed and experienced.

9. *They were continually in the temple, praising and blessing God.*

The days of their mourning had ended, and as the Temple had been associated with Israel's glory, and with much of their departed Master's ministry, the apostles returned to the sacred shrine to testify of Messiahship. They knew that Temple sacrifices had been superceded by Christ's supreme sacrifice, but Temple songs continued and in such holy joy and praise they joined.

How simple and how reserved the whole scene was! There was no sound of heavenly music as at His descent to earth at His birth, no whirlwind — a fitting departure for One who would not strive nor cry, and who had come down on the mown grass as gently as rain. The story of the Acts can be told in three lines —

Christ going up to heaven;
The Holy Spirit coming down from heaven;
The disciples going out to the ends of the earth.

And as they went out to proclaim the crucified, risen, ascended and exalted Lord in the power of the Spirit, the world around them was turned upside down. They knew Christ was with them still; that He and they would never be parted again. A short time before they could not believe for joy. Now they were joyful in service just because they believed.

C. *Fruits of His Ascension.*

Preparing His disciples for His death and departure, Jesus uttered a somewhat hard saying — "It is expedient for you that I go away" (John 16:7). "Expedient" means profitable, advantageous, but where was the benefit in the going away of such a marvelous Master and Friend? Could He possibly do more for them by His absence than presence? Yes, now highly exalted, He is able to do exceeding abundant above all we could ask or think. Let us try to enumerate the manifold blessings accruing from Christ's exaltation.

First of all, when He ascended on high, He led captivity captive (Psalm 68:18; Ephesians 4:8, margin, "a multitude of captives"). The image here is that of the victor with his long train of captives following him in triumph. It was thus that Roman emperors rode through the city in great state, having all spoils taken in war before them, along with the kings and nobles whom they had taken captive. By His death and resurrection, Christ spoiled His enemies, hitherto triumphant over men, and made an open show of the powers of sin and death (Colossians 2:15) when He ascended on high.

But is there not a further truth associated with Christ's triumphal ascension? Did He not liberate all prisoners of hope and take them with Him to glory? Up until the time of His death, there was the one abode for all departed spirits — an abode with its two compartments; one section named Abraham's bosom, or paradise (Luke 16:19-31; 23:43) to which all the righteous went, and in which Christ and the dying thief were found after their death at Calvary; the other section called hell contained the spirits of those who died in their sin. At His ascension Christ emptied paradise, translating the saints to heaven. He led captivity captive. But hell remained, and is still the abode of lost souls and will be until the Great White Throne when death and hell are destroyed and the Lake of Fire becomes the final and eternal depository of the wicked.

1. *He gave gifts unto men.*

Victorious rulers received tributes from the vanquished — costly gifts from those who had submitted to their sway. But here the heavenly Conqueror does not receive gifts but bestows them upon those who are His captives. What exactly is the nature of His ascension gifts? We have —

a. The Gift of Himself in a Richer Measure.

Think of everything His own were to gain by His visible absence from the earth! Preparing His disciples for His departure from them He said, "It is expedient for you that I go away" (John 16:17). But how would they be advantaged by His leaving them? Why, instead of having a *local* Christ, they were to have a *universal* One. Before His ascension, owing to His physical limitations His presence was localized, and could only be with some of the people some of the time. Now, by His Spirit, He is with all of His people all of the time. In the days of His flesh, He never traveled beyond the confines of His own land. Now, if we go to the uttermost parts of the earth, He is there. Commissioning us to go into all the world and make disciples of all nations, He assures us that He will go with us and work with us (Mark 16:20). The disciples only knew the physical Christ, the One they could see and handle (I John 1:1). They had touched Him, and they never forgot that touch. But now as the risen and ascending One they can touch Him no more. "Touch me not; for I am not yet ascended unto my Father" (John 20:17). The disciples had walked by sight, now they must walk by faith and believe that He indwells them and will never leave nor forsake them. While among men Jesus had nowhere to lay His head, now His resting place is in the hearts of those who love Him. His abiding presence wherever saints are found is one of the most profitable gifts of His ascension.

b. The Gift of His Throne — Power.

As Christ entered heaven His Father exalted Him, and, enthroning Him, gave Him all power and authority. "He sat down on the right hand of the Majesty on high" (Hebrews 1:3). The simile of "the right hand" suggests the delegation of all royal prerogatives. So our Lord returned to heaven to share His Father's throne (Revelation 3:21), and receive His glorification as the all-conquering Saviour (John 7:39; 12:16, 23; 13:31, 32; 17:1-5; Acts 3:13). And all His throne — power in heaven and in earth is at our disposal for service in a world of sin and need (John 1:12; Matthew 28:18-20). The dynamic witness in the Acts demonstrates how the early disciples appropriated power and authority from on high, or better still, how they were appropriated by Him, the exalted Christ, at the right hand of God.

c. The Gift of the Holy Spirit.

The third Person of the blessed Trinity is without doubt Christ's greatest ascension gift to His Church. Did He not promise to send the Spirit? He informed His own that His absence would be advantageous for them seeing that His "other Self," the gracious Spirit, would come to indwell them, reveal Him to their hearts, and guide them into all truth. Thus, on the day of Pentecost the effusion of the Spirit was experienced and the Church of the living God was born on earth. Existing as units before the ascension, the disciples were fused together and became the mystic fabric which Jesus called, "My Church," and throughout the Acts we have the manifestation of the presence, presidency and power of the Paraclete bestowed by the Father and the Son.

Lack of space forbids a more complete exposition of further benefits accruing from the ascension and exaltation of our Lord but we, herewith, group them together for further study by the reader.

Think of the gifts which are given for the enlightenment and edification of the Church, the Lord's Body! How varied they are (Ephesians 4:7-16)! Are we not apt to forget that every born-again believer received a regeneration gift for use in the service of the Giver? "Unto *every one* of us . . . the measure of the gift of Christ." Have you discovered your gifts or gift, and are they being used to the limit in the work of the ministry (Romans 12:3-8)?

Think of the high priestly intercession of Christ — an intercession continuous and ceaseless! He prayed while on earth (Hebrews 5:7), and now prays in heaven (7:25). The phrase, "He ever liveth," reveals the resurrection, not as an isolated fact of the past, but as a reality, present and continuous. One aspect of His triumph as the Son of man was the elevation of our human nature to the throne of the Godhead. As the exalted Jesus He knows all about our human needs, and as our great High Priest He can meet every one of them. He is our advocate (I John 2:1, 2). He hears our cries and silences all accusations against us (Romans 8:33, 34; Hebrews 9:24).

Think of all the preparation He is now able to make for those redeemed by His precious blood! Did He not tell the Father that it was His express wish that all His own should be with Him where He was going and behold His glory (John 17:24)? Did he not tell His disciples not to be troubled over His coming departure seeing He was going to prepare a place for them (John 14:1-3)? And because none can enter heaven apart from Him (14:6), we must be among the prepared people if we would have the hope of abiding in the place He is preparing for them in His Father's home.

Think of His supremacy as the result of His ascension on high! All are subject to Him (Ephesians 1:21-23; Colossians 1:18; I Peter 3:22), He fills all things (Ephesians 4:10), and awaits the rapture of His true Church (Hebrews 9:28). He also looks for the final subjection of all His enemies and the restitution of all things (Acts 1:11; 2:34-36; 3:20, 21). As we linger amid the shadows awaiting His return, may ours be the greater works which our glorified Lord seeks to accomplish in and through our lives (John 14:12; Ephesians 1:18-20).

For Pentecost – Whitsunday

For Pentecost
— Whitsunday

Lord God the Holy Ghost,
  In this accepted hour,
As on the day of Pentecost,
  Descend in all Thy power.

We meet with one accord,
  In our appointed place,
And wait the promise of our Lord,
  The Spirit of all grace.

Like mighty rushing wind
  Upon the waves beneath,
Move with one impulse every mind,
  One soul, one feeling breathe.

The young, the old inspire
  With wisdom from above;
And give us hearts and tongues of
    fire,
  To pray and praise and love.

Spirit of light explore,
  And chase our gloom away;
With luster shining more and more,
  Unto the perfect day.

Spirit of truth be Thou
  In life and death our Guide;
O Spirit of Adoption, now
  May we be sanctified.

— James Montgomery

MEDITATION FOR PENTECOST — WHITSUNDAY

THE GOSPEL OF WHITSUN
Acts 2:1-21

While Whitsunday is universally remembered in liturgical churches, it yet appears to be a most neglected day in evangelical, Bible preaching churches, just as the experience and power of Pentecost are sadly lacking in the lives of so many of their members. It is all too evident that the majority of evangelical Christians are destitute of the mighty unction and exuberant joy so characteristic of the early believers. Pentecost was an astonishing event in their lives, having more astonishing consequences. What a sensation that great day caused among a multitude of devout onlookers from many parts of the then known world who were in Jerusalem for the memorable Jewish Feast! The outcome of Pentecost, signalizing the birthday of the Christian Church, can be seen in all her subsequent history.

What, exactly, is the meaning of what is known as Whitsunday? This seventh Sunday after Easter, commemorating the descent of the Holy Spirit on the day of Pentecost, was originally called "White Sunday," when those who were baptized between Easter and Pentecost wore white and were referred to as "the white-robed ones." This last Sunday in the period which was also the occasion of the chief festival was named "Sunday in White" or "White Sunday," and so Whitsun is a contraction of this. On this Sunday in May, the Roman Catholic girls used to walk in procession to church, dressed in white. Also, "white" symbolizes purity, and the mission of the Holy Spirit is to make us holy, even as He is holy. Another interpretation is that Whit is actually "Wit" or "Wisdom" Sunday, the day reminding us of the apostles being filled with the wit or wisdom of the Holy Spirit. An ancient MS found in the Cambridge University reads —

> This day Wit-sonday is cald
> For wisdom and wit serene fald
> Was Ezonen to the Apostles as this day.

While we now think of wit as being something funny or witty, the term originally signified "wisdom from heaven" — an attribute which the enemies of the apostles were not able to resist. The Spirit came as the personification of the wisdom from above, so pure and peaceable.

The outstanding manifestation of the gift of Pentecost was power, as Jesus declared it would be. "Ye shall receive power, after that the Holy Ghost is come upon you" (Acts 1:8). The power is the Person Himself. Power is never divorced from the Paraclete. Power is not something we reach out to possess, but Someone who possesses us. There are many things we need but may not want, and other things we want but do not need. All who are the Lord's need power from on high, but left to themselves they are not able to be holy and victorious and fruitful. This is why we must consider "The Gospel of Pentecost" which is "The Gospel of Power." When we recall how the early saints turned the world upside down we can understand why we might easily change the title of the fifth book of the New Testament from the Acts of the Apostles to the Acts of the Holy Spirit Through the Apostles. Theirs was a supernatural power outside and above themselves, yet using them as the media of the salvation of countless numbers of sinners. How general is the need of this power of God!

If the inner life of a young man is subject to passions that defile, he must have power to make and keep him clean. Too many youths succumb before the tidal wave of temptation and are carried away until moorings snap and they become derelict on the ocean of life. Rudderless, they become moral wrecks. To ride masterfully over the perilous sea, they must have power to possess the white flower of a blameless life — a strength outside their own. To them the Gospel is preached, "Ye shall receive power," and as they fling open the avenues of their being to the Spirit of power, the shackles are broken. But if He is resisted as He strives to liberate the defeated life, and the yearning for higher impulses are stifled, how empty and destitute the life remains.

If a young woman is to be attractive, noble and winsome in her influence she, too, needs power from on high. If she is to shape her lips to utter a deliberate "no" when questionable matters are presented — if hers is to be a firm refusal to sell her honor and retain purity of character — if she is to stand firm against the subtle influences of moral degenerates seeking to betray her she must have the power of God. What young unmarried women need to keep them from having unwanted children is not a pill but power from on high. How we need another Pentecost to check the ever-increasing sexual immorality, broken marriages and the heartbroken lives of our lax age.

If the body is to be kept under control and made to function as the Temple of God, the possessor of it must have spiritual power. If the mouth is to be kept clean and sweet and filled with speech that elevates then the power giving utterance must be appropriated. If the eyes are to close instinctively to the sinful and seductive sights in the world — if the ears are to remain deaf to the luring voices ever striving to destroy inner peace — if the walls of imagination are not to have those pictures which we would never dare expose upon the walls of our home — if every organ of the body is to be pure functioning as the Creator meant, then power, more power, and still more power will be necessary. It requires a spiritual dynamic to deny oneself those habits harmful to mind and body — to be wide awake, no matter what our legitimate calling may be, and never allow the secular to supercede the spiritual — to bear the contempt of those who scorn consecration of life. Is it not encouraging to know that all the power needed is at our disposal and can be appropriated by faith?

If our homes are to be kept sweet and beautiful, then heaven's fragrant love must permeate them. It takes power, does it not, to be patient, kind, tender and cheerful amid adverse circumstances? The seamy side often appears at home. What a travesty it is when one tries to act as a saint abroad but is a devil at home! The omnipotent Spirit who came at Pentecost is well able to make our homes all they should be.

As the Spirit of love, He can possess all within the home, and combat all coldness, jealousy, harshness and estrangement.

As the Spirit of light, He can banish all ignorance or error, and bring the home into harmony with the Word He inspired.

As the Spirit of life, He can destroy all apathy and indifference, and unite all the members of the home in Christ.

As the Spirit of Liberty, He is able to snap the fetters of all enslaving habits and give to all the glorious liberty of the children of God.

If the businessman, surrounded by the sharp competition of the world, is to be straight and true, not yielding to the tricks of the trade, he must have the promised Power. If he is to retain his integrity even when markets are shrewd, and the stress is great, and refuse to traffic in forbidden or harmful products, he will have to gird himself with the whole armor of God.

If the man of God is to be used to bring the impact of God to bear upon a guilty world, power from above will be needed. It takes power to condemn practices alien to God's holy will — to proclaim with rare tactfulness and tenderness the great facts of sin and judgment — to preach a full Gospel as the only panacea for the world's ills. Eloquence, science, scholarship, culture and philosophy are all good in their place, but worthless in winning the lost unless there is the accompaniment of the enduement of the Holy Spirit. The one supreme requirement for effective witness is, "Be ye infilled with the Spirit." When so saturated we become mighty through God to the pulling down of strongholds, with or without acquired wisdom and knowledge.

As the result of Pentecost those early disciples became —

Anointed witnesses testifying to Christ and His power and glory.

Inspired witnesses not speaking from or of themselves, but channels of a divine revelation.

Effective witnesses, able to convince the world of sin, righteousness and judgment to come.

Prophetic witnesses revealing things to come.

Salvation, sanctification and service cover our life in Christ, and the unction of Pentecost is especially associated with the last of the three giving us spiritual discernment of truth and power, conviction and effectiveness in the utterance of that truth. Both Peter and Paul stand forth as conspicuous examples of heralds proclaiming the Word of God with all boldness.

Concluding our meditation on the significance of Pentecost there are two aspects we can further emphasize —

First of all, the presence and power of the Holy Spirit was so wonderful on that momentous day that even the dead walls of the upper chamber felt the impact of Him who had come as the Spirit of power. Matter responded to Spirit and the place was shaken where they were gathered together. Pillars and posts, wood and stone trembled at His presence. What a spiritual earthquake that must have been! Was it not a symbol of what the Holy Spirit was to accomplish through those who received such a baptism? Did He not lay hold of those weak and feeble disciples and shake the walls of their prejudices, and move them to the very foundation of their beings? A characteristic feature of the Acts is the breaking of fetters, the bursting open of prison doors, the shaking and disturbance of human hearts. The sudden deaths of Ananias and Sapphira, and of Herod, the miraculous deliverances of Peter and Paul from prisons, and a spiritual turbulence in the lives of multitudes all testify to the way the omnipotent Spirit is able to turn things — and persons — upside down.

The second thought is that the risen Christ thought of all the needs of His own when He promised, "Ye shall receive power." The question is, What do we know of a personal Pentecost? Because, as we have indicated, the power is the Person Himself, then seeing that every believer has the Spirit (Romans 8:9), the potential of manifested Power is ever present. It is only as we obey the Spirit and move in the line of His will, however, that He is able to demonstrate His power in and through our witness. Is it not partially true to say that knowledge is power? We may have exact knowledge regarding the Spirit's personality, activities and gifts yet be so destitute of His Power blasting the fetters of prejudice, pride, tradition and fear.

The solution of all our problems and the necessary strength and wisdom for a dynamic witness for Christ are to be found in the gift He bequeathed His own.

We read, do we not, that the Spirit "came suddenly" upon those who had waited for the fulfillment of the Master's promise. As they waited they prayed and created, thereby, the soul-atmosphere so necessary for the reception of the Spirit. Our obligation is to keep on praying, earnestly and believingly that everything displeasing to His holy will might be removed, that our personal spirituality may be intensified, that we may not grow weary in well-doing. Then, one day, our Pentecost will come, and we shall find ourselves caught up and borne along by the rushing, mighty wind, and as the result of a fiery baptism preach and testify as the Spirit gives us utterance. May this remembrance of Pentecost result in pentecostal blessing both in our hearts and churches!

> Wake, heavenly Wind, arise and come,
> Blow on the drooping field;
> Our spices, then, shall breathe perfume,
> And fragrant incense yield.

AN OUTLINE FOR WHITSUNDAY

Pentecost (Acts 2:1-4), referred to as "The Birthday of the Church," was indeed a day, displaying the miraculous power of God.

A. *The Conception and Manifestation of the Church Was a Miracle.*

1. Trace the oneness of purpose (Acts 1:4). There was no striving after unity, but the use of unity for service.

2. Trace how this oneness fused them together. There was a visible sign of invisible unity — community worship before community singing.

3. Trace the set day, place (probably the Temple), company, purpose, spirit.

B. *The Symbols of the Spirit Were Miraculous in Operation.*

1. Wind, fire, tongues. Irresistible energy — "rushing of a mighty wind." Transforming and purifying power. Mysterious Life. Divine Gifts — "as the Spirit gave them utterance."

2. Symbols by themselves produce nothing. "As of" suggests they were signs of the presence of the Holy Spirit. The sound "filled all the house." Yet the gift was personal — "sat upon each of them." Tongues represent an individual gift — "the wind bloweth where it listeth" symbolizes a world-wide ministry.

3. Symbols indicated divine power for service. Power was manifest in produced effects. The sound, so mysterious, drew the crowd — the "tongues" amazed them — the preaching transformed them for 3,000 were saved.

C. *The Spirit in the Church Makes Her a Miraculous Channel of Blessing.*

1. While there was unity at Pentecost, there was not uniformity. Gifts were varied. A Spirit-filled church is diverse in gifts and potent in her effect upon the world. John Wesley's conversion was far more epoch-making than Napoleon's conquests. Pentecost reversed the babble of Babel, and captured the language of the world for Christ.

For Mother's Day

For Mother's Day

I think God took the fragrance
of a flower,
A pure white flower, which blooms
not for world praise
But which makes sweet and beautiful
some bower;
The compassion of the dew,
which gently lays
Reviving freshness on
the fainting earth,
And gives to all the tired things
new birth;
The steadfastness and radiance
of stars
Which lift the soul above
confining bars;
The gladness of fair dawns;
the sunset's peace;
Contentment which from trivial
rounds ask no release;
The life which finds its greatest joy
in deeds of love for others . . .
I think God took these precious
things and made of them . . .
mothers.

— Author Unknown

MEDITATION FOR MOTHER'S DAY

THE MOTHERHOOD OF GOD
Isaiah 66:13

The other day I read, "The great annual homage to Mom is back this Sunday. It's Mother's Day, an anniversary that escalates year by year in commercial significance — youngsters alone are expected to spend a staggering £47 million on presents.

"For the greeting card companies, it's their best day apart from Christmas.

"The same goes for telephone companies, who are taking huge newspaper advertisements to urge readers 'to make sure nobody comes between you and your mother this Sunday.'

"If Mom lived in California, I could spend about £2 sending a 'Candygram' — a box of chocolates and a greetings telegram."

In the revelation of the blessing of Israel in the coming Millennium, God assures His people that "as one whom his mother comforteth, so will I comfort you" (Isaiah 66:13). In these homely words we have one of the sweetest and most tender pictures of the character of the God we seek to serve and follow. And that revelation is not in the New Testament, but in the Old! In the New Testament Jesus teaches us to think of God as our Father. Indeed, He uses this filial term more than all the inspired writers put together. But here in the Old Testament, God likens Himself to a comforting *mother*.

Some would have us believe in a progress of revelation regarding the character of God. At first His people had a vague and crude conception of Him. To them He was simply a tribal deity. But surely this word of Isaiah's makes us pause, for what fuller or more charming revelation of God's nature can we find than this descriptive one in which God likens Himself to a devoted mother?

Two introductory thoughts emerge for our consideration. The first is this: that the manifold relationship in which human beings stand to each other are all used to reveal the many-sided character of God, and it takes them all to unfold His fullness. He is our King, and we are His subjects (Revelation

15:3). As the King of saints He gives the saints laws, seeking thereby to govern them for their highest welfare. And from His own, He expects loyal allegiance.

He is our Father, and we are His children (Psalm 103:13; Matthew 6:8; 7:11; Galatians 4:6). As our Father He provides for our needs. He trains, corrects, and educates us in love and service as members of a great family.

Here we have something deeper. A mother is a ministering angel in times of pain and sorrow. She has the art to comfort better than a man, and this mother-love, inexpressibly beautiful and tender, is planted in her breast by the mother-heart of God. The Jews have a sweet saying to the effect that "God could not be everywhere, so He made mothers." And this is true, for a loving mother is God's tenderest image in humanity.

A mother is a mother still,
The holiest thing alive.

Mother-love of earth, however, is but a pale reflection of the feeling within the heart of God, as with unfailing tenderness He comforts the weary, wounded spirit of His child.

The second thought is that God combines in Himself all the virtues of a perfect character. The best, holiest, and sweetest persons are usually lacking in one or more graces. Male and female created He them, and the characteristic features are resident in His loving heart. He possesses in perfection the most gracious in noble manhood and the pure-heartedness of womanhood. He fuses together in His own person the strong, protective love of man, and the tender, brooding, comforting and sacrificial love of woman. This is why both men and women turn to Him for satisfaction and salvation — both are a part of Him.

As John Oxenham expresses it in his book of poems —

The Vision Splendid

Father and Mother, Thou
In Thy full being art —
Justice with mercy intertwined,
Judgment exact with love combined,
Neither complete apart.

And so we know that when
Our service is weak and vain,
The Father — Justice would condemn
The Mother — Love Thy wrath will stem
And our reprieval gain.

How full of consolation is the divinely-chosen figure of a mother, especially as we think of our Lord in whom was mingled the blood of a mother and the blood of God! If the Old Testament is God's picture book, and the New Testament His teaching book, then the latter reveals how, as a mother, He comforts His children. How apt the illustration is, for what can surpass the love of a devoted woman or the self-sacrificing love of a mother! What power a mother has to live in the lives of others, which power is her gracious prerogative and happiest attribute, yet sometimes her sharpest agony! It is the woman who suffers most and is able to hide her feelings more effectively than a man. How she struggles against much heartache, bleeding and sorrow, and who, as death shadows the home, strives to arrest the inevitable separation from a loved treasure.

How like God, who created motherhood, these virtues are! How silently He suffers, bears the pain of desertion and rejection, and strives in a thousand ways to avert the eternal doom of the sinner and win him for Himself! He speaks of Himself as "the God of all comfort" (II Corinthians 1:3, 4) and so He is! Did He not say that while a mother may cease to have compassion for the son of her womb, that He would never forget His children (Isaiah 49:15)? One wonders if Robert Burns, the Scottish poet, has the prophet's words in mind as he closed his lament for James Earl of Glencairn —

> The Bridegroom may forget his bride
> Who made his wedded wife yestreen:
> The Monarch may forget his crown
> That on his head an hour has been:
> The Mother may forget the child
> That smiles sae sweetly on her knee:
> But I'll remember thee, Glencairn,
> And a' that thou hast done for me.

A. *God Comforts by His Presence.*

We are all familiar with the motto, *What Is Home Without A Mother?* She is queen of her home, and the house is lost without her. Her presence means comfort, joy, love and service. It is worse still to have a heart and home without God. Yet He is not so far away from any one of us for He is always near to soothe and sympathize. He lifts His troubled child up into His everlasting arms, silently folds around him the deep sense of Himself, and so the heart is comforted.

This aspect of God's character bids us remember that the very grace we seek from Him depends upon our thought of Him and of His care. So many treat Him as a kind of convenience. He is a tower they run to for safety when the storms of life appear. And, let it be said, He is a tower into which the righteous can run. The tragedy is that as soon as the storms blow by, many depart from the tower and forget God until the storms break afresh.

How different is turning to God from turning to our mother! Remember, the prophet is not thinking of a little child, but of a grown man heartsore and broken, fleeing back for the comfort of his mother's presence. "As a man whom his mother comforteth, so will I comfort you." Many a man, weary and

broken by a pitiless world, with things against him and fortunes ruined, or with dear ones gone, or faith almost giving way, or entangled in the net of sin, has retreated in such dark, lone hours to the mother who gave him being. Many a man has crept back home like a wounded animal, and has cast himself upon the mother-love that warmed his heart in childhood days.

And here is God, the source of our being, the ancient home to which all belong, offering Himself to us as the divine, eternal mother. "I will not leave you comfortless: I will come to you" (John 14:18). Tenderly He draws near and gathers us up in his bosom, and by his very nearness, consoles and comforts us. "Fear not, I am with thee." And so we are "comforted by God."

> The watchful mother tarries nigh
> Though sleep has closed her infant's eye;
> For should he wake, and find her gone,
> She knows she could not bear his moan.
> But I am weaker than a child,
> And Thou art more than mother dear;
> Without Thee, heaven were but a wild;
> Without Thee, earth a desert drear.

B. *God Comforts Us by His Words.*

The child's first teacher is his mother. From her lips he receives his earliest and most sacred lessons of God, life and duty. When discouraged, mother's words comfort and inspire. When disobedient, her remonstrance brings penitence. When in doubt, her counsel leads to firm resolve. Think of the young men who, amid the strong temptations of life, have been encouraged to walk in the straight path by the remembrance of prayers and words they learned at mother's knee!

Yes, and is it not true that to a mother's heart her child never seems to grow up? To her, he is always the child who nestled near to her side. He may pass out into the world and meet honor or disgrace, but in her imagination he is always the little form that clung to her knee, and ran to her for comfort, and whose little aches and pains she soothed away.

The grown man, broken in the battle of life or by his own sins, may return to his mother, but it is not the grown man she sees. She sees only her child! Thus it is with God. To Him we can never be anything else but children — weak, foolish, inexperienced and erring. Man at his best is but an

> Infant crying in the night
> With no language but a cry.

And as he cries, God comforts as a mother by His gracious words. He utters "comfortable words." He exercises a mother's pity over our sin and folly, and makes every allowance for our circumstances. Then, with His own heart, pleads for us. What a pathetic scene that was when, as Jesus watched the retreating forms of those who were unwilling to face the cost of discipleship, He said to His own, "Will ye also go away?" How touching was the reply: "To whom shall we go? Thou hast the words of eternal life" (John 6:67, 68). May we cultivate the childlike ear and listen to His voice.

C. *God Comforts Us by His Silence.*

Several writers have expounded this gracious theme of the mother-love of God. To Dr. Charles Hordan and especially to Dr. J. Carroll am I indebted for many of my thoughts here. The remarkable fact is that all expositors make much of this feature of mother-comfort now before us. If her child is in trouble, the mother receives that child without asking many questions. A mother's intuition tells her what is wrong. It is enough for her to know that her child is in distress. She may guess much, and fear more, but comfort is her first consideration. Explanations can wait!

How like the motherhood of God! God our mother does not probe the wound when there is power to heal. How beautifully tender is the mother-comfort of God! He asks no questions, utters no reproach, demands no explanation. He does not use the scrutiny of a detective, but the sympathy of a devoted parent. He simply says, "Come unto Me and rest!" And it is so easy to carry our sorrows to Him as, with the tenderness and reticence of a mother, He is unwilling to touch the wound or draw aside the veil from our hidden grief. It is His glory to conceal things.

One phase, however, of this silent comfort is what Dr. Carroll calls the mother's "inarticulation." He agrees it is a poor word to express the meaning of the thought. When a child flees to his mother for consolation, with what or how does mother comfort her distressed one? Not with many words which often increase the child's grief. Mother is wiser, and catching up the child bends over him and smothers him with kisses of love. And, in the silence, his poignant pain is healed. Silent sympathy is a soothing balm. It was not anything mother said, but was simply her soothing touch and presence that brought relief.

Thus it is with God who, with a strange inarticulate comfort, calms the troubled breast. He asks no question, strikes no wounds. We carry to Him our torturing doubt, worldly loss, stab of heart, deep gashes of disappointment, and ruin of sin within the soul. And He comforts us with His forgiving presence. What we weep over may remain, yet in carrying all to the mother-heart of God we are comforted. We kneel before Him, but we cannot see His radiant form. We speak to Him, but receive no articulate answer. Yet we leave His presence calmed and consoled as a child folded within the breast in the silence of love. The sublime philosophy of this truth is wrapped up for us in the tender refrain:

> In the heart of Jesus there is love for you,
> Love most pure and tender, love most deep and true;
> Why should I be lonely, why for friendship sigh,
> When the heart of Jesus has a full supply?

D. *God Comforts Us by His Sympathy.*

A wise child tells about all his joys, sorrows and burdens without reserve into that most sacred confessional box — his mother's ear. And the need of a confidant is not only characteristic of childhood, for it belongs to us all. This is why those heartbroken men came back from the grave, and "went and told Jesus."

But to return to the child. Think of him as he scampers home from school and places his books in mother's hands, finding the chief award for his diligence in mother's approving smile! And, further, it is because of her gift of sympathy that he turns to her in pain and sorrow. The little son of the woman of Shunem was carried home from the harvest fields ill with sunstroke, and he sat upon his mother's knee till noon and then died.

God offers us the same motherly tenderness and sympathy. He heals, gladdens, sympathizes, loves, and cares as no mother could. Does He not give Himself the appealing name of Comforter? Yet is it not strange to think that men will seek for comfort almost anywhere else than in the Mother-God above? We can detect the sob of unwanted love in the lament over Jerusalem, where the sympathizing Jesus uses the figure of the mother-bird. "O Jerusalem, Jerusalem, . . . how often would I have gathered thy children together, as a hen doth gather her brood under her wings, and ye would not" (Luke 13:34).

Men try to escape from sorrow by drowning it in drink, in seeking a change of circumstances or surroundings, in harder work, in eager pursuits, in the distractions of sin and pleasure. And all the while God stands open to every sufferer. This truth regarding His motherhood means that He strives to soothe, relieve, cleanse and emancipate. What fools we are to cut ourselves adrift from the God who made all mothers, and who waits to do far more for us than the best and holiest mother is capable of doing!

> As trustful as a child who looks
> Up in his mother's face,
> And all his little griefs and fears
> Forgets in her embrace;
> So I, do Thee, my Saviour, look,
> And in Thy face divine
> Can read the love that will sustain
> As weak a faith as mine.
> — J. D. Burns

For Father's Day

For Father's Day

Your Father knoweth all the crowding
  needs
    That make a burden for the anxious
      heart,
And He who ev'ry chirping sparrow
  feeds
    Will not forget to play a Father's
      part:
Who doubts His love a needless sorrow soweth:
Your Father knoweth.

Your Father knoweth of the hidden
  way,
    Where mists cling low about His
      children's feet.
To Him the darkness shineth as the
  day,
    And He shall guide them by the
      path most meet:
Who fears, forgets that all the way he
  goeth
His Father knoweth.

Your Father knoweth all the hosts of
  sin
    That round the souls of men in
      ambush lie.
And how to send His reinforcements
  in
    "Changing defeat to vict'ry's ringing
      cry":

To hold in leash the wind that fiercely
  bloweth
    Your Father knoweth.

Your Father knoweth all the troops of
  fears
    That lurk with His children's
      trembling hearts,
Fears of their weakness, mourned
  with bitter tears,
    Fear lest they should not fear sin's
      hidden darts:
And how to give the strength that
  mighty groweth
Your Father knoweth.

Your Father knoweth; then shall perfect peace
    Guard like a sentinel each coming
      day,
For fears are put to flight, and doubt-
  ings cease,
    And joy goes singing on its home-
      ward way
When like a morning star this sweet
  word gloweth,
Your Father knoweth.

— Anonymous

"I do always those things that please
him" (John 8:29).

MEDITATION FOR FATHER'S DAY

THE FATHERHOOD OF GOD
Ephesians 3:14, 15

While Father's Day is of later origin than Mother's Day, and is not so extensively recognized, it is nevertheless increasing in popularity. Commercially, these special "days" are profitable to many merchants who have come to exploit them to the full. It is fitting, however, to have such occasions, for we can call special attention to our indebtedness to others.

Comparisons and contrasts come to mind as we bring the Fatherhood of God alongside the human relationship of fatherhood. Paul brought the two together when he bowed his "knees unto the Father of our Lord Jesus Christ, of whom the whole family in heaven and earth is named" (Ephesians 3:14, 15). The title of Father is attributed to God in a fourfold way —

1. *God is the Eternal Father of our Lord Jesus Christ,* who came as the only-begotten Son (I John 1:3; Ephesians 1:3). In the days of His flesh, Christ frequently used the filial term "Father." When only twelve years of age, He knew He was in the world to accomplish His Father's business, and as He came to die, He expressed the same unbroken, intimate relationship in His committal to the Father's hands.

2. *God is the Father of Adam,* and of all his natural offspring (Luke 3:38). It is only in this sense that God is the Father of us all. Job asks, "Hath not the rain a father?" (38:28). The modernistic concept of the Fatherhood of God is foreign to Scripture. Only in respect to creation is God the Father of all mankind. He it was who made us, and not we ourselves. "Have we not all one father? hath not one God created us?" (Malachi 2:10).

3. *God is the Father of Mercies* (II Corinthians 1:3). Material as well as spiritual mercies flow from His bountiful hand to all His creatures. Wordsworth, the noble poet, gave us the lines —

Father! — to God we cannot give
A holier name.

Alexander Pope uses the designation in similar fashion —

Father of all! in every age,
In every clime adored,

113

By saint, by savage, and by sage,
  Jehovah, Jove, or Lord!

God is merciful to the just and the
unjust alike. The Father's heart embraces all His sons, whether of creation or of grace.

  Father of mercies! in Thy Word
    What endless glories shine!
  Forever be Thy name adored
    For these celestial lines.

4. *God is the Father of all regenerated by the Spirit's work.*

Modernism exalts the Fatherhood of
God and the brotherhood of man, but
omits the Saviourhood of Christ. None,
however, who are destitute of divine
grace within the heart, have the right
to call God, Father — or their fellowmen, brothers. It is only those who are
accepted in the Beloved, who know
Christ as Saviour, who have the privilege of sonship an l can cry, "Abba,
Father!" (Galatians 4:6). The term
Abba, meaning "will" or "acquiesce," is
only found three times in the New
Testament (Mark 14:36; Romans 8:15;
Galatians 4:6), and means "Father."
The repetition signifies paternal emi-
nence. Jesus taught His own to approach God as Father, in the prayer
"Our Father, which art in heaven," a
truth emphasized by Paul in the Epistles (Romans 15:6; II Corinthians 1:3;
I Thessalonians 3:11; II Thessalonians
2:16). God is *not* the Father of unregenerated men and women, irrespective
of any religious affiliation they may
have. Jesus said of the religious leaders rejecting His claims as the Son of
God, "Ye are of your father, the devil"
(John 8:44). "Thou art my Father,
my God, and the rock of my salvation"
(Psalm 89:26), is the cry of the regenerated heart.

How applicable are the expressive
words of Keble —

  Father to me Thou art, and mother
    dear,

And brother, too, kind husband of my
  heart.

As we come to recall all we owe to
our fathers in the flesh, we may find
it profitable to place the human relationship alongside the divine.

A. *A father transmits his being to his
children,* who are known as his issue or
offspring, or seed (Acts 7:6, 8). In like
manner, God is the Author of our
spiritual being. We are His offspring,
spiritually as well as creatively. We
are His, having been begotten by His
Spirit and His Word (James 1:18; I
Peter 1:3). From God, the Source of
life, we have received life forevermore.

B. *A father makes provision for the
nourishment and upbringing of
those whom he brings into the
world.*

A French proverb has it, "A father
is a banker given by nature." Lifting
our thoughts heavenward, God as our
father, is an unfailing Banker. He is
able and willing to supply all the
needs of His children. Having created
and redeemed us, He delights in shoul-
dering the entire responsibility of our
lives. He exercises paternal tenderness
in bringing up those who have become
His children through the work of the
Spirit (Isaiah 45:3; I Peter 2:2).

C. *A father clothes his children for
necessity and ornament.*

Jacob made his son Joseph a coat of
many colors (Genesis 37:3). What
proud father does not like his child or
children to be well and properly clad!
Is it not so with God our Father? Does
He not adorn His children with graces
of the Spirit and with holiness? He
provides a well-stocked wardrobe for
His sons and daughters (Isaiah 61:10;
Matthew 6:30).

D. *A father, dearly loving his children,
highly esteems them and greatly*

pities them if they are afflicted with need.

If one is overtaken with sickness, the parent quickly tenders help or sympathy. God, however, is more solicitous of His own than an earthly parent could be. Being perfect, perfection of thoughtfulness and sympathy is His (Psalm 103:13; John 15:9; 17:23).

> A father's hand will never cause
> His child a needless tear.

E. *A father will go to any length to protect and defend his child from injuries and abuses.*

To the utmost of his power he will vindicate the innocency of his own. Any evidence of guilt breaks a parent's heart. God as our Father is more eager and alert than any human father could be in the defense of His children against the foes of sin and Satan. Spiritual wickedness abounds on every hand, but God shields His blood-bought ones with His wings from the rage and malice of persecutors (Psalms 59:9,16; 62:2; Ephesians 6:11).

> Father of peace and God of love!
> We own Thy power to save,
> That power by which our Shepherd rose
> Victorious o'er the grave.

F. *A father gives particular attention to his weakest child.*

If he has one who, because of physical infirmity or sickness, cannot care for his or her own personal needs, parental compassion abounds. What love is bestowed upon a child who is not as normal as others in a household! Scripture reminds us that God is exceeding thoughtful and tender toward His weak children. His compassion is unparalleled. As a Father, He is merciful (Luke 6:36). It is not His will that the weakest of His little ones should perish (Matthew 18:14; Isaiah 40:11; I Thessalonians 5:14).

G. *A father deems it his duty to provide sufficient food for his children, and if sick, healing medicines.*

Because of a father's love for his own, he will sacrifice personal delights in order to secure what is essential for his needy offspring. Too often, children are ignorant of what their parents sacrifice on their behalf. Stones are never given for bread. What a provider our Heavenly Father is! He it was who commanded the ravens to feed His hungry prophet. Every redeemed child of His can claim with confidence the declaration of the Shepherd Psalm, "The Lord is my shepherd; I shall *not* want" (Psalms 23:1; 34:8, 10; 132:15; Matthew 7:9).

H. *A father is thrilled when his child begins to lisp "daddy."*

How delighted he is when the young one tries to speak. He is also ready to listen to the requests of a dear child. Devoted parents do not find it hard to understand baby language. Isaac cried unto his father (Genesis 22:7). Our God and Father loves to hear His babes as they learn to pray. Petitions may be crudely expressed at first. Even the most advanced of His children do not know how to pray as they ought. Our Father, however, understands and answers our prayers, not according to our intelligence, but His own (Proverbs 15:8; 12:22; Isaiah 61:1; Matthew 7:7; Luke 4:18). Shakespeare, in *The Merchant of Venice*, reminds us that, "It is a wise father that knows his own child." Is it not a consolation to remember that our wise Father above knows us completely and is ever ready to answer the Spirit-prompted petitions of His children? A prudent father knows when to deny a request. Because of his superior intelligence, he knows what will be hurtful and harmful for his child, and in kindness he

116

says "No!" And God, because of the perfection of His wisdom, knows what is best for His own. He never refuses what is good for them (James 1:17; 4:3).

I. *A father who is loving and discreet, is careful to set a good example for his children to imitate.*

He realizes how closely he is watched, and therefore endeavors to live honorably. Good and godly fathers continue to speak when dead. They live on in noble sons and gracious daughters who gain their inspiration for Christian living from those who gave them birth. Paul urged his spiritual children to emulate his example and follow him, even as he followed his Lord. Our Father in heaven offers us His Son as our holy pattern (Matthew 5:48; Luke 6:36; Colossians 1:4). As a father may have a deeper love for the child who seeks to be like him, so God is favorable toward those of His children who strive to resemble His holiness (II Peter 1:4; Acts 13:22). John was the disciple whom Jesus loved. The apostle enjoyed a sweeter union, seeing his was a closer likeness to his Lord.

J. *A father is solicitous as to the right deportment of his children.*

He will instruct them in all points of good manners toward superiors, and in precepts of good learning whereby they can qualify themselves for the responsibilities of life. It is tragic that when some children grow toward maturity they have a tendency to think their parents a trifle behind the times! Alexander Pope must have had this thought in mind when he penned the lines —

> And still tomorrow's wiser than today;
> We think our fathers fools, so wise we grow.
> Our wiser sons, no doubt, will think us so.

When it comes to God our Father, who can teach like Him? He has given us rules to walk by and precepts of behavior to follow, whether we are with friends or foes (Nehemiah 9:14; Psalms 25:4; 27:11; John 1:17; Ephesians 4:1; II Timothy 3:15; I John 3: 2, 3).

K. *A father is considerate of the common weaknesses of his child.*

While he never condones wrong, a good father makes every legitimate allowance for unworthy acts, and pardons the erring one if he repents in sorrow. Sinfulness, rebelliousness, ingratitude on the part of a child, all are grievous to the heart of a parent. Doubtless Isaac Watts had the proverb of Solomon in mind, "The eye that mocketh at his father, and despiseth to obey his mother, the ravens of the valley shall pick it out, and the young eagles shall eat it" (Proverbs 30:17) when he wrote —

> What heavy guilt upon him lies,
> Now cursed by his name;
> The ravens shall pick out his eyes
> And eagles eat the same.

Other Bible writers express the fact that he who honors his father shall have long life (Malachi 1:6; Ephesians 6:2). Our Heavenly Father pities the frailties of His children (II Samuel 18:33; Psalm 103:13).

Willingly He forgives those who sin against Him (Psalm 22:5; Hebrews 8: 12). He never belittles sin. Loving His children, He chastens them (Isaiah 1:2; Proverbs 22:18; 23:13). If there is persistence in stubbornness and perversity, God deals firmly with rebellious children (Psalms 1:6; 89:31, 32; Micah 6:13). Thomas Campbell, a 17th century poet, declared —

> I'll meet the raging of the skies
> But not an angry father.

But God's erring children have no need to be afraid of coming before Him.

Correction hurts Him as much as it does His child. He is never overindulgent like Samuel (I Samuel 3:13). He would be unkind, however, never to reprove His sinning child (Proverbs 3:11; 13:1; Isaiah 27:7; Jeremiah 31:18-20; Hebrews 12:9, 10).

L. *A father provides for the future of his children.*

The father of Luke 15 divided his portion with his two sons. It is the duty of parents, if at all able, to lay up for their own. How bountiful is the provision of our Heavenly Father, both for the present and future of His redeemed children! What an inheritance He has reserved for them! (Psalm 31:19; II Timothy 4:8).

God as the Father of all fathers, has a Fatherhood superior to that of an earthly father. An earthly father is subject to earthly passions, and can be justly hard and cruel. But God can never act in this way. His dealings are always consistently just, and in harmony with His character (Jeremiah 31:3). An earthly father, although he may be the best who ever breathed, has not the greatness and glory of God, who has no superior in quality, nor equal in dignity (Revelation 5:13).

An earthly father, in spite of the best of intentions, may not be able to help his child in time of need and difficulty. God, however, is equal to any crisis that may emerge in the life of His own. He never fails. He is ever a present help in trouble (Isaiah 49:8; Philippians 4:19). Earthly fathers are sometimes reduced to beggary, and cannot thereby assist their needy children. Not so God for He is never impoverished (Psalm 34:8-10; Isaiah 54:10).

An earthly father, although he is able to accomplish many beneficial things for his child, does not have the power to convert him from the error of his ways. He can, of course, be the means of leading his children to Christ, but he is powerless to save them from sin. God alone is able to give a sinner a new heart, and make that one His child (Jeremiah 24:7; Ezekiel 36:26).

An earthly father, no matter how long he may remain with his dear ones, is, after all, only mortal and dying, and someday will leave his children fatherless. Death dissolves many precious relationships. Our Father in heaven, who offers Himself as the Father of the fatherless, is immortal. He is the Father of eternity (Isaiah 9:6). He will remain our gracious Father, forever.

An earthly father, although the best of men, is only a man at the best. He can never be perfect. There is always a fly in the ointment. The most wonderful father often has a defect in his qualities. Not so God, who has all perfections and excellencies of the divine being. He always presents His children with the pattern of perfect holiness. Apart from the Son and the Spirit, He has no equal in holiness.

The spirit of heavenly sonship is the greatest and chiefest of all blessings and privileges. Nothing is comparable to that of being children of the living God, through faith in His Son. And as children, it is our duty not to debase our birth by sinful, reproachful actions. As God is the best of fathers, so we must be the best of children.

> Father, I know that all my life
>   Is portioned out for me,
> The changes that will surely come
>   I do not fear to see;
> I ask Thee for a present mind,
>   Intent on pleasing Thee.

For Independence Day

For Independence Day
— July 4th

The patriotic hymn *America* was composed by the Rev. Samuel Francis Smith, in February, 1832, and was first sung the following July 4th in Boston. Each recurring Independence Day has found millions of voices lustily singing its verses.

My country, 'tis of thee,
Sweet land of liberty,
Of thee I sing:
Land where my fathers died,
Land of the pilgrim's pride,
From every mountain side
Let freedom ring!

My native country, thee,
Land of the noble, free,
Thy name I love:
I love thy rocks and rills,
Thy woods and templed hills;
My heart with rapture thrills,
Like that above.

Let music swell the breeze,
And ring from all the trees
Sweet freedom's song:
Let mortal tongues awake;
Let all that breathe partake;
Let rocks their silence break,
The sound prolong.

Our fathers' God, to Thee,
Author of liberty,
To Thee we sing:
Long may our land be bright
With freedom's holy light;
Protect us by Thy might,
Great God, our King!

MEDITATION FOR INDEPENDENCE DAY

THE LAND I LOVE
Philemon

The celebration of the Fourth of July as a national holiday is one that every Christian and all citizens should take cognizance of, seeing it is the most conspicuous day in American history. The signing of the Declaration of Independence in Philadelphia in 1776 revealed the highest form of patriotism, for the principles contained in such an historic document proclaims the right of the individual to think for himself, and to fashion his life without outside compulsion.

Such freedom is akin to the Reformation under Martin Luther. In fact, as Paul Lindemann points out, "There is the relation of cause and effect between the principles of the Great Reformer and those laid down later in the Constitution of the States. For this reason the Church may with special propriety celebrate Independence Day. The holiday also has a special significance for the Church because the principles on which our government has been founded have been conducive to the Church's health and prosperity, and furthermore, because the Church is the most valuable contributing agency to the country's welfare and stability. The greatest patriots are not the most vociferous platform shouters and flag-wavers, but that quiet element in our American constituency which puts into daily practice the principles of Jesus Christ and acts as a conserving salt in our national life."

Benefits accruing from the Constitution are constantly expounded by preachers and politicians, and cannot be declared too often. Let us remind ourselves of a few of these, noting their spiritual counterpart.

A. *Equal Rights for All.*

Caste or class has no claim in America. Any American-born boy can become President of the United States. Abraham Lincoln went from a small log cabin to the White House. Royalty or aristocracy are foreign to our democratic republic. Talent, ability and perseverance can take a poor lad and make him a Rockefeller. Because of the principles of individual liberty and equal rights for all, many immigrants reaching America with hardly a cent to their names, rose to positions of great influence in finance, science, politics and religion.

Christianity and the Constitution are alike in the gospel of equality. Paul desired the converted runaway slave, Onesimus, to be received by his rich master, Philemon, as his brother. Before God all men are equals. When it comes to the blessings of the Gospel of Christ, equal terms of possession are offered to all, irrespective of who and what they are.

B. *Separation Between Church and State.*

America recognizes no state church. Our founding fathers left a land where religious leaders sought to enslave the minds of men, and, landing at Plymouth Rock, determined to be free to worship God according to the dictates of their own Spirit-enlightened consciences. Roger Williams, Baptist preacher and founder of the city of Providence, Rhode Island, also fought for non-interference in religious matters by the State. He saw, as did the originators of the Constitution after him, the evils of a church governed by civil authority, and of a state or nation controlled by ecclesiastical powers.

America, as a nation, protects all religions and favors none. Whether this constitutional law is fully observed is another matter. How grateful we should be for freedom from the tyranny of clerical dominance and ecclesiastical influence so disastrous in European countries and South America! State-controlled churches always mean darkness, spiritual deadness and ritual hypocrisy. In America, Christianity thrives because men are free to worship God as their conscience prescribes. The tragedy Americans face is the loss of

this doctrine of separation of church and state. Roman Catholicism deems itself to be above the state and is subtle in its meddling with governmental affairs and its insistence upon special recognition. Catholics, whether American or any other nationality, are first of all Catholics, not nationals. If the choice had to be made between state or church, the church would come first. From the prophetic point of view, we know that Rome is to control things religiously and politically. The Romish Church is notorious for its abuse of the principles of separation of church and state. America stands for the protection of all religions, even the somewhat unpatriotic religion of Jehovah's Witnesses. Long may freedom reign!

C. *Differing Functions of Separate Spheres.*

Accepting the constitutional principle of separation of church and state, we yet affirm their interdependence. They are two separate areas, ordained for different purposes, operating along different lines. The state is to preserve order, to see right and justice prevail, to protect the weak and punish evil-doers. The state is the official upholder of morality and decency. The church has a purely spiritual function of saving immortal souls by the preaching of the Gospel. It is to confine itself to this area and not to overstep its boundaries into the realm of the state. To the foregoing summary as set forth by Paul Lindemann in *Festival Days* we can add that the state is only prosperous and beneficial in operation as it recognizes that righteousness alone exalts a nation. The church also only functions as the conscience of the state as she remembers and adheres to her spiritual constitution. When the church fully witnesses for her risen Lord, mantled with Pentecostal power, she is the state's greatest ally. The prestige and influence of a state are never higher than the spiritual power of the church. The early church knew how to turn the world around her upside down.

D. *Christians Make the Best Citizens.*

Recognition of the principle of separation of church and state does not free Christians from definite obligations toward the state. There are those who feel that as Christians they should not vote, have anything to do with politics, or engage in the defense of their country in the event of war. Paul, however, makes it clear that we are to be subject to the powers that be. Further, is it not unchristian to enjoy the benefits of a free civilization and all the bounties of a land like America, and not endeavor to preserve them? "To the Christian, the matter of obedience to governmental regulations and the maintenance of civic righteousness is not a matter of expediency," to quote Lindemann again, "but a matter of duty and compulsion laid upon his conscience by the command of the Lord. We are to render unto Caesar the things that are Caesar's."

True patriotism and a nation's moral influence are not dependent upon legislation, but upon spiritual forces such as the church represents. This is why Christians make the best citizens. Although their eternal citizenship is in heaven, they are not so heavenly-minded as to be of no earthly use. The Christian so lives, as he obeys the laws of his land, acts as conserving salt, having as his objective the preservation of the moral health of his nation. The Church of Jesus Christ does not primarily exist to produce loyal, law-abiding citizens. She labors to transform sinners into saints, knowing that spiritual regeneration always results in national purity. Alexander Blackburn's impressive poem is clear on this point —

What Makes a Nation Great?

Not serried ranks with flags unfurled,
Not armored ships that gird the world,
Nor hoarded wealth, nor busy mills,
Not cattle on a thousand hills,
Not sages wise, nor schools, nor laws,
Not boasted deeds in freedom's
    cause —
All these may be, and yet the State
In the eye of God be far from great.
That land is great which knows the
    Lord,
Whose songs are guided by His Word;
Where justice rules 'twixt man and
    man,
Where love controls in art and plan;
Where, breathing in his native air,
Each soul finds joy in praise and
    prayer —
Thus may our country, good and
    great,
Be God's delight — man's best estate.

Racketeers and crooks, who flood the country with their evil, soul-destroying schemes and practices, are not true Americans. They are traitors to the Constitution and deserve to be denaturalized. Avaricious politicians, who place self-interests before state-interests, and fatten on unjust practices, are likewise enemies of the Constitution and earn the limit of punishment their greed and lack of conscience demand. Spies, selling their country down the river and ever working against their nation's welfare and safety, are despicable. Americans who are communists are unworthy of citizenship. If they believe Russia to be a better paradise than America, they should go there and free America of their dangerous influence. As long as they remain here they are a menace to the grandest and freest country in the world. Un-American Americans need to learn this "New Flag Salute" which a loyal citizen conceived —

I am a citizen of the United States of America, and I hereby pledge myself to live my life to the glory of my country.

I will be honest, because my country has no need of a thief.

I will speak the truth, because my country has no need of a liar.

I will be brave, because my country has no need of a coward.

I will work, and not beg, because my country has no need of an idler.

I will be one to prove my country the greatest nation on earth in industry, wisdom, honor and goodness.

On this Independence Day, let us bless God again for America. It is a land of bountiful natural resources — the paradise of plenty — the breadbasket of the world. Within its domains can be found the most varied and beautiful natural beauty anywhere in the world. Amid the expansion of cruel communism, and nations lost to godless aggressors, America is the land of the free. We have a free democracy, freedom of religion, freedom of speech and press, and freedom to vote as we please.

E. *Liberty Is the Watchword.*

The Liberty Bell in the old Independence Hall in Philadelphia is symbolic of all that the magnificent Constitution stands for. Because the Constitution is founded upon the Word of God, we can praise Him anew for the spiritual freedom He has made possible. It avails little, although we have political freedom, if the heart is destitute of the freedom Jesus spoke about (John 8:36).

> He is the freeman whom the truth sets free
> And all are slaves beside.

Paul emphasizes the necessity of this freedom bought by the precious blood of Christ:

> Now the Lord is that Spirit: and where the Spirit of the Lord is, there is liberty (II Corinthians 3:17).
> Stand fast therefore in the liberty wherewith Christ hath made us free, and be not entangled again with the yoke of bondage (Galatians 5:1).

Can we say that this blood-red freedom is ours?

This historic day will mean little if we use it only as an outlet for the patriotic love of our country. If we are grateful to God for all America is and has, let us also praise Him for our Christian heritage and dedicate ourselves anew to His service, that as Christians first and Americans second, we may fulfill His work and will as His servants, and as citizens of these United States. Let us also plead for a God-honoring land. Then will be answered this prayer, as it arises from many a loyal heart on this Independence Day —

> God bless our native land;
> Firm may she ever stand
> Through storm and night;
> When the wild tempests rave,
> Ruler of winds and wave,
> Do Thou our country save
> By Thy great might.

For Vacation Days

For Vacation Days

Among the most unique poems I love
to read are those by William L. Stidger
in, *I Saw God Wash the World* which
includes his reaction as he returned
from a vacation among the mountains.

I have come back from the mountains,
    Back from the snow-white peaks,
Back from the crimson sunsets
    With opal and golden streaks.

Back from the glacial torrents,
    Tumultuous, mad moraines;
Back from the twilight canyons
    And whispering wind refrains.

Leaving behind the horizons
    And waterfalls whipped to spray;
Back from the cliff's sheer reaches
    Where shadows of eagles play.

Back from the pine tree's incense,
    Back from the river's songs;
Back to the beat of traffic
    And surging of human songs.

Back — but I'm bringing with me
    Vision, and song, and scent;
Visions of glacial canyons
    And aspens in worship bent.

Highways of far horizons
    Forever my feet have trod —
For I have come back from the
    mountains
    And climbing the trails with God.

MEDITATION FOR VACATION DAYS

THE SECRET OF A HAPPY VACATION
Mark 6:31

As vacations are much in our minds at the beginning of the summer season, so at this time it may prove helpful to have a simple talk on their need and best use. All of us realize the necessity of employing our annual vacation time wisely and well, so that we can return refreshed and fully strengthened for the manifold tasks ahead.

What sympathy and tender care the Lord Jesus revealed when He exhorted His disciples to "Come . . . apart . . . and rest awhile" (Mark 6:31). He recommended rest after fatigue, and suitable relief from the toils of life. He knew that if His followers did not "come apart," they would not be very long in *coming apart*, or breaking up altogether. Having bodies and minds requiring rest, we need periodical vacations. We shall not be able to serve God day and night without ceasing until we reach heaven. Christ, then, as Lord of the body, considered the weary frame of His own, and al-

lowed His tired workers a time of relaxation or consecrated rest. The reason for a well-earned vacation is stated. The little band lived in a whirl. With so many people coming and going, the disciples hardly had time to eat. An unceasing stream of needy souls arriving and departing, all eager to hear and see the great Teacher, made a short break from such activity imperative.

No matter how happily we may be situated today, or how fortunate we may be in our work, the time comes when the mind is jaded, the brain is weary, and we need to retire from the heat and burden of the day. Consecrated businessmen, hard at it the year round — devoted wives and mothers, accustomed to the daily routine and the common tasks of home life — children who have studied hard at school — all alike need physical and mental rest. Let us therefore discover how we can use our vacations, both pleasurably and profitably.

A. *Accept Them Rightly.*

There are some foolish people who

127

scorn the necessity of taking a vacation. They point to the devil, affirming that he never takes a vacation, so why should they? But who in his right senses wants to copy the devil? It would be better for the world if he did take a long vacation. Before long, however, he will be compelled to take a forced vacation for a thousand years, and how peaceful the earth will be then.

In Glencoe, Scotland, there is a seat with the inscription "Rest and be thankful." So may the soul, through powers that faith bestows, win rest and ease, and bliss that angels share.

It has been pointed out that nature herself makes provision for resting. This appears in the vegetable world when "in winter, seeds are resting in the ground, buds are resting on the boughs." The animate world also takes its rest, when fresh energy is accumulated. So it is with human nature. Medical men tell us that the alarming increase of nervous troubles, insanity and heart disease is due much to the negligence of those who refuse to take necessary rest periods. As the intensity of life increases, rest becomes more vital. So the supreme end of a vacation is to repair the waste and injury of months of strenuous labor. The constant and often monotonous activities of daily life involve the wear and tear of our physical machinery, so we must rest up for repair.

Vacations are necessary from the spiritual point of view. In the rush of life and the stress of work we have not as much time as we should have for meditation upon the deeper things of life. We have to rise early, and work long, so we retire late at night, weary and tired. A vacation enables us to store up the batteries of body, soul and spirit. Physicians remind us that "the

wear and tear" is "greater as life becomes fuller." How true this is of the believer! In the spiritually-minded person, life reaches an intense pitch if lived in the fear of the Almighty, and in the light of eternity. The constant fight with sin, the incessant struggle against those forces alien to God, the persistent attack upon the spiritual life by Satanic influences, the unchanging atmosphere of antagonism to spiritual things where we live and labor, all tell upon the soul. Thus we must have a season of seclusion when we can turn aside for a period from the vitiated atmosphere to which we are accustomed, and repair our wasted bodies and refresh our spirit. And if a vacation is rightly used, we can return to our work and homes with our secret wounds healed, our jaded minds revived and our hearts doubly energized for conflicts ahead. The charm and beauty of nature can minister to tired minds and quicken our desires to serve the Lord with greater devotion.

B. *Take Them Heartily.*

If we would gather gain and gladness from a vacation, we must use it heartily without any trace of a bad conscience. There may be some great souls who feel it more noble and heroic to remain at their post and deny themselves a rest. But if our work is carried through in an upright and honest way, no matter how humble and insignificant our task, then a season of rest can be looked upon as a call of God to recuperate and revitalize our spiritual, physical and mental powers.

C. *Spend Them Unselfishly.*

Vacations have a social aspect as well as a personal one. If we ignore this fact, they will never be beneficial. In the exacting duties of an active life, when so many legitimate things claim our time and attention, there is a tendency to become engrossed in our own battle. We fail to give ourselves up to the happiness of others, as much as we would like to. So if we go away with loved ones and friends, let us strive to live for each other's comfort and joy. If we are selfish, thinking only of our own enjoyment at the expense of inconveniencing others, then the true Christian spirit of the vacation will be missed. Kindly thoughtfulness must be ours. Paul, the champion of Christ, yet urged the limitation of personal liberty in the higher interest of others. Possibly there is no time when we need to remind ourselves of this self-sacrificing principle more than at vacation time, when change of environment throws us among people we have never seen before.

As we pack up and go away, let us determine to be kind, courteous, thoughtful and grateful to those who may serve us. "Evil is wrought for want of thought, as well as want of heart." A vacation, then, will never be well spent, no matter how great the sights we see, or how exhilarating the air we breathe, if we leave behind an unkind memory. Let us ask God to guard our lips and life, so that nothing will escape us while among strangers, causing them to think ill of the Saviour we love and serve.

D. *Consider Them Spiritually.*

The word "holiday" is actually an abbreviation of "holy day," that is, consecrated day. Thus the ultimate end of a holiday or vacation is not only to make us healthier, but also holier men and women. To get the utmost good out of a period of rest should not be a difficult matter. Alas, however, there are some clever people who can get the most out of their *vocation,* but so little out of their *vacation!* When they go away, they seem ill at ease — the hours drag — it is hard for them to while away the time, so they appear happier when back at the old grind again. Such restless souls lose the sweetest ministries of God, whereby strength is gathered for the long days of winter. If rest days are to be profitable, there are three secrets to be observed:

1. *Go with Christ.*

When the Master invited his weary disciples to turn aside for relaxation, He did not say, "Go," but "Come," suggesting that He went with them. They had been with Him in the thick of things, amid the crowds who claimed so much time, energy and thought. Now He wanted to get away with them from the pressure of everyday labor. Evidently the disciples were not disappointed or chafed at the thought of Christ's going with them on their brief vacation. To have Him with them was not galling or a restriction of liberty. They felt that the season of rest would be a failure without the tireless Worker who would also be their best holiday Companion.

Is it not unspeakably foolish to try to leave Him out of our pleasures? Doubtless you have heard of the little girl who, the night before the family went away for the annual vacation, in saying her prayers, said, "Good-by, God, we are off on our vacation." If we forget Him, it does not matter where we go, for sin will have its opportunity and spoil the sunshine of our vacation. If we take Him with us, every leisure hour will be twice blessed, every flower will be more beautiful, every brook will sing sweeter music to our ears. Not only so, but we shall return to the monotonous tasks with added joy, conscious that our leisure was not secularized.

2. *Learn to know God better.*

Tennyson, kneeling beside a brook, watching the movements of the weeds and running water, remarked most reverently to his friends, "How beautiful God is!" He felt the outer and inner stimulus of natural beauty. If, like the poet, we use our eyes, our vacation can be hallowed by finding God everywhere. If we muse upon His handiwork, money saved for and spent on a vacation will be worthwhile. Relaxing amid scenes of beauty and peace, we learn that God is the unhurried One. Leaving behind the fret and fever of a busy, bustling life and drinking in the quiet, patient, yet unconquerable mood of nature, we come to see how God carries on His work silently but surely. The peace brooding over the landscape grips our troubled heart and acts as a healing medium and we are refreshed. Our mind and body react healthily to life and beauty all around. Beholding the fascinating variety of nature, we remember that the storm and sunshine, producing so much loveliness, mirror life itself. Moral beauty cannot be woven out of monotony and smoothness. Our joys and sorrows, adversity and prosperity, combine to produce strength of character and beauty of spirit. How enriching are such holiday reflections!

If we go to the ocean, with its life-giving breezes, changing tides, and rolling waves, we can meditate upon the majesty of God, for "the sea is his, and he made it" (Psalm 95:5). If we go to some quiet country spot, with its soft, balmy air, we can follow the footprints of our Creator as we walk the lanes and roam the fields.

One remarkable feature of the American way of life is the summer Bible conference ministry, whereby all ages can combine vision with a vacation.

There are hundreds of Bible conferences over the land, among mountains, by lakes, in areas noted for their scenic beauty, where believers can relax and feed their souls at the same time. Eternity alone will reveal what the cause of Christ owes to these summer conferences, at which physical strength is renewed, and life is blessedly transfigured.

3. *Shun the Devil.*

It is to be deplored that far too many people look upon a vacation as the time when all religious restraints and influences can be cast off. They do things in strange places, where they are not known and where familiar eyes cannot see them, things which they would not do at home.

Satan continues to be active when saints are on vacation. Often he succeeds, during this time, in undermining the consecration of those who are not watchful. Attractive amusements and questionable enjoyments are plentiful, and if time is not guarded and truly spent well, the devil has plenty of mischief for idle hands to do. If we simply kill time while away, instead of our vacation recreating us, it destroys our energies and desires.

When away from home we must be careful to preserve our Sundays and seek out God's house where His Word is faithfully preached. May we never be guilty of desecrating the Lord's Day while on our vacation! "Being let go, they (Peter and John) went to their own company" (Acts 4:23). The company we seek on a vacation is always a true indication of our spiritual life.

Take one or two good, wholesome books in your suitcase, and use the spare hours to store the mind with noble thoughts. In the course of a busy life there is not much time for the reading of great books. A restful vacation, however, provides us with opportunities for enriching the mind. Of course, in packing all that is necessary, the Bible will not be forgotten. Any kind of vacation is misspent unless there are quiet moments every day for meditation on the Book. Linger awhile in the King's meadows of Holy Writ, where the grass is ever green, and the water as clear as crystal, and every part of you will be refreshed. In the ordinary course of life, when the soul is agitated by cares, tormented by problems, absorbed by insistent duties, we are not always able to see clearly the deeper things of God. This is one reason why He ordains a time of rest, a cessation of toil, when we can enter more fully into His secrets.

As you take your vacation, then, guard against the devil who walketh about seeking those whom he may devour. Respond to the Master's invitation, and go apart with Him. Let Him be your Companion, Guard and Guide, and all will be well. No regrets will be yours when you return to the everyday toils of life.

A Prayer for Vacation Days

Loving Father, who didst make this earth so fair, open our eyes to see its wonders and our hearts to feel its beauty. In our days of refreshment and recreation, draw us nearer to Thee through the things which Thou hast made. May the joy of Thy sunshine, the quiet of Thy forests, the murmur of Thy streams, and the steadfast strength of Thy everlasting hills teach us the deep secret of Thy peace. Calm our fretful spirits. Deepen the current of our shallow lives. Renew in us faith and courage, physical strength and spiritual vision, that we may know ourselves to be safely held in Thy strong hands, and that we may joyfully conform our lives to Thy great purposes.

From this life, so near to nature's heart, may we drink in new strength to help us reach the restless hearts of men. Give us Thy secret and the power to share it with our fellowmen, that we may go back to the world and its duties, stronger, simpler, sweeter. Thus may we become more worthy messengers of Him who saw His Father's goodness in the sparrow's flight, and His Father's love in the beauty which clothes the lilies of the field. We ask it for His dear sake. Amen.

For Labor Day

For Labor Day

This is the gospel of labor, ring it, ye
    bells of the kirk
The Lord of Love came down from
    above to live with the men who
    work,
This is the rose that He planted, here
    in the thorn-cursed soil —
Heaven is blessed with perfect rest,
    but the blessing of earth is toil.

           — Henry van Dyke

Work for some good, be it ever so
    slowly,
Cherish some flower, be it ever so
    lowly,
Labor — all labor is noble and holy.

         — Frances Sargent Osgood

O God, Thou mightiest Worker of the
universe, Source of all strength and
Author of all unity, We pray Thee for
our brothers the industrial workers of
the nation. As their work binds them
together in toil and danger, may their
hearts be knit together in a strong
sense of their common interests and
so fulfill the law of Christ by bearing
the common burdens. Grant the
organizations of labor quiet patience
and prudence in all disputes. Raise
up leaders of able mind, and large
heart, and give them grace to follow
wise counsel. Bless all classes of our
nation and build up a great body of
workers strong of limb, clear of mind,
glad of labor, striving together for the
final brotherhood of all men; through
Jesus Christ our Lord. Amen.

           — W. Rauchsenbusch

MEDITATION FOR LABOR DAY

THE DIGNITY OF LABOR
Psalm 104:23

Longfellow wrote of "The nobility of labor — the long pedigree of toil." A similar sentiment was expressed by the 16th century writer, Charles Swain —

> There's a dignity in labor
> Truer than e'er pomp arrayed.

Around the world Labor Day is recognized at different times. In many European countries the first day of May, "May Day," is observed as Labor Day. In America it falls on the first Monday of September, and is a legal holiday in honor of, or in the interest of, working men as a class. Such a day means more in those countries where the masses were held in slavery, but came to their deliverance through the sacrifice and untiring efforts of noble labor leaders.

Samuel Gompers, famous American Federation of Labor leader, wrote in 1898 a message that leaders of labor, as well as of industry, should never forget —

> Labor Day differs in every essential from the other holidays of the year of any country. All other holidays are, in a more or less degree, connected with conflicts and battles, of man's prowess over man, of strife and discord for greed or power, of glories achieved by one nation over another.

> Labor Day, on the other hand, marks a new epoch in the annals of human history. It is at once a manifestation of reverence for the struggles of the masses against tyranny and injustice from time immemorial; an impetus to battle for the right in our day for men, women and children of our time, and gives hope and encouragement for the attainment of the aspirations for the future of the human family.

> It is devoted to no man, living or dead; to no sect, sex, race or nation. It is founded upon the highest principles of humanity, is as broad in its scope as the universe.

As a carpenter, Jesus taught the world the dignity of labor. There, at His bench, we have the toil of divinity revealing the divinity of toil. For something like fifteen years, He knew what it was to earn His own bread by the sweat of His brow. And this we know — His work was the best. He was never guilty of turning out anything shabby or shoddy. He gave

135

manual labor a dignity it has somehow lost. By example, He taught men, as Isaac Watts expresses it in *The Thief* that —

Hands were made for honest labor,
Not to plunder or to steal.

Thomas Dekker of the 15th century wrote — "Honest labor wears a lovely face." The laboring Christ, who invited all who labor to come to Him for rest, certainly exemplified such a sentiment (Matthew 11:28).

A. *The Obligation of Labor.*

All men must work. The Bible tells us that if man fails to work, he cannot eat. Charles Lamb asked —

Who first invented work and bound the free
And holiday-rejoicing spirit down?

God's Word tells us that because of his sin, man would have to labor in the sweat of his face until he returned to dust (Genesis 3:19). Paul tells us that we must work with our hands the thing which is good (Ephesians 4:28). So we live in a world in which "Man goeth forth unto his work and to his labour until the evening" (Psalm 104:23).

An unnamed ruler of the synagogue said, "There are six days in which men ought to work" (Luke 13:14). And all through the Bible, work, spiritual and secular, is commanded. No man can believe in the Bible and yet not believe in work. Horace, the Latin philosopher, wrote that "Life gives nothing to mortals except great labor." Several proverbs echo a similar truth —

Man is born to labor, and a bird to fly.
No sweet without some sweat.

A Scotch proverb expresses it —

Naething is got without pains
Except dirt and long nails!

Dr. Walter Chalmers Smith gave us the lines —

Dusting, darning, drudging, nothing is great or small,

Nothing is mean or irksome, love will hallow it all.

And this proves that women, as well as men, must work. It is only partially true that "men must work and women must weep." Men weep as well as work, and a woman's work is never done.

An Oriental proverb has it that the devil tempts every man except an idle man who tempts the devil. Legitimate labor is noble and beneficial in every way, and it was because of this that Ovid prayed, "When I die, may I be taken in the midst of my work." How fitting it is to die in harness, no matter what sphere we represent.

B. *The Idolatry of Labor.*

While God has ordained that man ought to work and must work, He never commanded him to overwork, which is always the danger of industrious workers. Don Vaughan wrote of "The Idolatry of Work," and too many make a god of their work.

All work and no play
Makes Jack a dull boy.

What a disastrous blunder it is to be so lost in labor, as to be negligent of other important phases of life. To be obsessed in business and forget home, social and church obligations is to court ruin. It is, of course, serious for a nation when it loses its zest for work. Lack of love for labor makes for decline of national character. Idleness is also disastrous for the individual. In a lazy hour David stained his noble character. Some, however, swing to the other extreme and are so greedy for work and the material gain it may bring, that all desire for necessary rest and refreshment wastes away. "Come unto me, all ye that labour . . . and I will give you rest." Sir Lewis Morris has reminded us that —

This of old is sure,

That change of toil is toil's sufficient cure.

It is here that we can appreciate the limitation suggested by the synagogue ruler, "There are *six* days in which man ought to work." Six days — not seven. God claims only one day out of seven for Himself, but man is guilty of infringing upon the example and commandment of God. The day of rest is menaced, if not by physical toil, then by exhausting pursuits and pleasures. The average working man of today forgets that —

A Sabbath well spent
Brings a week of content
And strength for the toils of the morrow.
But a Sabbath ill spent
What e'er may be gained
Is a certain forerunner of sorrow.

C. *The Abuse of Labor.*

Such abuse takes on many forms. Great nations like America and Britain have traveled far in advantages for workers. Not too many years ago the average worker had little opportunity to regain expended energy. Many worked a ten to twelve hour day, with only Sunday off, and sometimes not even that. They had no paid vacations, no fringe benefits. Gradually, however, with the growth of labor unions, the majority of workers now have an eight-hour day, five days a week, and advantages men and women of seventy years ago would never have dreamed of. Wages are at an all-time high and conditions are unsurpassed. All of this is to the good, if the worker gives an honest day's work for an honest day's pay. A common complaint, however, is slackness on the part of the well-paid laborer. Many employers feel they are not getting their money's worth. John Webster of the 15th century wrote —"Laboring men count the clock oftenest." Many who have to work with their hands are not clock watchers, nor are mothers who toil when others play or sleep. Wherever, or at whatever we labor, let us never be guilty of giving less than we are paid for. Let us never abuse the improved labor conditions of our advanced age (Proverbs 13:4).

Another form of the abuse of labor is cheap foreign labor, or the slave camp for which Communism is notorious. Forced labor, with hardly enough to keep body and soul together, is diabolical. What a paradise America is compared to Siberia, where untold thousands are broken in spirit and body because their masters were ignorant of the dignity of labor.

The labors of the poor make the pride of the rich;
The pleasures of the rich are bought with the tears of the poor.

The masters of the Kremlin continue to fatten on the despair and degradation of the enslaved captives who toil without rest or reward. In his Labor Day speech, 1953, President Eisenhower hailed the freedom of American workers today, and said that they give the lie to the sly evil of the promises of totalitarianism —

We contemplate with renewed appreciation the principles that make and keep us a free people. The workers of America are witnesses before the world of the strength, the pride, and the prosperity that alone can be won by free labor.

They are strong in their independent unions. They are proud beyond the temptations of political subservience. They are an indestructible bulwark of free government. These witnesses to freedom's blessings give the lie to the sly evil of the promises of totalitarianism. They mock the false insinuation that economic well-being can be purchased only at the cost of political freedom. They are the final answer to those who prate freedom and practice slavery, who excuse terror and aggression in the name of concern for the very workers whose lives they stifle.

Free American labor has won for itself the enjoyment of a standard of living unmatched in history. The contemporary world knows no comparison with it. There is only brutal contrast to it.

To this, there is no more pitiful and dramatic testimony than the food which this free people has been able to send to feed hundreds of thousands suffering the peculiar torments of the proletarian paradise of eastern Germany.

This is a day sincerely to salute American labor: its freedom, its dignity, its matchless productive genius — and the lesson it records for all men to read, for all time to come.

There is another form of abuse of labor the prophet warns against. "Wherefore do ye . . . labour for that which satisfieth not?" (Isaiah 55:2). Robbers, gamblers, tricksters, and all who live off their crime and evil ways, scheme and labor in unprofitable ways. They bring no satisfaction to themselves or to others. Many of the rich who never work with their hands, labor hard and long at their pleasures and pursuits for killing time without profit to society. "Labour not for the meat which perisheth," said Jesus, "but for that meat which endureth unto everlasting life" (John 6:27). Full accomplishment is always the portion of those who have a mind to work in an honorable way for honorable ends (Nehemiah 4:6).

D. *The Reward of Labor.*

Noble labor brings its own reward. The laborer is worthy of his hire (Luke 10:7; I Timothy 5:18). If our task is honorable, the Lord God blesses us in all the work of our hands (Deuteronomy 14:29). "He that gathereth by labour shall increase" (Proverbs 13:11). Solomon asked, "What profit hath a man of all his labour which he taketh

under the sun?" (Ecclesiastes 1:3). There is much profit. The Greeks had a saying, "The gods sell us good things for hard work." A Dutch proverb reads, "Labor warms, sloth harms."

While labor organizations have secured the reward which labor deserves, we must not forget the teaching of the Bible in respect to contentment with wages (Luke 3:14; Matthew 20:1-16; Hebrews 13:5). If we are the Lord's, no matter what secular work may be ours, if we are underpaid for what we do, our righteous Master will see to it that what is just will be forthcoming.

That labor itself compensates has been the theme of poet and philosopher. A Latin proverb has it, "If doctors fail you, let these three be your doctors: a cheerful mind; labor; and moderate diet." George Meredith wrote that "Work is both food and medicine." Rousseau expressed it, "Temperance and labor are the two true physicians of man." Shakespeare, in *Macbeth*, says that, "The labor we delight in physics pain." Carlyle wrote of the man who sings at his work. Isaac Bickerstaff, of the 18th century, gave us the verse —

> There was a jolly miller once
>   lived on the River Dee;
> He worked and sang from morn till
>   night;
> no lark more blithe as he.

In his *Maid of the Mill* he expresses a similar thought —

> 'Tis a sure sign work goes on merrily,
> When folks sing at it.

To this agrees the old Latin proverb, "Labors accomplished are pleasant." Paul has the exhortation, "Whatsoever ye do, do it heartily, as to the Lord, and not unto men" (Colossians 3:23). When he wrote this, it was to those who were more or less slaves, and knew nothing of well-paid labor and beneficial labor conditions.

If we do with our might what our hands find to do, diligent labor will bring us divine and human approval. A day of honest toil, although tiring, will produce a night of restful sleep and gathered strength for yet another day's work. Shakespeare in *Macbeth* speaks of —

> Sleep that knits up the ravellid sleave of care;
> The death of each day's life, sore labour's bath.

E. *The Exemplar of Labor.*

All who labor can find an ideal model in God the worker. He is not an inert, inactive deity, but a *working* God — One who is ceaselessly active. The Incarnate Son revealed this aspect of the Almighty Father's being when He said, "My Father worketh" (John 5:17). God Himself works! It is therefore ungodlike not to work if able. Jesus tirelessly labored, and in doing so He reflected God's diligent labor. Godliness and sloth cannot coexist. Through the centuries Christ has inspired men to work — it is one of His social achievements. His example constrains men to fill their hands with honest, beneficial toil.

Because of our physical make-up, we find labor wearying. Even Jesus was "weary with His journey." God, however, is ever at it — is never weary — never slumbers nor sleeps. He has always worked, and works "even until now." The ancient Greeks pictured their gods as living in a distant Olympus, quaffing their nectar, pursuing their own pleasures, but aloof from and unconcerned with the affairs of men. How different is the God of the Bible!

The deist of the eighteenth century treated God as a kind of absentee landlord. He had made the world: He had set it going — as a watchmaker might set a watch going — and then left it to itself. This, however, is not the Spirit's revelation of God, even though there are those who think of Him as remote, aloof, unwatchful and unconcerned.

The God of the Christian is an active God, an ever-present God, the mighty, invisible Worker in the world. The materialistic outlook is that the only forces at work in the world are those forces we can feel and see. Tangible and visible powers claim our attention. God does not seem to count. Alliances of nations, armies and navies, stockpiles of bombs — these are the materialistic forces to reckon with. The active, working, practical God is not considered. Napoleon, although a supreme military genius, continually forgot the laboring God. When he set out on his Russian campaign, he took everything into account save God. He did not reckon with the frost and snow, and with his grand army ruined, he confessed: "God Almighty has been too much for me."

Looking around, it would seem as if dictators and politicians are trying to run God's world. But amid the distress of nations, let us not give way to panic or unbelieving anxiety. God is still on the job. "My Father worketh even until now." Forces of evil are rampant. Iniquity abounds all over the world. It would seem as if the devil is the only one at work. Amid the deadly handiwork of hell, however, our hope is in God who is working out His purpose. Godlessness is everywhere apparent, but ours is not a godless universe. God is still busy at His saving and redeeming labor. How constant and untiring is He in such a sacred task! The great object of His mighty, costly, ceaseless labors is the deliverance of souls from the tyranny of sin.

What a picture Jesus gave us of the unwearying work of God! *Even until now.* He never takes a holiday. He never works by the clock. He is no time saver. His redeeming ministry never ceases. With man, disappointment sometimes leads to abandonment of labor, but God never gives up. He is long-suffering. When Sir Isaac Newton finished his *Principia*, he left the precious manuscript lying about the room. The next morning the maid, thinking the bundle of manuscript was but waste paper, used it to light the fire. The great scientist simply had to begin all over again. This is what God is constantly doing. Disappointed, He never abandons hopeless cases. With infinite patience He resumes and continues His work. Laboring in His cause, His workers are inspired by His unwearied patience. John Milton would have us live and labor —

"As ever in my great Taskmaster's eye."

For Harvest Festival Day

For Harvest Festival Day

Sowing and Reaping

He bids me go forth in the morning
  When everything seems so bright,
And scatter the seed all day long
  Till evening and oncoming night.

And when come the evening shadows
  And the day is almost gone —
"Thou knowest whether shall
      prosper" —
  Keep on with the sowing — Keep
  on!

Some seed will fall by the wayside,
  And some where the rocks abound,
And some mid the thorns and briars,
  But some will fall on good ground.

Sometimes the load seems heavy,
  Sometimes in sorrow I weep;
But I know if in tears I am sowing
  In joy and gladness I'll reap.

What joy at the final ingathering
  With Christ in the "Harvest Home,"
When the reapers from all the great
  fields
  Bringing their sheaves shall come!
                — Frank A. McGaw

Sow a Thought — Reap an Act
Sow an Act — Reap a Habit
Sow a Habit — Reap a Character
Sow a Character — Reap a Destiny

MEDITATION FOR HARVEST
FESTIVAL DAYS

THE HARVEST HOME
Jeremiah 8:20

An outstanding feature of the Bible is its use of natural objects in the declaration of divine truths. The entire realm of nature is ransaked for fitting symbols of our spiritual life. For example, when the Master illustrated His own work and ours, He spoke of sowers going out to sow.

He spoke of lilies, vines, and corn
The sparrow and the raven;
And words so natural yet so wise
Were on men's hearts engraven.

For a description of Christ's own beauty we are taken to the rose of Sharon and the lily of the valley (Song of Solomon 2:1).

As a root out of a dry ground, we have a foreshadowing of His humility (Isaiah 53.2); the brevity of life is pictured in the fading leaf (Isaiah 64:6).

For a reminder of God's care and provision we go to the lilies of the field (Matthew 6:28).

Thorns and thistles are expressions of the ugliness of sin (Genesis 3:18).

A lifeless, formal religion is before us in the barren fig tree with nothing but leaves (Mark 11:13).

The true nature of sinners is portrayed as tares among wheat and fit only for burning (Matthew 13:25-40).

Saints, on the other hand, are wheat among tares (Luke 22:31).

The devil, because of his subtlety, is likened unto a wicked sower — an enemy (Matthew 13:39).

In many parts of the world, this is the season when harvest is recognized. The Jews celebrated the Feast of Tabernacles at harvest season. Many churches have a Harvest Festival Sunday, when with fruits and flowers displayed in the church, gratitude is expressed to God as the giver of every good gift. Waving fields of golden corn, valleys clothed with flocks and orchards with their fragrance of flowers and luscious fruits, all alike proclaim the liberality of God.

In many a country homestead a custom is observed called "Harvest Home." With all the harvest gathered in, workers and friends gather together for a feast. Perhaps it was something like

143

this that Jeremiah the prophet had in mind when he wrote, "The harvest is past, the summer is ended, and we are not saved" (8:20). Such a "harvest" test resolves itself into two parts:

Seasonable Opportunities: Harvest — Summer

Slighted Opportunities: Past ended, not saved.

Seasonable Opportunities

The prophet refers to summer and harvest. All seasons, however, are necessary to produce a full harvest.

A. *The Four Seasons.*

As there are four evangelists represented by the four gospels, so there are four evangelists of nature, or four seasons, each speaking with a loud voice to the soul of man. Four, it is said, is the number of grace.

1. *We have Spring!*

With the magic touch of spring, insects awaken, seeds rise from the dead, trees put on their lovely dress, the birds become vocal with praise.

O to be in England,
Now that April's there!

But any place is beautiful when this welcome season comes around. Everything is so fresh, as the voice of heaven cries, "Awake, thou that sleepest!" And spring answers to childhood, which is life's fair morning.

2. *We have Summer!*

There is glory all around when the sun blazes forth in all its meridian splendor and produces a riot of colors, banishes our sicknesses and gladdens our hearts. And, at the zenith of its power, the Sun can represent youth with all its beauty and strength. "The glory of a young man is his strength."

3. *We have Autumn!*

Autumn is the season when the leaves change color and drop; the time of shorter days and darker nights. And as autumn chases summer, we witness the ingathering of the fruits of the earth. Here we have a simile of middle life, when the years seem shorter and decay sets in.

4. *We have Winter!*

As the year ends we come to cold, ice, snow, frost and chilly winds. And if our years be "four score" they are often labor and sorrow. Ultimately, like the old year, we expire, only to begin life anew in God's beautiful country where they have no seasons and we never grow old.

B. *The Four Secrets of Harvest.*

It is a fascinating sight, indeed, to watch the ingathering of harvest, or the "leading in," as it is called. And any harvest proclaims God's faithfulness to His own promise, for did He not declare, "While earth remaineth, seed time and harvest shall not cease"?

Outlining the four chief elements in a good harvest, we have —

1. *Prepared Soil!*

For days farmers are active in plowing, turning and breaking up hard soil. All fallow ground must be deeply stirred. Thus is it with the deep, convicting work of the Spirit. His plow is necessary for our correction and sanctification, so we have the trials and upheavals of life.

2. *Buried Seed!*

Next in order comes the scattering of precious seed over the bare, brown soil. Seeds are of all kinds, and are planted with care. And this is our solemn and constant responsibility. The seed of the Word must be scattered far and wide. Alas, some hearts are full of buried gospel seed which has not taken root or come to fruition.

3. *Diligent Toil!*

In turn there follows the labor and anxiety of farmers and gardeners. Long days and anxious night all help to produce a bountiful harvest. So we think of the tears, prayers, anxieties and efforts of godly souls over the salvation of lost men and women. Often we find ourselves dismayed and discouraged for, although we plow and sow, we seldom reap. Yet we have the assurance that if we are faithful, we shall come home rejoicing, bringing our sheaves with us.

4. *Goodness of God!*

All the forces of nature work harmoniously together under the guidance of God for the harvests of earth. Wind, rain, sun and atmospheric forces are all necessary if man is to gather a harvest. Farmers, no matter how diligent and thorough, are ultimately dependent upon God. Thus is it with the spiritual harvest. Our very best is useless apart from the influences of the Holy Spirit. We may pray, labor, weep and give. The increase, however, comes from God.

C. *The Fourfold Spiritual Application.*

Jeremiah used the figures of summer and harvest in a spiritual sense. Therefore let us seek to discover what these illustrations from the realm of nature represent in our own lives.

First of all, we think of our contact with Christian and spiritual privileges. We live in a land of open Bibles, religious liberty and godly influences. Multitudes are surrounded with abundant opportunities of being saved. But the tragedy is, in spite of all inducements to salvation, countless numbers are not saved.

Then there are those who have been through revivals when the Spirit of God was tremendously active. Harvests of souls have come and gone, yet they are not saved. And men are harder to win if they have passed through many a reaping time when the gospel sickle gathered in the sheaves.

Further, we are never without solemn reminders of death and eternity. The grave is gathering in a sad and terrible harvest. Death, the reaper, is bringing in his sheaves, and yet so many are not saved. Solemn warnings pass unheeded.

Again, farmers always rejoice in extra sunshine and unusual harvesting weather. If rain and storms do not hinder in the "ingathering of summer fruits," reapers are happy indeed. And do we not bless God for the lengthy day of grace, which has already lasted for over 1,900 years? But somehow the goodness of God for the lengthy day is not leading the majority to repentance. The door of mercy is still open, but sinblinded souls fail to take advantage of a harvest time which soon will cease.

Slighted Opportunities

How poignant is Jeremiah's phrase, "And we are not saved." In spite of all subtle and outright influences, the saving grace of God was resisted. We think of the concern of the farmer to secure his harvest and of how he works with feverish haste to reap his fields before soaking rains and fierce storms overtake the crops. Would that souls were as anxious over their eternal safety! The rains of judgment and the storms of divine wrath are about to break over a guilty world — yet so many are indifferent.

God grant that those of us who are preachers and Christian workers may catch something of God's passion for the lost. The day of salvation is growing shorter and the world is heading up for the great harvest of tribulation. Oh, for grace to labor with consecrated enthusiasm and unabated devotion for the salvation of those who, if they die in sin, must be gathered in bundles and burned in fire.

From Jeremiah, the weeping prophet, as he has been called, we can learn much regarding the evangelical truth of salvation.

A. *Why We Are Not Saved*

There are at least seven reasons why many are not saved. For example, there is the unwillingness to repent. "No man repented," or "every one turned to his own course" (8:6). These unrepentant souls were unashamed in their sin. They had ceased to blush (8:12). Sin was gloried in, treated as a joke.

Ignorance is another reason why some are not saved. They "know not the judgment of the Lord" (8:7). And because of lack of knowledge they are destroyed (Luke 19:42; John 4:10).

There is also rejection of a divine testimony. "They have rejected the word of the Lord" (8:9). Too often, truth is listened to but not applied. Or, doped with unbelief, the devil persuades us that what we hear is not true.

Harkening to false voices is another barrier to salvation. "Peace . . . no peace" (8:11). Preaching that never makes us feel uneasy or uncomfortable lacks divine unction. God help us to function as true prophets!

Jeremiah also mentions a wrong conception of salvation. "We looked for peace but no good came; and for a time of health, and behold trouble" (8:15). And the difficulty with many is that they want an easy time. They will become disciples if they can walk with Christ in silver slippers or on the sunny side of the street.

Dependence upon wrong methods is before us in the words, "The snorting of his horses . . . his strong ones" (8:16). Expected help from Egypt was a common fault of Israel, and punishment was hers for leaning on such a broken reed. As a chosen nation, Israel was also guilty of depending upon her privileges and position. Similar folly is ours if we rest upon our ceremonies, prayers, morality, church membership and Christian parentage.

As the result of Israel's unwillingness to turn from her ways, God was provoked to anger (8:19), and persistence in sin and rebellion occasions the displeasure and judgment of God.

B. *Why We Should Be Saved.*

Men should be saved because God wills their salvation. All the while souls remain lost, the divine heart is hurt (8:21). God mourns when He is robbed of those created by His power. Another reason why men should be saved is because of coming judgment. What desolation will be experienced when the Lord thrusts in His sickle and reaps! (Revelation 14:15). Let us pray unceasingly that unheeding multitudes may be led to repentance as they think of the lake of fire.

C. *How We Can Be Saved.*

Jeremiah pleads with the people to turn from all false hopes to healing balm in Gilead (8:22). Such balm, however, could only heal bodily bruises and diseases. The precious blood of Christ provides a healing balm for all spiritual ills. Thus we must look away unto the Lord if we would be saved (Isaiah 45:22).

If you are unsaved, my friend, remember that the cold, dark winter of judgment is coming. Before long the summer of grace will end, and if you die in your sin, then in hell you must reap what you have sown. The only harvest for you then will be that of a sinful life and despised opportunities. Will you therefore not repent and turn to the Saviour? As farmers rejoice over a bountiful harvest, will you not allow the Spirit to gather you in? Let the hearts of those who have sown many a prayer and tear for your salvation

rejoice because of your definite acceptance of Christ as Saviour.

> Whether sown in the darkness, or
>   sown in the light:
> Whether sown in weakness, or sown
>   in might:
> Whether sown in meekness, or sown
>   in wrath,
> In the broadest highway, or the
>   shadowy path:
>> Sure will the harvest be!

For Reformation Day

For Reformation Day

A mighty fortress is our God,
　A bulwark never failing;
Our helper He, amid the flood
　Of mortal ills prevailing.
　　For still our ancient foe
　　Doth seek to work us woe;
　　His craft and power are great,
　　And, armed with cruel hate,
　　On earth is not his equal.

Did we in our own strength confide,
　Our striving would be losing,
Were not the right Man on our side,
　The Man of God's own choosing.
　　Dost ask who that may be?
　　Christ Jesus, it is He;
　　Lord Sabaoth is His name,
　　From age to age the same,
　　And He must win the battle.

And though this world, with devils
　filled,
　Should threaten to undo us,
We will not fear, for God hath willed
　His truth to triumph through us.
　　The prince of darkness grim —
　　We tremble not for him;
　　His rage we can endure,
　　For lo! his doom is sure,
　　One little word shall fell him.

That Word above all earthly powers —
　No thanks to them — abideth;
The Spirit and the gifts are ours
　Through Him who with us sideth.
　　Let goods and kindred go,
　　This mortal life also;
　　The body they may kill:
　　God's truth abideth still,
　　His kingdom is forever.
　　　　　　　　　— Martin Luther

MEDITATION FOR REFORMATION DAY

THE MONK WHO SHOOK THE WORLD
Romans 1:17

Many of the Reformed and Lutheran churches recognize in their calendar what is known as "Reformation Day," usually observed on the 31st of October. Sermons are preached during this day on the significant religious movement in Western Europe, early in the sixteenth century, which resulted in the formation of various Protestant churches.

On the eleventh day of November, 1483, in the small town of Eisleben, Germany, Hans and Margaret Luther gazed proudly at their firstborn, but they little knew what a potent force he was to become in the religious world. The entire world was shrouded in spiritual darkness because of the tyrannical power of fanatical churchmen, whose yoke Martin Luther was to break. In those dark Middle Ages it pleased God to lead one great soul through a spiritual experience of sin so deep and abiding that there was awakened in him an intense craving to know the truth of the Gospel. It was then that Martin Luther was chosen of God to be the harbinger of light to the Rome-ridden people of Europe. The conflict between the two opposing forces of light and darkness had first to be fought out in his own soul. God first shook the monk, and then the monk shook the world. That the Reformer was detached from the ways of the world is summarized, caustically, for us in the lines of Thackeray —

> Then sing as Martin Luther sang,
> As Doctor Martin Luther sang,
> "Who loves not wine, woman and song,
> He is a fool his whole life long."

Thomas Carlyle remarked that "Luther is one of our spiritual heroes, a prophet to his own country and time." Browning wrote of him as "Grand rough old Martin Luther." Matthew Arnold, in his *Mixed Essays* gives us the suggestive contrasts —

We have the Philistine in Religion —Luther;

The Philistine in Politics — Cromwell;

The Philistine in Literature — Bunyan.

But in the Christian world at large, we

151

owe much to his dynamic witness, and it may prove profitable to remind ourselves of his life and labors.

A. *His Birth and Boyhood.*

As already indicated, Martin Luther saw the light of day in Saxony, in the year 1483. His parents were poor but pious. Hans, his father, was a mine laborer, who earned about enough to keep the beast of poverty from the door. Hans and his wife attended a Winter Fair in Eisleben, and while there she was taken with travail pains. Refuge was sought in a nearby house, where she bore the child whom Rome would come to fear. As Carlyle expresses it, "In the whole world that day there was not a more entirely unimportant-looking pair of people than this miner and his wife. And yet what were all the emperors and popes and potentates in comparison? There was born here, once more, a mighty man, whose light was to flame as the beacon over long centuries and epochs of the world, the whole world and its history was waiting for the man." Such a lowly birth takes us back to another Who was born in still more humble surroundings. The Christ born in the manger was the One for whom Luther lived and fought.

Luther's earlier years were characterized by constant privation. Carlyle tells us that he had to beg, as the school children in those times did, singing for alms and bread, from door to door. "Hardship, vigorous necessity, was the poor boy's companion; no man nor no thing would put on a false face to flatter Martin Luther. It was through hard days, and not among the show of things, that he had to grow." He was a boy of rude figure, yet with weak health. His was a large, greedy soul, full of all faculty and sensibility, and he suffered greatly. Like his Master

before him, Luther was a stranger to affluence. Hans gave his eager son the best education he could. Endowed with a great intellect, Luther had a hunger for knowledge. He set out to study law, but his ways were not God's ways.

B. *His Spiritual Experiences.*

The experiences of Martin Luther were as varied as they were fascinating. He had a quest for God. With Job he could say, "Oh that I knew where I might find him!" (Job 23:3). God, of course, has different methods of dealing with different men.

1. *Luther the Monk.*

Alexis, a companion of Luther's, was struck dead with lightning during a thunderstorm at Erfurt. When he fell dead at Luther's feet, the future reformer, then only nineteen years of age, was so impressed that he determined to devote his life to God and His service. It thus came about that, against his father's wishes, he entered the Augustine Convent to become a monk.

Although this can be thought of as a wrong step in Luther's spiritual history, it was yet overruled by God for the good of the Christian faith. Carlyle says of this decision, "This was probably the first light-point in the history of Luther, his purer will now first decisively uttering itself; but for the present, it was still as one light-point in an element of darkness. He says he was a pious monk: faithfully, painfully struggling to work out the truth of this high act of his, but it was to little purpose. His misery had not lessened, had rather, as it were, increased into infinitude."

Drudgeries, penances and prayers did not relieve the burden of his soul. Although he traveled far in religious orders, his soul lived in misery. He was made a professor of philosophy at Wittenburg University, and was the recognized preacher there also. He had a form of godliness but was destitute of its power.

2. *Luther as a Christian.*

In the Convent Library at Erfurt, there is a picture of the young monk, then twenty-four years of age, portraying a face full of yearning for the light. In those days the Word was precious. There was no open vision. One day, however, while in the library, his eyes lighted upon a large, old copy of the Bible, chained to the wall. He read and read, and reaching Romans, read that the just could only live by faith. Immediately a new world was opened to Luther, and he determined to accept all he had discovered in the blessed Book.

A deep, spiritual crisis overtook him in the Benedictine Convent, Bologna. While here he was overtaken by illness and was forced to remain. Darkness and despair overtook him. Remorse filled his soul. The sense of his sinfulness troubled him. The prospect of judgment filled him with dread. When the terrors reached their highest pitch, however, the words of Scriptures he had memorized comforted and restored his soul. Health was regained and his journey to Rome resumed.

It was in 1511, at the age of twenty-seven that this young German monk first saw Rome. He had come with fierce conflict of soul to see the pope and obtain an indulgence. But as he climbed the holy stairs, Scala Sancta, made up of the twenty-eight marble steps of the Lateran Church, one of Rome's principal churches, the miracle happened that stands out as the most important epoch in Europe. Luther started to ascend the stairs, believing that if he reached the top, an indulgence of a thousand years deliverance from the fires of purgatory would be his. But what happened can be best told by Luther himself. In a glass case in the library of Rudolstadt, is a manuscript in the handwriting of his son, Dr. Paul Luther, reading thus —

> In the year 1544 my late dearest father, in the presence of us all, narrated the whole story of his journey to Rome. He acknowledged with great joy that, in that city, through the Spirit of Jesus Christ, he had come to the knowledge of the truth of the everlasting Gospel. It happened in this way. As he repeated his prayers on the Lateran staircase the words of the prophet came suddenly to his mind, "The just shall live by faith." Thereupon he ceased his prayers, returned to Wittenburg and took this as the chief foundation of all his doctrine.

Shocked by what he saw on those stairs, he was suddenly arrested by God who said to his soul, "This staircase can never be the ladder of salvation." He was immediately ashamed of himself at being a victim of such superstitions, and he fled from Rome. He left Wittenburg believing in justification by works — he returned believing in justification by faith.

During these years, Luther was subject to attacks of depression, fear and doubt. Naturally he was temperamental. "The devil has often cast up against me the whole cause that I carry on; against me and against Christ." In the room he occupied at Wartburg, where he sat translating the Bible, guides will point out a black spot on the wall. This is there because the devil appeared and forbade Luther to continue his work, and Luther threw the ink well at his satanic intruder.

C. *Outstanding Characteristics.*

Volumes have been written on the many-sided character of Luther. Of his varied gifts Carlyle wrote: "I will call this Luther a true, great man; great in intellect; in courage, affection and integrity; one of our most lovable and precious men. . . . A right spiritual hero and prophet; once more, a true son of nature, for whom these centuries and many that are yet to come will be thankful to heaven."

1. *As a Father.*

After his conversion, Luther broke with the Roman Catholic Church. His was a complete renunciation. Discarding the vow of celibacy, he married a nun, Catherine von Bora. This step was taken as a practical testimony to the change of heart he had experienced. For years he had longed for domestic happiness. From the outset the Luther home was a happy one. "Kathe, you have a good husband who loves you and you are an Empress." He also told his devoted wife that he held her dearer than the kingdom of France and the Dukedom of Venice.

Affectionate as a husband and a father, he was yet strict. Upon one occasion he would not allow his son to appear before him for three days. Any approach was denied, until the erring child wrote an apology and sought forgiveness. When Luther's wife and friends pleaded for leniency, he said, "I would rather have a dead than an unworthy son."

2. *As a Reformer.*

As we come to another Reformation Day observance, we remind ourselves how the mighty work of Luther saved Europe from Romish dominion. The darkness of the Middle Ages was scattered and the lamp of Protestantism lit which still burns brightly. Luther's struggle against an enraged and cruel papacy was hard and long, but he faced the conflict with superb courage.

His first challenge took place in October, 1517, when a monk named Tetzel was exposed for selling indulgences. Antagonism became intense and Luther wrote against all popish practices, so much so that the then pope issued a Bull on December 10, 1520, forbidding Luther to continue his fight. The Reformer, however, feared no pope. He took the Bull and, amidst a great gathering of people at Elster Gate, Wittenburg, burned it to ashes.

The next and more notable challenge came on April 17, 1521, known as the famous Diet of Worms, of which Carlyle said, "Luther's appearance there may be considered as the greatest scene in modern European history." The one-time monk had spent the previous night in prayer that he might be guided aright. The next day he was brought before the young emperor, Charles V, the princes of Germany and the papal authorities. As the spokesman for the Reformation movement, Luther was ordered to recant. The tense scene has been dramatically described by Carlyle — "the world's pomp and power sits there on this hand; on that, stands up for God's truth one man, the poor Hans Luther's son." Friends had urged Luther not to go to the trial, reminding him of the burning of John Huss. Luther's reply to all entreaties was, "Were there as many devils in Worms as there are roof-tiles, I would go."

Standing bravely before his accusers, he met their command to recant with a renowned reply: "Confute me by proof of Scripture, or else by plain, just arguments. I cannot recant otherwise. For it is neither safe nor prudent to do aught against conscience. Here stand I: I can do no other. May God help me, Amen!" The emperor dismissed Luther, deeming him to be a madman, one possessed by the devil. From then on strong measures were taken to check Luther's influence and work.

Further challenges in 1526 and 1529 at the Diets of Speier were met in the same courageous fashion. Firmly maintaining his ground, Luther said: "We are resolved with the grace of God to maintain the pure and exclusive preaching of His only Word, such as it is contained in the Biblical books of the Old and New Testaments, without adding anything thereto that may be contrary to them." Thus obeying his Spirit-enlightened conscience, Luther defied all threats.

3. *As a Teacher.*

Giving himself to a close, prolonged study of Scripture, Luther gained a clear insight into its fundamental truths. He became a man of one Book. "Through so many commentaries and books, the dear Bible is buried so that people do not look at the text itself," he once wrote. "It is far better to see with our own eyes than with other people's eyes."

Coming to see that the Word could not be bound, he fought to have it widely and freely read. "To be free — to live in the kingdom of truth and to confess as truth whatever he saw to be truth," was his ambition. "A layman," said Luther, "who has the Scripture is more to be trusted than pope or council without it." Luther himself has given us valuable expositions of the Word. He translated the Scriptures into the language of his people. "You have now the Bible in German. Now I will cease from my labors. You now have what you want. Only see to it and use it after my death. It has cost me labor enough. What an unspeakable grace it is that God speaks to us."

His outstanding commentaries were on *Romans* — the reading of which, in London, was used for John Wesley's conversion — and *Galatians*, which Luther called the Epistle of Catherine von Bora, after his wife. He regarded it as the spouse among the books of the Bible, seeing it unfolded the Protestant doctrine of justification by faith.

On Reformation Day fresh emphasis is given to Luther's doctrinal creed. He was the champion of justification by faith, and by faith alone. "In my heart this article reigns alone," said Luther, "and shall reign, namely, faith in my dear Lord Christ, who is the only Beginning, Middle and End of all my spiritual and divine thoughts." He said that Christ in His death became "a Sacrifice, satisfying for our sins; in His resurrection, a Conqueror; in the Ascension, a King; in His intercession, a High Priest."

The forgiveness of sins by God alone was another truth he preached with great power and effect. He wrote to a soul concerned about forgiveness, "It is God's command that we should believe our own sins are forgiven. Hear what Saint Bernard says, 'The testimony of the Holy Spirit in thy heart is this — thy sins are forgiven thee'."

In these days, when both in America and Europe, Roman Catholicism is rapidly increasing its stranglehold on religion and politics, what a need there is for a hundred Martin Luthers with courage enough to expose the great gulf between the beliefs and practices of Romanism and the clear teaching cf God's infallible Word.

4. *His Closing Days.*

Martin Luther was an old man before his time. At sixty, his bodily frame was diseased and he had an irritability so trying to those around him. He had an intolerance on doctrinal matters that hindered his influence. Writing to a friend, he described himself as "a worn-out, lazy, tired, cold and now one-eyed man." Yet he remained active to the end, which came on the 18th of February, 1546. During the day Luther complained of pains in his chest. His two sons, Paul and Hans, then 13 and 14 years of age, respectively, sat up with him through the night. Awaking from sleep in the early hours with sweat on his brow, he turned and said, "It is the cold sweat of death. I must yield up, spent, for my sickness increaseth." After receiving medicine, his thrice-repeated words were, "Thou hast redeemed me, Thou faithful God. Truly God has so loved the world."

A loyal follower asked, "Venerable Father, do you die trusting in Christ, and in the doctrine you have constantly preached?" Luther's reply was a joyful, "Yes," which was his last word on earth.

Reformation Day will find many a preacher expounding the text, thrice repeated in Scripture, which resulted in Luther's conversion and enabled him to pass from a religion of fear into one of faith. "The just shall live by faith," was the powerful phrase exercising such an important and mysterious influence in the life of Luther. "It was a creative sentence, both for the Reformer and the Reformation." Of this great verse Luther himself remarked, "Before those words broke upon my mind, I hated God and was angry with Him because, not content with frightening us sinners by the Law and by the miseries of life, He still further increased our torture by the Gospel. But when, by the Spirit of God, I understood these words — The just shall live by faith — then I felt born again, like a new man. I entered through that open door into the very paradise of God. . . . In very truth, this text was to me the true gate of paradise."

Among the many Luther gems of "faith" which all true Protestants must never fail to stress are —

1. "Faith and human understanding are one against another."
2. "Faith dependeth upon the Word."
3. "Faith is a Christian's treasure."
4. "Faith in Christ destroyeth sin."
5. "Faith maketh us Christ's heritage."
6. "Faith is to build certainly upon God's mercy."
7. "To doubt is sin and everlasting death."

There is a German proverb to the effect that "Doctor Luther's shoes don't fit every village priest." When God made Luther, He broke the mold, and there has never been another like him. All who love the truths which the Reformer loved can, however, occupy his shoes in respect to his allegiance to the unadulterated, basic foundations of the Christian faith.

We cannot do better than quote the expressive lines of Marianne Farningham as we conclude our brief survey of the life and labors of Martin Luther —

That which he knew he uttered,
Conviction made him strong;
And with undaunted courage
He faced and fought the wrong.
No power on earth could silence him
Whom love and faith made brave;
And though four hundred years have gone
Men strew with flowers his grave.
A frail child born to poverty,
A German miner's son;
A poor monk searching in his cell,
What honors he has won!
The nations crown him faithful,
A man whom truth made free;
God give us for these easier times
More men as real as he!

For Memorial – Veteran's Day

For Memorial
— Veteran's Day

Stainless soldier on the walls,
    knowing this — and knows no
        more —
Whoever fights, whoever falls,
    Justice conquers evermore,
    Justice after as before;
And he who battles on his side,
    God, though he were ten times
        slain,
Crown him victor glorified
    Victor over death and pain.
                    — Ralph Waldo Emerson

Bravely to do whate'er the time
    demands,
    Whether with pen or sword, and
        not to flinch,
This is the task that fits heroic hands;
    So are Truth's boundaries widened,
        inch by inch.
                    — James Russell Lowell

MEDITATION FOR MEMORIAL — VETERAN'S DAY

LEST WE FORGET
I Corinthians 11:26

It is only fitting to commemorate our national memorial days when we pause and remember the freedom from tyranny and oppression which the sacrifice of millions of our fighting men have made possible. Through the perils, toil, pain and slaughter of countless numbers of our nation's finest fathers and sons, free nations rejoice in liberty of religious worship, of conscience and of political choice. What better poem expresses the feelings of free men on a Remembrance Day than Rudyard Kipling's *Recessional.*

> God of our fathers, known of old,
> Lord of our far-flung battle-line,
> Beneath whose awful Hand we hold
> Dominion over palm and pine —
> Lord God of Hosts, be with us yet,
> Lest we forget — lest we forget!

Remembrance Day, recognized yearly on November 11 or on the preceding Sunday, commemorates the fallen dead of the two World Wars. *Memorial Day,* or *Decoration Day,* which is observed on May 30, is kept primarily in honor of the men killed in the U. S. Civil War (1861-1865). But *Veteran's Day,* or *Armistice Day,* taking place on November 11, commemorates the signing of the armistice of 1918.

Since the world wars, lesser wars have brought an increasing number of dead to remember such as the Korean War, as well as the disastrous war in Viet Nam and the Israeli conflict. The threat of another universal holocaust of war troubles the nations of the world, and well it might, for if it comes, nuclear weapons will annihilate countless millions all over the world.

The pre-eminent Memorial or Remembrance Day, however, is when the saints gather around the Table of the Lord to remember His supreme sacrifice on behalf of a lost world. What a blessed "Memorial Feast" this is, as in symbol, we "Remember Him, and all His pains."

Calvary's Memorial

While "the heart has its reasons," the Israelites desired to know the significance of the annual Passover Feast which they observed. When approached with the question, "What mean ye by this service?" they had to have a satisfying answer (Exodus 12: 14-28).

It is both necessary and profitable to pause and ask ourselves what we mean by the observance of the Lord's Supper, not only for our own satisfaction but also for the enlightenment of those outside the church who are anxious inquirers. As Christians, we cannot get the utmost spiritual benefit out of the Christian Passover if we do not fully realize all that our Lord means by it.

It is to be regretted that many look upon the Supper as a matter of form — as a necessary part of Christian worship that should be engaged in. Church members with little or no contact with Christ feel themselves obligated to "take Communion." But no value accrues from observing it if it is a mere, unintelligent habit — a church ceremony to be observed at certain periods of the year. Even with those who have experienced God's saving grace and power, familiarity is apt to breed indifference. Unless love for the Saviour is kept fresh and warm, remembrance will be mechanical and unbeneficial.

Further, it is sad to see how many treat the Supper as if it were a fetish or charm, containing some wonderful virtue. Church life and work have little appeal for them, but when Communion comes around they must be there, as if it conveyed some special grace to keep them going until the next Communion. On the other hand, there are those narrow-minded people who think more of the Table than the Lord. They exercise the prerogative to admit or exclude from the Table. When Christians bar other true Christians from the Table, they make it "Man's Table."

How necessary, then, to ask the old question: "What mean ye by this serv-ice?" What is it to us? How do we value it? As God has beautifully pictured gospel truths in Old Testament scenes, symbols and sacraments, perhaps we can trace a few parallels between the Passover and the Table.

A. *A Commanded Service.*

The Passover was ordered and arranged by the Lord, not by Moses. "The Lord said unto Moses" (Exodus 12:1). In like manner, the Lord's Table is a divinely instituted ordinance. "I have received of the Lord" (I Corinthians 11:23). In the upper chamber Jesus merged the Passover into the Supper (Luke 22:11). "Where is the guestchamber, where I shall eat the passover?" Thus our Lord orders us to observe this rite. "This do." And as a command it must be obeyed without question. "The children of Israel went away, and did as the Lord commanded Moses and Aaron, so did they" (Exodus 12:28).

It is, therefore, in loving obedience that we remember all that Christ accomplished by His death. Religious organizations that make no provision for the Lord's Table are guilty of disobeying a divine command, and of also denying themselves a source of spiritual refreshment and strength.

B. *A Memorial Service.*

Each time the Israelites feasted on roast lamb and unleavened bread they looked back to that divine deliverance from Egypt. "This day shall be unto you for a memorial" (Exodus 12:14). The Passover was a reminder of redemption by the blood of a lamb. "It is the sacrifice of the Lord's passover, who passed over the houses of the children of Israel" (Exodus 12:27). All the people in houses covered by blood were safe from death without.

Christ our Passover was sacrificed for us (I Corinthians 5:7). The Table points back to the cross, and is our "Cenotaph" or Calvary's War Memorial. On "Memorial Day" thousands gather at Memorials over the land and cbserve a moment or two of silence in honor of those who died in battles. On the Lord's Day we gather at the Table to remember the grim battle at the cross, when Christ, by dying, slew death and conquered once and for all His and our great enemy. He vanquished death and all its powers.

C. *An Experimental Service.*

All who partook of the first Passover and several subsequent feasts, knew what the rite signified. The participants were those delivered from death by blood. "Draw out and take you a lamb . . . and kill the passover" (Exodus 12:21). No other could participate. Who should participate at the Lord's Table? All believers irrespective of their spiritual experience. Participation is limited to those who have been delivered from the bondage and death of sin. Jesus said to His disciples, and to *disciples only* — "Take, eat."

Participation is a sign of faith, an evidence cf the appropriation of Christ as Saviour. Those who eat and drink without any saving knowledge and experience act a lie, and eat and drink condemnation to themselves (I Corinthians 11:29). The Lord's Table is for the Lord's people, and for *all* the Lord's people. Thus, when it is spread, *all* who know they have been redeemed by the blood should be lovingly invited to remember their Redeemer.

D. *A Holy Service.*

The holy nature of the Passover is indicated by these requirements, "The first day ye shall put away leaven out of your houses." "Ye shall observe the feast of unleavened bread" (Exodus 12:15, 17). Thus the people were taught that holiness of heart was essential if the Feast was to act as a means of spiritual grace on behalf of the participant.

"The first day." How suggestive this is of "The first day of the week," observed by the early disciples! We dare not come to the Table with conscious, unconfessed sin in our heart. Leaven was to be put away. Being then pure, we can worthily participate. Personal examination will reveal all that is alien to the Lord's holy mind, and, cleansed from all defilement, our remembrances cf Him will be rewarding. Hands and mouths receiving the bread and wine must be clean.

> The cause of God is holy
> And useth holy things.

E. *A Temporary Service.*

As the people partook of the Passover they were reminded of the fact that they were a pilgrim people. "Thus shall ye eat it; with your loins girded, your shoes on your feet, and your staff in your hand; and ye shall eat it in haste; it is the Lord's passover" (Exodus 12:11). The Feast, then, was taken on the march. Is there not a deep truth here then for our hearts to meditate upon? The Passover was meant to be engaged in until the cross, when all it typified, was fulfilled. The Lord's Table was instituted by the Master when He merged the Passover into His own memorial Feast, and, like the Passover, it is only temporary: "Ye do shew the Lord's death *till he come*" (I Corinthians 11:26).

As this Day comes and goes we eat and drink with our loins girt, our feet shod, our hands equipped for service for we are but pilgrims and strangers. Soon the Lord's Supper will give way to the Marriage Supper of the Lamb (Revelation 19). The Passover was a memorial of *power* — the Table is a memorial of a *Person*. Before long, ours will be the joy of sitting down with Him and drinking of the fruit of the mystic vine. But until He gathers us around His heavenly board, let us reverence the sweet memorials of His death for a world of sinners lost and ruined by the fall.

For Thanksgiving Day

For Thanksgiving Day

If God forgot the world for just one
day,
Then little children would not laugh
and play;
Birds would not in the leafy wood-
lands sing,
And roses would not beautify the
spring.
No gentle showers throughout the
summer long,
No autumn fields to cheer the heart
with song,
No rising sun, no moon to give its
light,
No placid lake reflect the stars of
night.
No friend to help us on the toilsome
road,
No one to help us bear the heavy
load.
No light to shine upon the pilgrim
way,
No one to care, or wipe the tear
away.
No listening ear to hear the lost one
call,
No eye to see the righteous battler
fall.
No balm of Gilead to dull the throb-
bing pain,
No one to comfort and sustain.
Millions would die in unforgiven sin,
With none to bring the lost and stray-
ing in;
Yea, this great universe would melt
away,
If God forgot the world for just one
day.

            — Dr. James M. Gray

MEDITATION FOR THANKSGIVING DAY

THE GRACE OF GRATITUDE
Luke 17:15, 16

Few Americans who engage in the festivities of Thanksgiving Day stop to ascertain the origin of this commendable national institution. It is a fact of recorded history that the first Thanksgiving took place in the Plymouth Colony some time during November, 1621. A year before, the Pilgrims had landed from the Mayflower. What hard days they had had to face! Their first winter was most severe, but spring came at last and they planted crops which, to their joy, flourished. As autumn approached, these exiles from Holland and England desired to celebrate their good harvests. In their respective countries they had observed the traditional Harvest Festival, which possibly had its origin in the Feast of Tabernacles when the people of Israel rejoiced before the Lord for the fruits of the earth.

Governor William Bradford is credited with proclaiming a three-day celebration when fifty-five colonists and one hundred Indians gorged themselves with fish and "a great store of wild turkeys." Bradford later wrote:

Famine once we had —
But other things God gave us in full store;
As fish and ground nuts to supply our strait,
That we might learn on Providence to wait;
And know by bread alone man lives not in his need.

Since then Thanksgiving Day has had a wandering career. Here is a summary given by one of our daily papers several years ago in a fitting editorial.

"In 1623, the date was July 30. In 1631, the Pilgrims were in a bad way again, and set February 22 as a day of fasting and prayer. Luckily, a ship arrived with provisions and February 22 became Thanksgiving Day. In 1633, the Massachusetts Bay Colony held two Thanksgiving Days — June 19 and October 16. From then on until the Revolutionary War, when Congress interested itself, the dates varied from June to October and November. Congress was just as undecided as the Pilgrims and the various colonies, which had celebrated Thanksgiving whenever their Governors felt the urge.

"During the Revolutionary War period (1775-1781), the dates fixed by Congress skipped from July to May to April to May, etc. There wasn't an Autumn Thanksgiving during that period. In 1789 Congress (with a few chronic squawkers objecting to this 'mimicking of European customs') asked George Washington to proclaim the first national Thanksgiving Day, which he did.

"Washington issued another Thanksgiving proclamation, this time on his own, in 1795. He picked Thursday, February 19. One phase of the proclamation sounds strangely apropos in view of current developments abroad. He wrote:

'Render this country more and more a safe and propitious asylum for the unfortunate of other countries.'

"After Washington left office, Thanksgiving was an off-and-on affair. Some Presidents and Governors issued proclamations, some did not. By 1830, however, the custom was pretty general."

It is Sarah Josepha Hale, the Boston widow, who worked at getting a set observance of Thanksgiving Day. For twenty years Mrs. Hale, who was one of America's first women journalists, fought for a recognized day. She pestered President Abraham Lincoln until, in 1864, he declared that thereafter, by annual Presidential proclamation, the last Thursday in November be observed as a national Thanksgiving Day. However, in 1941, President Roosevelt and Congress changed the term "last Thursday in November" to "fourth Thursday in November." Since some

Novembers have five Thursdays, Thanksgiving is celebrated the fourth Thursday every year now.

As we come to another Thanksgiving Day there are many blessings for which to praise God, blessings which have become increasingly precious as war drums continue to beat. Here we are, with plenty to eat in a starving world, with shelter over our heads in a world of unhoused millions. Seeing that each of us possesses so many benefits for which to praise God, may the grace of gratitude be manifested not only on one statutory Thanksgiving Day, but on every day of the year. As Christie Lund has expressed it:

> I would indeed give thanks,
>   I am so rich today,
> Rich in the things that count the
>   most —
>   Love and a child at play.
> Home and those who are near and
>   dear;
>   Health and strength of limb;
> Courage and comradeship and peace,
>   A faith in Him.

Turning to the spiritual side of gratitude, it was at Calvary in His cruel death that the Lord suffered the base ingratitude of man in all its fullness. In a measure of preparation for this sorrow, on His last pilgrimage to Jerusalem, Christ tasted the bitter thanklessness of man. That His heart was stung by the action of the cleansed lepers is evidenced by His question to the one grateful leper: "Were there not ten cleansed? but where are the nine?" (Luke 17:17). As this narrative contains several impressive truths worthy of our prayerful meditation at this Thanksgiving season, may the Holy Spirit guide us in our study.

A. *The Ten.*

All ten men were lepers, being smitten with the same loathsome, hopeless disease. All were afar off. All cried for mercy (Luke 17:12, 13). What a picture of sin-stricken humanity! Thank God that the Saviour who cleansed the lepers can cleanse from the more terrible leprosy of sin.

All ten went to the priest in response to the command of Christ. All acted in the spirit of obedience and faith. As they walked, something happened — new life shot through their withered, corrupted frames. Their halting steps were made firm. Loathsomeness vanished, and pure white flesh was theirs again (verse 14). The ingratitude, therefore, of nine of these lepers was the ingratitude of men who had been cleansed and healed by divine power.

B. *The Gratitude of One.*

Ten were healed, but only one, when conscious of the gift received, turned and fell at the feet of his Healer. Only one rendered immediate gratitude for immediate healing. This one cleansed man turned back; the other nine turned their backs and walked off with new, clean bodies, forgetting the One who had made their restoration possible. With a once croaking voice now clear and musical, only one of the lepers glorified God for the mercy and miracle of healing (verses 15, 16).

The phrase "giving him thanks" indicates the necessity of expressing our gratitude to the Lord — a gratitude for which He looks and which He misses when it is not forthcoming. Such gratitude is commanded specifically: "abounding therein with thanksgiving" (Colossians 2:7); "be ye thankful" (Colossians 3:15); "giving thanks always for all things" (Ephesians 5:20). It also glorified God: "whoso offereth praise glorifieth me" (Psalm 50:23). The cleansed leper by his thankful spirit gave glory to God (Luke 17:18). Natural gratitude is the natural pleasure felt in prosperity, but gracious

gratitude — gratitude filled with grace — blesses God. Job could do this in adversity because of his faith in God's wisdom and goodness.

1. *Thankfulness in Action.*

Gratitude is one of the foremost blessings and the parent of all graces. It produces contentment in all conditions, and it places a bridle on all one's desires. It checks gloom, it destroys envy, and it returns with blessings upon the head. We taste the sweetness of a gift twice over when we are grateful for it.

Gratitude likewise fits us for greater blessings. God is always ready to give more abundantly when previous gifts are properly valued, appreciated and enjoyed. Often the added gift is far more precious than the material benefit for which we have thanked Him. To the grateful leper Jesus gave a still greater blessing, a "second blessing" if you like. He was told that his faith had saved him (Luke 17:19, RV margin). A cleansed soul now resided within a cleansed body. Valuing blessings as they fall upon our unworthy heads, we receive further tokens of divine favor.

Again, gratitude is a remarkable discoverer. It can find causes for thankfulness in the most ordinary and sometimes unwelcome things of life. If you set before me a tray of sand containing some small particles of iron or steel, clumsy fingers would never be able to separate the two. But give me a magnet to swing over the tray, and in a moment of time the invisible particles of metal will be drawn by the power of attraction to the magnet. The unthankful heart is like a finger in the sand searching for filings. It can find no mercies for which to praise God, but as the magnet attracts the metal, so gratitude finds in every hour some heavenly blessings to sing about.

> Count your many blessings, name them one by one,
> And it will surprise you what the Lord hath done.

The Arabs put the case of gratitude and contentment very plainly in the shape of a proverb: "I had no socks and complained . . . until I saw a man who had no feet."

Think and thank! If hitherto you have lived on Grumbling Street or in Whining Lane, move to Gratitude Terrace or to Thanksgiving Corner, where the air and the district are of the best and the rent is no higher. As this moment, close your eyes and exclaim: "Bless the Lord, O my soul, and forget not all his benefits" (Psalm 103:2).

C. *The Ingratitude of the Nine.*

Being Himself the perfection of a grateful Man in His relation to His Father, Jesus was saddened when the nine healed men failed to return to say "Thank you." This is the reason why, with a stung heart, He asked: "Were there not ten cleansed? but where are the nine?" Ah, where were they? Why did they push on with no overmastering remembrance of Him to whom they owed everything? We are often in the company of the ungrateful nine, for, like them, we, too, take all we can get from God, but offer Him very little in return.

1. *Ingratitude — What It Is.*

a. Ingratitude! *It is a sin.* The Apostle Paul would have us know that ingratitude is one of the characteristic features of heathenism. We read that men "glorified him not as God, neither were thankful . . ." (Romans 1:21). Ingratitude is a sin against God, against society, against ourselves.

b. Ingratitude! *It is robbery.* Can a man rob God? Yes, he certainly can.

The other nine lepers robbed the heart of Jesus of the gratitude His miracle of healing deserved. Often we rob our friends of joy and happiness simply because we forget to say "Thank you." Only one out of ten gave thanks, and the proportion remains the same.

c. Ingratitude! *It is cruel.*

> Blow, blow, thou winter wind;
> Thou art not so unkind
> As man's ingratitude!

Robert Burns, the Scottish bard, declared that "man's inhumanity to man makes countless thousands mourn." Yes, we live in an ungrateful world. Heartlessness is the haunting shadow in many a heart and home. Few wounds so deeply enter the noble and generous spirit as those caused by ingratitude. The greater the kindness and compassion shown, the greater the weight of unmindfulness seems to be. Ingratitude has broken many a kind heart — it ultimately broke the Saviour's. How could men be so cruel!

d. Ingratitude! *It is selfishness.* Thankless lives are usually selfish lives. Ingratitude withers the finer qualities of the soul. The constant, thankless reception of the benefits of God and man makes one greedy. Rivers of goodness flow into the life, but nothing in the way of praise flows out.

It may be that "the nine," when cleansed, felt they had received only what was their due. Alexander Smellie suggests what their erroneous reasoning may have been: "The loathsome disease was an injustice and a grievance, and health was their right, and they need not be profoundly thankful." How we need to guard ourselves against such self-conceit and pride! Because gratitude is the atmosphere in which the fairest flowers bloom, may we ever strive to live in such rarified air.

2. *Social Ingratitude.*

What a happier, sunnier world this would be if people only knew how to be grateful for the blessings of civilization, the comforts of home, the amenities of life! At this Thanksgiving season let each of us *think* and *thank*. In Philippians 4:6-8, there is a close relationship between the words "think" and "thanksgiving." May grace be ours to *pause* and *praise!*

Gratitude is sadly needed in the intimate associations of life. How miserable we feel when we remember the deeds of those to whom we ought to have been grateful! There is a striking phrase in the story of Joseph: "Yet did not the chief butler remember Joseph, but forgat him" (Genesis 40: 23). Luke reminds us that the one cleansed leper whose lips became vocal with praises was a stranger, a Samaritan (Luke 17:15, 16). The rest were Jews; so Jesus got more from a stranger than from His own. How like life this is!

Think of broken hearts — broken by the ingratitude of children!

> How sharper than a serpent's tooth
> To have an ungrateful child!

Our Father above knows something about this, for we hear His grieved reproach: "I have nourished and brought up children, and they have rebelled against me. The ox knoweth his owner, and the ass his master's crib: but Israel doth not know, my people doth not consider" (Isaiah 1:2, 3).

Sometimes people have to die before they are appreciated, but instead of covering dead bodies with beautiful wreaths, let us impart a little more cheer while our friends are with us. Yes, and gratitude might help them to live longer! Often tombstones are silent liars. "Gone, but not forgotten" is a favorite epitaph, One feels like stealing out some midnight and changing those words on a stone or two whose story he knows. They might better be, "Gone, but soon forgotten," because of the lack of gratitude to, and loving remembrance of, the departed one. Many a grave is filled before its time through thoughtlessness and base ingratitude. God deliver us from causing an early grave!

> Over the casket pitiful we stand
>   And place a rose within the helpless hand,
> That yesterday mayhap we would not see
>   When it was meekly offered. On the heart
> That often ached for one approving word
>   We lay forget-me-nots; we turn away
> And find the world is colder for the loss
>   Of this so faulty and so loving one.
> Think of that moment, ye who reckon close
>   With love — so much for every gentle thought —
> The moment when love's richest gifts are naught,
>   When a pale flower upon a pulseless heart
> Like vain regrets exhales its sweets in vain.

Friend, is there a mother's or a friend's heart that you could cheer by a kind word of thanks? Have you forgotten to say "Thank you"? Well, delay no longer. Take your pen and write to that one who deserves your gratitude. A postage stamp may save a soul from despair.

3. *Spiritual Ingratitude.*

The Bible speaks about offering the sacrifices of thanksgiving, giving thanks to the name of the Lord (Hebrews 13: 15). Let our response be: "O my soul . . . forget not all his benefits" (Psalm 103:2). If only men, yes, even cleansed men, would praise the Lord for His goodness, how happy His heart would be! There may be some excuse for the heathen as they manifest a thankless spirit, although Romans 1:18-21 holds every man responsible for a message of gratitude. Those blessed by the knowledge of God, however, are doubly without excuse. As we have seen, it was nine cleansed, healed men who took the gift of health without thanking the Giver. God always suffers more when ingratitude is shown by those who dwell beneath His shadow.

Do you praise Him continually for Himself, for His transcendent attributes, for His beloved Son, for His Holy Spirit, for His infallible Word, for His grace and salvation, for His Day, for His Church? May our thanks ascend to Him for these unspeakable gifts!

Yes, and may our "thanksgiving" lead to "thanks-living." God grant that lips and life may be in complete harmony. A tongue of praise is always sweeter when behind it there is a heart of purity. A hallelujah from the lips of an inconsistent Christian is but a sounding brass and a tinkling cymbal. By lives of loving obedience and earnest consecration, may we express our sincerest gratitude to the Master, who, by His sacrifice for us, deserves praise forevermore.

For Sunday Observance Day

For Sunday Observance Day

Prayerful Preparation for Sunday

"O Lord, we would now dismiss the cares of the world with the week. May we rise in the morning with refreshed bodies and renewed strength, and be in the Spirit on the Lord's Day. And do Thou send out Thy light and Thy truth, that they may lead and guide us to Thy holy hill and to Thyself; through Jesus Christ our Lord. Amen."
— Rev. Fielding Ould (1864)

"O Almighty God, who, after the creation of the world didst rest from all Thy works, and, as an image of Thine own, didst sanctify a day of rest for Thy creatures, grant us that putting away all earthly cares and anxieties, we may be duly prepared for the services of Thy sanctuary; and that our rest here upon earth may be a preparation for the eternal Sabbath promised to Thy people in heaven, through Jesus Christ our Lord. Amen."
— Archbishop Benson of Canterbury (1829)

"O God, the Author of Eternal Light, do Thou shed forth continued day upon us who watch for Thee, that our lips may praise Thee, our lives may bless Thee, and our meditations on the morrow glorify Thee, through Jesus Christ our Lord. Amen."
— Sarum Missal

MEDITATION FOR
SUNDAY OBSERVANCE DAY

A SABBATH DAY'S JOURNEY
Psalm 122:1

It is not the purpose of this homily to discuss the connection of the name Sunday with ancient sunworshipers, nor to prove that the Jewish Sabbath is not the Lord's Day which the Christian Church observes, nor to elaborate upon the technical distance between the Mount of Olives at Bethany and Jerusalem. The phrase which Luke the historian uses, "A Sabbath Day's Journey," gives us an insight into a custom recognized by Jews from early times. In Jewish reckoning the distance to be covered on the Sabbath was 2,000 cubits (Numbers 35:5), or equal to almost one mile by our measure. Weymouth translates it "about a mile off." This measure, imposed for journeys outside the city — there was no limit to walking inside the city — is supposed to have been borrowed from the space left between the Israelites and the Ark when they passed over Jordan (Joshua 3:4). The same distance was used by Rabbinical Law to indicate how far Jews could travel on the Sabbath with-out transgressing the Mosaic Law in respect to travel on the holy day (Exodus 16:27-30). It was practically impossible to travel beyond the limit subscribed seeing the gates of the city were closed (Nehemiah 13:19). If all exits from our modern cities and towns were closed on a Sunday the day would be a purgatory for those who use cars, trains and buses for pleasure. Many who have to travel considerable distances to churches would likewise find the old-time law inconvenient.

The Jews thought more of their Sabbath than they did of the Saviour, and, as He revealed, many of their Sabbath restrictions were heartless and foreign to the character of God. For the Christian, limitation of Sunday travel is self-imposed and directed by the requirements of the divine will. As we live under grace, Sunday should be a blessing not a burden — a delight not drudgery. But while we do not slavishly follow Rabbinical restrictions we are not to change liberty into license. We cannot journey where we like on the Lord's Day. In our more privileged dispensation, it is our obligation to use His Day as He would have us. Thus we come to a spiritual application of the phrase relative to a Sabbath day's journey. Matthew Henry, commenting on this verse, says (Acts 1:12) — "A sabbath day's journey, is no further than devout people used to walk on a sabbath evening, after the public worship was over, for meditation." While many still use the term Sabbath for the Lord's Day, as the Lord's people our responsibility is to employ all the day, no matter how we describe it, for His honor and glory.

A. *A Journey in Heart Preparation.*

The stretch allowed was from Bethany to Jerusalem, and both places are symbolic. Bethany means, "house of song or obedience" — Jerusalem, "possession of peace." What better journey can we take on a Lord's Day than one from a personal obedience to the possession of peace? As we approach each Sunday may its opening moments be occupied in definite heart preparation for all the day may hold for us in worship and service. If, like John of old, we too are in the Spirit on the Lord's day (Revelation 1:10), then the whole day will prove to be honoring to God and spiritually beneficial to ourselves. Alas! too often we begin the day in a wrong spirit and rob ourselves, thereby, of all God waits to bestow. We go to God's house and are disappointed with the preacher, not because he did not have the right message but because we lacked previous heart-examination and prayer, creating, as they do, the inner spiritual atmosphere so necessary for the reception of truth. Before officiating at the laver the priests had to wash their hands and feet whether they were dusty or not. Often we reach the close of a Sunday conscious of barrenness and loss all because

we neglected to seek cleansing of heart in its opening moments. A wrong beginning often results in a day robbed of blessing.

B. *A Journey Into His Secret Presence.*

While it is true that Sunday is a divine provision for the exercise of the ordinary means of grace and spiritual succor through the worship and ministry in the sanctuary, as George Herbert emphasizes in the lines —

On Sundays, heaven's gates stand
ope
Blessings are plentiful and rife,
More plentiful than hope

— yet we must not neglect our personal, secret communion with the risen Lord whose victory over the grave the day commemorates. Availing ourselves of all the ministrations of the church of our conviction and choice, and diligent in any public responsibilities we may have, we must not neglect a frequent journey to the secret place. Abraham said to his servant, "Abide ye here . . . I will go yonder and worship and come again unto you" (Genesis 22:5), and the Lord's Day will only be the gate of heaven to our hearts as we say to our duties and to outward activities whether in church or home, "Abide here, while I go yonder to worship alone." It was only when Daniel was left alone that he had a great vision (Daniel 10:8). Your accommodation may be severely restricted for you to get alone with God, but love will find a way to hold a private audience with the King.

C. *A Journey Into His House.*

Dr. A. T. Pierson would have us know that "about the Sabbath cluster all religious interests. It is linked with an open Sanctuary, and an open Bible, with the worship of God and the work of piety." How privileged we are to live in a land where there is no restriction on a journey into the house of the Lord! Atheistic Communism succeeds in seriously curtailing such a joyful journey. May we not be guilty, in a land of open Bibles and of open churches, of forsaking the assembling of ourselves together! Mutual worship and fellowship exercise a wonderful spiritual influence over the lives of the participants. We must come together —

1. In the spirit of true reverence with no other thought in mind save the worship of God in sincerity and truth.

2. With expectant hearts, for the Lord has something for each heart. There were many things in his life which the psalmist could not understand until he came into the sanctuary (Psalm 73:17). What heavenly light is ours upon many spiritual problems and difficulties as we wait upon the Lord!

3. Regularly, if it is at all possible. Trivial and unnecessary matters should not be allowed to hinder our journey to the temple where the Lord waits to meet us. How much Thomas missed when he absented himself from the rest of the apostolic fellowship! (John 20:24). May we be found following the custom of Jesus who, with delight, journeyed on the Sabbath to God's house! The psalmist was glad when asked to accompany other worshipers to the sanctuary (122:1). Our journey to church should never be irksome or undertaken as a mere duty, but always taken as a blessed privilege.

D. *A Journey Into His Book Divine.*

The best book to read on the Lord's Day is the incomparable one which He gave the world. The old custom of laying aside all other books and concentrating upon the Bible on the Sabbath, is dying out with tragic results. "What should I read on a Sunday?" is a question no true Christian should ever ask. For him there is only one Book to read, namely the one revealing the Master. Our Sunday reading should never distract holy thoughts of Him who claims one day out of seven for Himself. It was while he was in the Spirit on the Lord's Day that John received a deep insight into the final purposes of God set forth in the Revelation. Avoiding trashy literature, we must delight in devotional portions such as the Psalms, and feed faith and devotion and quicken love thereby.

E. *A Journey Into the World for Souls.*

Essential though it is, to foster our own spiritual life in spiritual exercises, we must not only journey to the house cf God, but also journey out into the community on errands of mercy. We must seek out those who are journeying to hell and persuade them to travel with us to heaven. Evangelism, it has been said, is simply one beggar telling another beggar where to get bread. It was on a Sabbath Day that Jesus cast out demons and performed other miracles (Luke 4:33; 6:6). His Day is a great day for service as His own journey to the sick, the aged, the lonely who are unable to journey to church and cheer their hearts. Then there are the demon-possessed and withered lives awaiting the Saviour's touch through our witness. Visitation of homes and institutions, tract distribution and open-air ministry on the Lord's Day continue His Sabbath benefits.

Thus, if we journey on the Sabbath Day from the stains of the past week to definite heart-cleansing and preparation; from the sordid, mundane things of earth into His secret presence; from our accustomed spheres and homes into His dwelling place; from the broken cisterns of earth's literature into His Book divine; from our own selfish de-

sires and religious enjoyment into a
world of lost souls then we shall prove
most definitely that —

In holy duties let the day
In holy pleasures pass away:
How sweet a Sabbath thus to spend,
In hope of one that ne'er shall end.

For Missionary Day

For the Annual Missionary Day

O Thou who didst so love a lost world as to give Thy only begotten Son for its salvation, we pray Thee to bless the activities of all missionary societies. Teach us to realize that the command to go into all the world and preach the Gospel to every creature is binding in measure to each individual. Show us what we ought to do. Increase our zeal, our interest, our service, our supplications. May we help in sending others, if we cannot go ourselves, by our prayers and offerings; for the sake of our Lord Jesus Christ. Amen.

— Church Missionary Society (1799)

How appealing are the verses which the renowned missionary statesman, Oswald J. Smith, has given us in his poem *The Cry of the Lost*.

I've heard of a land far away
    Where millions in darkness are
        dying,
And they sadly moan as they pass
    alone
    Through years of endless sighing:

"Oh! we're lost! we're lost, and at
    awful cost,
    For we heard not the Story old
Of a Saviour's love and a Home above,
    A shelter within the fold."

I see them in anguish and tears
    Unable to stifle their moaning;
But in vain they plead, not a soul
    gives heed,
    Nor hearkens to their groaning.
Yet, they'll stand at last when their
    life is past,
    And they'll tell as they leave the
        throne,
That since no one came in the
    Saviour's name,
    They suffered and died alone.

Enough that the Master I love,
    In sorrow and pain has been calling;
That He bids me bear of their woe
    my share,
    For lo, the night is falling.
And they seek for light in their hope-
    less plight,
    For the Light that comes from
    above,
So I gladly go, leaving all below,
    To tell them of Jesus' love.

MEDITATION FOR ANNUAL MISSIONARY DAY

GOING AS HE COMMANDED
Acts 1:8

The spread of Christianity to the ends of the earth received its impetus from its Founder who commissioned His disciples to go out into all parts of the world preaching the Gospel which His death and resurrection made possible. Although in the days of His flesh Jesus limited Himself to the small country of Palestine, He became the Saviour of the world, and left His disciples a message that has found its way into a thousand languages. True though it is that Jesus was born a Jew, He was not bound by the bigoted nationalistic spirit of Judaism. His declaration was that "God so loved the world," and that His death upon a cross would manifest such a universal love.

When Jesus became the risen Lord, He summarized His own preaching in its missionary intentions in the two great imperatives to which world evangelization owes so much: "Ye shall be my witnesses . . . unto the uttermost part of the earth" (Acts 1:8). Jerusalem was the point of departure because this city had been the center of Jewish national life and religion. The initial point of service now is the home of each disciple, for if they cannot win souls for Christ where they live, they are not likely to win any if they go to Africa or elsewhere. "All power is given unto me in heaven and in earth. Go ye therefore, and teach all the nations" (Matthew 28:18, 19; Acts 1:8). With the *Go* of commission there was the *Lo* of companionship — "I am with you alway."

For decades the church has been unhindered in her missionary enterprise, but now many doors have closed and others are closing. The advent of Communism and the upsurge of nationalism in heathen lands have brought about a lamentable curtailment of missionary activity. We can no longer sing —

From the fields and crowded cities,
China gathers at His feet,

because the 600 millions in China are under the heel of a tyrant who has abolished all foreign missionaries. Neither can we sing —

Coming, coming from afar,

179

From the steppes of Russia dreary
From Slavonia's scattered lands,

for the simple reason that these vast areas once open to missionaries are now closed. This is because at the heart of Communism is the destruction of Christianity. While vast continents like Africa and India are still fields of service, it is becoming increasingly difficult for missionaries to enter, unless they go as teachers or doctors. Yet in these critical days for missions, the church has never had so many dedicated young men and women preparing for missionary work in those lands still willing to welcome heralds of the cross.

The scope, nature and methods of world missions are changing, and such a change constitutes a challenge to the church in these critical times so heavy with prophetic significance. A fresh assessment of the missionary situation and of how life, talent, sacrifice, gifts and prayer can be harnessed to meet the need of our time is most urgent, if non-Christian lands are to be widely evangelized. Multitudes are yearning for the full satisfaction which the Gospel of grace alone can impart. People are calling in their hunger and privations, in their emptiness and unrest, in their weariness and sin, in their delusions, in their awakening, but the question is, How is the church answering the cry of a lost humanity? Dr. J. H. Jowett asks:

> Is the Church thrilling to the call? Is she staggering in unbelief? Or is she leaping forward to the inspiration of her quenchless hope. Men and women, the Lord Jesus Christ is alive! His grace is still abounding! Our resources are all-sufficient! We are not the first to face a difficult road, and the children of faith have always been justified in their most audacious ventures. "O Zion, that bringest good tidings, lift up thy voice with strength:

lift it up, be not afraid; say unto the cities of Judah, Behold your God."

What better theme could we have on a Missionary Sunday than —

A. *A Missionary Conversion.*

You may ask, "Well, now, what exactly is this kind of a conversion?" It is a conversion downward from head to feet, the reverse to the conversion of those in the gutter of sin who, once their feet are on the straight way, grow in grace and knowledge. A missionary conversion pre-supposes a previous experience of regeneration. We must *come* unto Christ before we can *go* into the world for Him. What, then, are the elements of the conversion we are considering?

1. *The Head Is Converted.*

The adage has it that "Knowledge is power." So if one is to become a power for God in the mission field there must be knowledge of its requirements and problems, as well as challenge. This means saturating the mind with facts derived from missionary literature. Studying books and maps of India in his cobbler's shop fired the soul of William Carey to go there and become the father of modern missions. After her conversion to God, Mary Slessor devoured the records of missionary activity as reported in church magazines and never rested until she reached West Africa there to become "The White Queen of Calabar." Scores of missionaries testify to the fact that it was through reading missionary biographies or books and magazines that the conviction was begotten in their hearts to dedicate their lives for service in the regions beyond.

2. *The Heart Is Converted.*

Once the mind is fully informed as to the appalling need of multitudes in heathen darkness, the heart is moved to do something to meet such a need.

Thought leads to action, that is, if we do not scan superficially the denominational or general missionary material sent out by missionary societies. Through the vision gained by reading, love is created for the millions of souls waiting for the light of the Gospel. If our hearts are not moved as we read missionary appeals there is something wrong in our spiritual experience.

3. *The Hands Are Converted.*

A mind enlightened and a heart touched with sympathy prompt the hands to take the cause of missions in many practical ways. This is why women's missionary societies greatly aid work abroad, not only by caring for collecting boxes, but also by making bandages and garments so necessary for hospital work. A woman had a friend in Dundee who became so interested in missionary work she read about, that her heart was stimulated to play her part in meeting the appeal for money. She was too old to become a missionary, and did not have very much money of her own to give, so she hit on the plan of making toffee and candies and selling them to neighbors and friends and among her fellow church members. All money accruing from the sale of her products was divided among various missionary projects in which she was interested. If we could catalog all efforts of human hands to raise money for work abroad, endeavors would prove to be amazing.

4. *The Pockets Are Converted.*

Too often this is the last part of a Christian to be converted. A close-fisted kind of a man who was asked to contribute to some worthy cause growled and said, "My hand is never out of my pocket," to which the friend who was collecting replied, "True, I wish it would come out and bring something with it." How tragic it is to think

cf urgent missionary plans having to be scrapped because too many hands remain in pockets and purses! Stirring appeals for help from those in the front lines of the battle fall upon deaf ears. What a contrast there is between what we spend on ourselves and what we surrender for Christ's cause in distant fields!

5. *The Knees Are Converted.*

Reading and hearing of the gallant, sacrificial service of the few among so many in heathen darkness moves our knees to bend in intercession for missionaries, native workers, and for the millions without the knowledge of a Saviour's love. When William Carey decided to go to India, he said to his fellow church members in his home church, "I will venture to go down but remember that you must hold the ropes." Thus, there developed "Rope-Holders," bands of Christian people who organized prayer groups in homes and churches to intercede for those who had gone forth to far-off fields of service. How true it is in respect to missions that "more things are wrought by prayer than this world dreams of." The most heartmoving appeal for missionary intercession is the poem by my revered friend of long standing, Charles B. Bowser, of Shamokin, Pa., entitled Because You Prayed.

> God touched our weary bodies with
>   His power,
> And gave us strength
>   For many a trying hour
> In which we might have faltered,
>   Had not you, our intercessors,
>   Faithful been and true.
> Because You prayed
> God touched our eager fingers with
>   His skill,
> Enabling us to do
>   His blessed will
> With scalpel, suture, bandage;
>   Better still

He healed the sick, the wounded,
    cured the ill.

Because you prayed
God touched our lips with coals from
    altar fire,
    Gave Spirit fullness, and
      Did so inspire
        That when we spoke, sin-
          blinded souls
      Did see;
        Sin chains were broken;
        Captives were made free.

Because you prayed
The "dwellers in the dark"
    Have found the light,
    The glad, good news has
    Banished heathen night.
The message of the cross
    So long delayed
      Has brought them life at last
      Because you prayed.

6. *The Feet Are Converted.*

In the experience of many consecrated young people this is the last
phase of their missionary conversion.
The need of millions came to their attention through literature or appeals, and their hearts were moved. Then hands became active in different ways, even in the matter of personal giving. An unceasing prayer burden followed, and at last the response to the divine call, "Whom shall I send?" came and without hesitation the answer was, "Here am I, Lord, send me," and their feet took them to some of the loneliest and most benighted places on earth. May those of us at home never fail to hold the ropes as consecrated men and women live and labor in hard and difficult spheres separated from their loved ones, home comforts and church fellowship! Let us never forget that they are our representatives, our substitutes, and that by our unceasing prayers and gifts we are laborers together with them in the bringing of the other sheep into the Shepherd's fold.

For Church Anniversary Day

For Church
Anniversary Day

Lord God, we pray for Thy church. Thou hast called Thine own *Body*, Thy *Bride*, Thy *Household*, Thy *Fold*, Thy *Vineyard*. We pray, Holy Father, for this Thy Son's work, the fruit of His blood, this newborn world living through His death. We pray for its increase, that all nations may be gathered into it, the utmost ends of this earth: that all the heathen may be brought to a knowledge of the truth, that the church may do her work of evangelizing the world: that her borders may be enlarged, the fold widened. We pray for its unity, that all who are called by Thy Name, Lord Jesus, may be one, even as Thou and the Father and the Holy Spirit are one: even as there is but "one faith, one baptism, one God and Father of all."

We pray for its purity, that it may be "the salt of the earth," purifying the world, destroying the power of Satan, manifesting holiness, preparing a holy people for the Lord. We pray for its order, that it may approve itself the work of Thy hand, for Thou art not the Author of confusion, but of peace. We pray for its peace that it may be the peacemaker of the world, and accomplish Thy work of peace, for Thou hast spoken peace to them that are afar off and to them that are near; Thy peace hast Thou left with us. We pray for its doctrine, that it may be sound, that it may keep the spirit of truth. We pray for all the branches of this Tree, all members of this Body, all the sheep of this Fold, all the brethren of this Household of Faith; for the whole company of faithful people, friends and strangers, our own countrymen and foreigners; for all that are called by Thy Name. We pray for the healing of wounds, the mending of nets, the destruction of heresies, the reformation of manners, the salvation of all men; through the merits of Thy most precious blood. Amen.

— Bishop Armstrong (1813)

MEDITATION FOR
CHURCH ANNIVERSARY DAY

A Story That Thrills
Psalm 90:9

Having reached another chapter in the history of our church, an occasion such as this can only be profitable as we pause and ponder. On this anniversary day it is incumbent upon us to reflect, rejoice, repent and then renew our vows. As we turn back the pages of the past year and recall all we have experienced as a church, our hearts are filled with praise to God for all that He has made possible. "Not unto us, O Lord . . . but unto thy name give glory" (Psalm 115:1). How unfailing He has been in His provision for all the needs! Yet our hearts are sad over opportunities lost, over our lack of fuller dedication to the service of the Lord, over our failure to bring a greater impact for Him upon the souls of many around us. True repentance is ours because of what we might have accomplished in the extension of our influence as a church.

Another anniversary day, however, presents us with the challenge of renewal for He who has promised to do more for us than at our beginnings is in our midst to forgive the sins and failures of the past and to baptize us with power from on high as, in His mercy, we face another year of service. As this broken world has yet to see what God can accomplish through us who are completely yielded to Him, may all of us who form this church place ourselves anew upon His altar. For each of us, a message of warning yet of encouragement can be found in the prayer of Moses, the man of God, who used the somewhat descriptive simile of life whether communal or personal, "We spend our years as a tale that is told" (Psalm 90:9).

It is common at certain seasons of the year to take stock, and, scrutinizing our record, determine to live better lives. Thus we hear especially at the end of the year, the frequent expression, "I mean to turn over a new leaf," and such an expression indicates that there is a desire within us to live a different life and to magnify God as He has never been magnified before in our lives. But so often when people talk

185

about turning over a new leaf, what they need is a new life. Nevertheless, the idea of a new leaf implies that we think of life as a book and the passing years as leaves of such a volume. The Bible refers to life in many aspects, and the metaphors used to indicate the brevity of life, for the majority of metaphors or emblems are associated with speed. Life is as a watch in the night, as a flood, as a sleep, as the withering grass, as a fading leaf, as a flying shuttle of the weaver, as a vanishing vapor. And here in the passage before us life is likened unto a tale quickly told and soon forgotten.

We must remember that in the days of Moses they did not have books such as we possess today. One means of conveying news was by the employment of a news carrier. The carrier would gather together from a community all the outstanding current events, and then he would run on to the next community. Standing before the people, he would recite all he had heard. As he unfolded the story the enthusiasm of the people would rise as they stood and listened and drank in every word. Then, when he reached the end of his recitation of all that he had brought to this community, he would pass on to another town. When the story was over, the interest quickly evaporated and died away, and what the carrier had reported was soon forgotten.

Probably this is the idea back of the simile, "We spend our years as a tale that is told." Here, then, is one of the most fascinating cameos of life. There is no need to engage a biographer to write our story. We are daily penning a volume, marvelous or miserable in nature, depending on our lives. Let us try to work out and extract a few spiritual suggestions from such a metaphor of our communal church life or our own personal existence.

A. *Has a beginning.*

"We spend our years as a tale (or a story) that is told." First of all, every good story has a beginning. There is always a Chapter One to a story, and in like manner life and churches have a beginning. All life begins with God. What a majestic statement that is, stamped on the forehead of the infallible Word of God. "In the beginning, God." What a grand opening to this wonderful story of redeeming love!

Our entrance into this world differs. What kind of a beginning did we have, what kind of an opening chapter to the story of our life? Possibly we were born into a Christian home and from earliest years have been surrounded with spiritual influences. On the other hand, possibly we were born into a home where God was not recognized, and we were handicapped because of the lack of a religious background. The first beginning of life is of little consequence. The great question is this: Have we had a new beginning? Do we know what it is to be born anew by the Spirit of God? Possibly we look back over our past and as the result of our beginning find ourselves subject to influences that militate against holiness. There are desires and propensities within that cripple us, but it does not matter how we have been handicapped as the result of our entrance into life. We can have a new beginning. "Behold, I make all things new," and through the incoming of the Holy Spirit and the work He makes possible in regeneration, the past can be blotted out and the power of heredity checked, so that life can function for God.

B. *Grows in Interest.*

"We spend our years as a tale that is told." A good tale grows in interest, and we like stories, do we not, that lead us on? One or two fascinating, gripping sentences at the beginning, and then as we journey on with the writer and follow him in the unfolding of his plot we find our interest deepening. Some stories are, indeed, very fascinating. Others are so dull and uninteresting, that we are not through the first chapter before we are disgusted and throw the story aside, having no further use for it. Life is like a story — it grows in interest.

How fascinating some lives are. Who can read the story of D. L. Moody and remain the same? I think of my first visit to Chicago, when I quickly found my way down to Lake Street, and tried to find the spot where D. L. Moody used to work as a salesman. Knowing that it was somewhere near at hand that he sold shoes for a living I thanked God for such a man who wrote a story of such absorbing interest. We think of records like the lives of William Carey the cobbler, the father of modern missions; of David Livingstone who blazed a trail for God in dark Africa; of Mary Slessor, Dundee mill girl who became the uncrowned queen of Calabar. Why, such stories lay hold of us and exercise a definite influence upon our lives! We cannot read them without feeling the impact of God upon our own characters.

On the other hand, there are lives so drab and commonplace, nothing out of the ordinary, lived on a very low plane indeed. What is the story of our church and our lives like? Have they grown in interest? Has life become more fascinating? Has life yielded greater glory to God with the passing days, and is it telling upon other lives as we journey on to the end of the road?

C. *Divided into Chapters.*

"We spend our years as a tale that is told." A good story is divided into several chapters which we find tantalizing if we have not very much time to spare as we sit down before a good book. If the story grips us we can hardly lay the book down, and those chapters annoy us. Yet, they are convenient, for one can stop at the end of a chapter and then resume reading at a more convenient time. Some chapters are short, others are longer, and it would seem as if the changing years and circumstances of life are similar in pattern to the chapters of a book. Think of the way in which the story of life is broken up and divided. We have the opening chapter of birth; second chapter, youth; third chapter, love and courtship; the succeeding chapter of marriage, and then the chapter of sorrows and trials and disappointments, and finally, the chapter of tears and graves.

"We spend our years as a tale that is told," and the tale is divided into chapters. What new chapter have we reached in life and experience.

Man's life's a book of history;
The leaves thereof are days,
The letters, mercies closely joined,
The title is "God's Praise!"

If we are coming to the end of a dark chapter, a chapter of life we are not proud to look back upon, it is blessed to know that "the blood of Jesus Christ his Son, cleanseth us from all sin" (I John 1:7). Although we began the present chapter of life in a most unworthy way, we can finish it knowing that the hand of God is well able to erase everything in that chapter unworthy of Himself.

D. *Describes Various Characters.*

"We spend our years as a tale that is told." A good story describes various characters, and a gifted author will contrive to have the most unique, outstanding, surprising characters in his story. We all love a plot in which there are those characters who cross the stage and somewhat thrill us with their exploits. We all admire the hero and we hate the villain, and like to see the hero victorious at the end of the story and the villain conquered. We are further gratified when the hero and heroine happily marry. Yes, a good story is made up of differing characters.

What an incomparable story we have in that ever fascinating book from the pen of Robert Louis Stevenson, *Dr. Jekyll and Mr. Hyde* — a book devoted to the unfolding of these two characters which were found in one person! It seems as if the story of our life is as complex, for what are we but a mixture of Dr. Jekyll and Mr. Hyde? At times we find ourselves doubting our Lord like Thomas, denying Him like Peter, loving Him like John. The devil and the angel are within each one of us. Often we find those who can pray like saints while at church, and then go home and act like demons. What a mixture the story of life is. Sometimes people see one side of our character, and at other times they see another, and they wonder if we can be the same person. But it is the work of the Holy Spirit to make us like one character, even like the Lord Jesus.

E. *Differ in Quality and Worth.*

"We spend our years as a tale that is told." Stories differ in quality and worth. Some are cheap and inexpensive, and we never give them room on our book shelves. The curse of modern life is right here—our book stalls are loaded with trashy literature having a most unwholesome influence upon young men and women today, novels which are poisoning the springs of life. We cannot develop saintliness by living upon yellow novels.

Books do differ in quality and worth.

Not so long ago some $35,000 was paid for a few leaves of *Pickwick Papers,* coming as they did originally, from the pen of Charles Dickens. Are there not books priceless in value because of their authorship and influence? Some of these are secured at great cost, and are counted as literary treasures. Other books pour from the press and have a very short life because they are of a putrid character.

"We spend our years as a tale that is told." Some lives are worth more to God and man than others. Mary Slessor was worth more to God and humanity than her drunken father. What is our life worth? It is perfectly true that lives are like books. They differ in quality. Life is only valuable as it serves God and a lost world and fits us to enjoy His Presence forever.

While living in Dundee, Scotland, one came under the influence and spell of Robert Murray McCheyne, whose "Memoirs" are revered next to the Bible in many a Scottish home. Think of this dedicated young man, moving Scotland for his God, and dying at the early age of 28! But it is not the length of life only that tells the quality of it. One may reach one hundred years and achieve very little for God. Others may die at a very early age indeed and fulfill the divine purpose in their brief span. Murray McCheyne only ministered the Gospel in Scotland for something like five years, but Scotland has never lost the impact of God brought to bear upon it through the saintly life of Murray McCheyne.

One day, while actively preparing his diary and memoirs, here is what he wrote: "O God, help me to live so as to be missed." And missed he was!

I would be missed when gone!
I would not — my life done —
Have no eyes wet for me,
No hearts touched tenderly,

No good of me confessed;
Dead — and yet not missed!

There is not a more poignant, tragic phrase in God's infallible Word than that one describing Jehoram, who "departed without being desired" (II Chronicles 21:20). There are those who would be better off dead, better for the world if they were out of the way because of the evil influence they exert. Will we be missed when gone? May the passion of Robert Murray McCheyne characterize each one of us. By divine grace let us live so as to be missed! God grant us a life of quality and of worth because of the fact that it is fully yielded to Him and thereby fit as a channel of blessing to a weary world!

F. *Sometimes Continuous.*

"We spend our years as a tale that is told." Many stories are continuous. We are sorry to get to the end of some books, and annoyed as we come to the two little words "The End." At other times, if a story is printed as a serial, when we get to the end of one chapter and read, "To be continued in the next," how impatient we are for the appearance of the next installment.

There is never "the end" at the conclusion of the story of life, for life is to be continued. The sky, not the grave is our goal. There are those who would have us believe that death ends all; that as we reach the conclusion of our earthly pilgrimage out we go into oblivion; that when we die we are like dogs — done with. But death is not the end — it is an episode. Death is the opening of the gate into another life, a story continued beyond the close of the earthly chapter. How and where is the story of our life to continue? We are immortal, whether saved or lost, and the continuation of life in another realm depends upon our relationship to the Lord Jesus in this world. For the saint there will be the continuous story of grace and glory, a never-ending story of wonder and joy, and of service in heaven. There is eternal progress for the saint. But for the sinner there is no progress after the tomb, for in hell the sinner will go back over the old pages of life with remorse. "Son, remember!" Memory of the past can be torture when we think of how the story of life could have been romantic, and how that continuation of the story could have been in the realms of eternal bliss.

G. *Ends in Different Ways.*

Finally, a good story usually has a most interesting ending. Of course, stories end in different ways. We all prefer those stories with a good ending. Sometimes we are very disappointed with their conclusions. We anticipate the end and, reaching it, find the author has come to a different finale altogether. Some stories finish on a very sad note. The Old Testament ends its story with a curse, for the last word in the Old Testament is "curse"; but the end of the other story in the New Testament is totally different. The New Testament ends with a benediction. Stories end in different ways — so do human lives.

How are we going to reach the chapter of death? We should not be too concerned about dying. The end chapter of death need not concern us. If we live well, God will give us grace to die well. What we need now is not dying grace. Such will be ours when we come to pass through the valley of the shadow of death. What we do need is grace to live even though we must face the fact of the end. How is life to end? In bitterness or blessing? In glory or gloom? In tragedy or triumph? In heaven or hell?

Voltaire, the famous French infidel who died in 1778, had a very tragic ending to the story of his life. In the closing moments he could be heard blaspheming the name of the Lord and crying out, "O Christ! O Jesus Christ!" And he ended his moments in torture, crying, "I wish I had never been born!" No wonder another closed his career in the very same way, saying:

Out, out, brief candle!
Life's but a walking shadow, a poor player
That struts and frets his hour upon the stage
And then is heard no more: it is a tale
Told by an idiot, full of sound and fury,
Signifying nothing!

— Macbeth

What an end! But by the grace of God many have been enabled to come to the end with a different testimony. We think of Charles Wesley, the sweet singer of Methodism, who died ten years after Voltaire, and what a lovely climax we have to the sweet story of his marvelous life. As his eyes closed upon this world and opened upon another, friends around him heard him say, "I shall be satisfied when I awake in Thy likeness! *Satisfied! Satisfied! Satisfied!*"

May we come to the end of our earthly story in triumph and not in tragedy. There are one or two things to remember if, as we live our lives and pass through the world, others around are to be blessed through our influence. We must allow God to write upon the pages of our lives His sublime story, and when God pens the volume we have a story the world can read with profit. Paul caught this thought when he said that we are "living epistles," letters, stories, known and read of all men (II Corinthians 3:1, 2), and that as we are influenced by books, so men

and women around us will be won for God by the lives we live.

The next thought is this, that if we are conscious that some of the past pages of the story of life have been spoiled by sin, let us not talk about turning over a new leaf. Let us ask God by His gracious Spirit to undertake for us and apply the efficacious blood of the Lord Jesus to erase everything unworthy in the past. He always waits to take the sponge dyed red with His own blood and remove everything painful and sinful in the past.

We must always bear in mind that the story of our lives is to be unfolded at the judgment seat. "And the fire shall try every man's work of what sort it is" (I Corinthians 3:13). If we are a saint, then the story of life will be unfolded at the judgment seat of the Lord Jesus where believers are to be judged. If we lived in sin, and passed out in darkness, then there will be the Great White Throne with its terrible judgment, when the Judge will lay hold of the book of life and read the story. The grave works no miracle, for the person we are when we die, that person we are on the other side. Character remains fixed, and if we would escape the Great White Throne with its repetition of the shameful story of life — "For out of thine own mouth will I judge thee" (Luke 19:22), is what the Judge has already said — if we are to escape the terror of the Great White Throne, then we must fly to the arms of mercy and seek the forgiving grace of God. If we know what it is to walk with Him in white and to have a story that is made possible by His hand upon us, then, when "the day breaks and the shadows flee away" (Song of Solomon 4:6), stories will continue in another world with greater charm and fascination and sweetness. How true then, is the old simile — "we spend our years as a tale that is told."

Filling My Niche

I may not shine as others do,
  With brilliant gifts of intellect;
But even in my humble sphere,
  I may the greater Light reflect.

I may not speak with words of fire,
  Till men in crowds are strangely
    stirred;
But I may soothe some aching heart
  By just a simple, kindly word.

My talents may not number ten,
  Nor even five may I possess;
But I can use the one I have,
  And using it attain success.

I may not own some vast domain,
  Nor boast of rich reserves of gold;
But having Christ I'm heir of all,
And know the joy of wealth untold.

I may not move in circles high,
  Nor count my friends among the
    great;
But in companionship with Christ,
  I find the bliss of high estate.

I may not write with matchless skill
  Some epic that shall thrill the race;
But every day my life may tell
  The story of redeeming grace.

I may not paint in colors fair,
  Some wondrous scene of bygone
    days;
But day by day, in simple deeds,
  My life may witness to His praise.

I may not win the world's applause,
  Of fame for me there may be none;
Far higher will the rapture be,
  To hear my Saviour say — "well
    done."

For Annual Church Budget Day

For the Annual Church Budget Day

Give a proportion of thy gains to God,
And sanctify thy income. Set apart
A well-considered portion cheerfully
As thy thank-offering for His bounte-
ous love;
He is the great Proprietor of all,
Thou but His steward that must give
full account
For all that His great love hath lent to
Thee.

— Fred Mitchell

My house is Thine, Lord Jesus
And all that I possess;
Use it for whatsoe'er Thou wilt,
Thou comest but to bless.
The gold that came from Thee, Lord,
To Thee belongeth still;
Oh, may I always faithfully
My stewardship fulfill.

— J. Woodfall

"A steward is a person entrusted
with the management of another's
property"

— Concise Oxford Dictionary

Christian Stewardship means but
one thing — whatever has been entrusted to us by God — our time,
talents, treasures, prospects and possessions — belong to Him, and He has
the first claim upon them.

When God's work is done in God's
way for God's glory it never lacks
God's supply.

MEDITATION FOR THE
ANNUAL CHURCH BUDGET DAY

FAITHFUL STEWARDSHIP
I Corinthians 4:2

The necessity of budgeting one's resources in order to meet the obligations of a situation is forcibly illustrated for us in two of our Lord's matchless parables. Leaders in a community desirous of building a tower for its protection sit down and count the cost. If they try to build without sufficient money and material, then when both run out and they are left with a skeleton of a building, men will mock them for not accurately assessing their needs (Luke 14:28-30). The same principle faces a king going to war against another king. How can he expect to be victorious if he tries to fight 20,000 soldiers of the opposing army with only 10,000 of his own? (Luke 14:31, 32). In the same practical way a wife and mother knows that unless she works out the requirements of the home, and budgets her money accordingly she will find herself with a frightening debt through overspending. Wisely she will not order food or goods at the cost of ten dollars if she only

has eight dollars to spend.

While the church of God is a divine institution the militant part of it on earth is dependent upon human resources for its ministry in a world of need. The sword of the Lord is likewise the sword of Gideon. This is why pastor and officebearers of a church meet together and prayerfully plan for its continuance and expansion; its home needs and missionary commitments, and, preparing a budget for all monies required, presents the required amount to the fellowship of the church and appeals to every member to fulfill his stewardship. Then, as each member gives according to his ability, the budget is met, and the ministry of the church is not retarded.

How pertinent is the exhortation of Paul, as we come to our own personal responsibility in respect to church support. "It is required in stewards, that a man be found faithful" (I Corinthians 4:2). For those who fail to come to the help of the Lord in their share of the church budget, He has some solemn things to say in His parable of the Unjust Steward (Luke 16:1-13). Shakespeare, in *The Rape of Lucrece* has the couplet —

> They are the lords and owners of
>   their faces,
> Others but stewards of their
>   excellence.

What are we but stewards of the excellence of our blessed Lord and owner.

Stewardship, if rightly taught and understood, makes unnecessary the persistent drive to secure enough money to keep the machinery of a church in motion. Because of a widespread misconception as to the exact nature of Biblical stewardship we suffer from a wrong emphasis as to divine requirements. People are urged to give irrespective of any Christian experience. But —

> The cause of God is holy,
> And useth holy things.

Offerings of the unregenerated or of the carnally-minded do not earn the benediction of heaven. So let us examine closely how the Scriptures deal with stewardship.

A. *Faithful Stewardship Is Biblical.*

The term "steward," meaning "a person entrusted with another's property," is applied in different ways. Eliezer is said to have been a steward of Abraham's household (Genesis 15:2) and as such it was his responsibility to provide all the members of the family with food and raiment, receive all cash, and spend what was necessary to keep regular accounts. Without doubt this godly servant proved himself to be a faithful steward. In His parable of the Unjust Steward our Lord underscores the obligations of stewardship by using the term seven times in eight verses, an impressive fact seeing that He was never guilty of repetitious speech. The unjust steward was not condemned because he acted dishonestly, but because he acted wisely for himself. Thus, the

Master would have us act wisely and diligently with all we are and have in His service. Then all who are called to minister the Word of Life as Christ's representatives are "stewards of the mysteries of God" (I Corinthians 4:1). Such mysteries are the doctrines of grace — the divine treasures with which preachers are entrusted to trade. All who are overseers of the flock of God "must be blameless" as His stewards (Titus 1:7). They are "good stewards of the manifold grace of God" (I Peter 4:10), and as such all their gifts and endowments must be held as the Lord's property and employed to promote His glory.

Wherever stewardship is taught or implied, the emphasis is always the same, namely, the full or complete surrender of all to Him who is the giver of all. If we fail to use aright what we have then we lose it. "Give, and it shall be given you" (Luke 6:38). If we honor the Lord with our substance then our barns will be filled with plenty, but withholding what we have results in poverty (Proverbs 3:9, 10; 11:24, 25). It is ever the liberal soul who is made fat:

> There was a man, some thought him
>   mad,
> The more he gave, the more he had.

B. *Faithful Stewardship Is
    Comprehensive.*

A study of the "stewardship passages reveals that it relates not only to money, but covers every aspect of life. Included within its range are the spiritual, material and physical areas of life. Gold and goods are secondary. What God must first have is the person himself — possessions will follow. When He has our soul and service, our silver constitutes no problem, for once our time and talents are harnessed to His chariot, our treasures are viewed as

His. A matter of vital concern is not merely the devotion of our possessions on a vast scale, but the unreserved surrender of life in Spirit-inspired service. Too often the surrender of money is our effort to buy off God. We are tithers but not livers. In his discussion of the Macedonian Christians, Paul made it clear that they were to be commended because they gave their own selves first to the Lord (II Corinthians 8:5). Their deep poverty and afflictions were no excuse for not giving. Having yielded their lives they do not have to be urged to give their money. Neither did they content themselves with good resolutions, but performed cheerfully the surrender of their substance (II Corinthians 8:4-11). Life, then, must be viewed as a perfect whole, with the consecration of ourselves as the center, and the dedication of our possessions as the circumference. If God does not have our heart then the best we seek to give Him will be useless in influence.

> Fill Thou my life, O Lord my God,
>   In every part with praise,
> That my whole being may proclaim
>   Thy being and Thy ways.

C. *Faithful Stewardship Is Christlike.*

A blessed and beautiful trait of our Lord's witness while on earth is that He practiced what He preached. Exhorting His own to give and give, He led the way in sacrificial giving. Rich, for our sakes He became poor. He gave and gave until He became love's bankrupt. As a Jew, He taught tithing although He had little of His own to tithe, seeing He lived on borrowed things. But if He had no earthly treasures to surrender, He could spill His ruby blood — which He did, so freely, for the salvation of a lost world. He never saved or spared Himself. He gave Himself for our sins, and eternal enrichment is ours because of such an abandonment.

D. *Faithful Stewardship Is Apostolic.*

Having witnessed Calvary with its outpoured sacrifice, the apostles knew that anything they had was not their own. Their recognition of the Lordship of Christ involved a stewardship of a practical nature. "Neither said any of them that aught of the things which he possessed was his own" (Acts 4:32). Under the impact of the advent of the Spirit on the day of Pentecost they "sold their possessions and goods, and parted them to all men, as every man had need" (Acts 2:45). Thus they followed the self-imposed penury of their Master with Peter the leader saying, "Silver and gold have I none" (Acts 3:6). Personal claims of ownership were renounced for the benefit of others.

When Paul came upon the scene his support was made possible by the faithful stewardship of those he had been the means of leading to Christ. Writing to the Macedonian saints, Paul emphasized the *reason* why they should give; the *spirit* in which they should give; the *principle* regulating their giving, and the *reward* of giving (II Corinthians 8:2-13; 9:7, See I Corinthians 16:2; Matthew 6:20; Acts 20:36). Paul, himself, was a prodigal giver even to the hazarding of his life for the sake of the Lord whom he dearly loved. Like his Master, the apostle gave until there was nothing left to give.

E. *Faithful Stewardship Is Productive.*

When we *spend* our money we merely change the form of its value. For instance, if I need a good watch and have 50 dollars and buy the article, I still have the money in kind. When, however, we *give* our money, there takes place a change of the control over it, and it becomes God's. There is a sense in which it is His already for "what hast thou that thou didst not receive?" (I Corinthians 4:7). Strange, though it may seem, consecrated stewardship is productive of the highest dividends and of unusual 100% interest. "He shall receive an hundred fold now in this time" (Mark 10:28-30). God's rate of interest for investment in His service is never low. No depression can affect such an investment, and thieves can never steal it.

Further, sanctified stewardship rebounds in blessing and is productive of joy. God, who is well-pleased with such giving and always loves a cheerful giver, always gives good measure in return. Good *livers* are usually glad *givers*, and are made to rejoice through surrender. While we do not give to get, eternal rewards await those who are altogether the Lord's. Treasure is laid up in heaven (Matthew 6:20) in which our faithful stewardship on earth will result in heavenly responsibilities. "Who then is that faithful and wise steward, whom his Lord shall make ruler over his household?" (Luke 12:42). God does not want to deprive us of our possessions, but He urges us to send them on before, or to convert our cash into treasures in heaven.

The story is told of a godly farmer who was known as being most generous and who was asked why he was able to give so much away and yet remain so prosperous. "We cannot understand you," they said, "you give more than any of the rest of us and yet you always seem to have more to give." The farmer replied, "Oh, that's easy to explain. I keep shoveling into God's bin and God keeps shoveling more and more back into my bin, and God has the bigger shovel." How true this is! *God has the bigger shovel.* The most generous among men can never out-give God, the Giver of every good and perfect gift. As we come to covenant our share in the church's budget for another year we must remember that God loves hilarious givers, and that if we give as unto Him, He will repay us in good measure, pressed down, shaken together and running over (Luke 6:38).

For Youth Challenge Day

For Youth
Challenge Day

Go thou in life's fair morning, go in
the bloom of youth:
And buy for thine adorning, the precious pearl of truth:
Secure this heavenly treasure, and
bind it on thine heart,
And let not earthly pleasure e'er cause
it to depart.

Go, while the day-star shineth, go,
while thy heart is light;
Go, ere thy strength declineth, while
every sense is bright:
Sell all thou hast, and buy it; 'tis
worth all earthly things —
Rubies, and gold, and diamonds, scep-
tres and crowns of kings.

Go, ere the clouds of sorrow steal o'er
the bloom of youth;
Defer not till tomorrow, go now, and
buy the truth —
Go, seek thy great Creator, learn early
to be wise;
Go, place upon His altar a morning
sacrifice.
— Sankey's Sacred Solos

Remember now thy Creator in the
days of thy youth,
While the evil days come not, nor the
years draw nigh,
When thou shalt say, I have no
pleasure in them.
— Ecclesiastes 12:1

Youth, what man's age is like to be
doth show;
We may our ends by our beginnings
know.
—Sir John Denham (1615-1669)

MEDITATION FOR
YOUTH CHALLENGE DAY

A Rich Young Man's Regret
Matthew 19:16-22

Eternity alone will reveal how the efforts of organizations like *The Children's Special Service Mission, The National Young Life Campaign,* both British movements functioning for over half-a-century, and the American-conceived *Youth for Christ,* begun a quarter of a century ago, have influenced countless numbers of young people for Christ and His church. At a time when it seems as if Sunday school activities are on the wane, all concentrated attempts to reach youth with the truth should be welcomed and prayerfully and practically supported.

It is most interesting to study the Bible from the standpoint of youth, and discover its emphasis upon young men and women following the example of godly parents, and also upon the necessity and value of a personal commitment to the claims of God. Have you ever thought of the momentous decisions Scripture records, and of the different way in which some young people acted when faced with the great crises of life? The record of the rich young ruler, for example, one of the saddest in the gospels, is one of perennial interest, and was the inspiration of the pathetic picture, *The Great Refusal.* The Old Testament counterpart of this youth's decision is that of Orpah, who thought more of her gods and her people than of Naomi's God and, like the young ruler, went away. Each of the first three evangelists preserve the incident of Christ's encounter with this commendable youth, each providing some original touch thereby presenting us with his complete picture. Drawing all facets of his character together we can discern two inescapable aspects, namely, Things Possessed, and Things Unpossessed.

A. *Things Possessed.*

Several noble, admirable qualities mark this young man out as one with all his powers fresh and full. Evidently a lovable man, with many fine virtues, he was attractive and winsome. Yet with all his gold and graces, he was not satisfied. If only he had surrendered to Christ, all that was good about him would have been enhanced.

1. *He had a knowledge of Christ.*

He called Christ "Good Master" (Matthew 19:16). He saw in Jesus a good man, a teacher, yet only approached Him on the human plane as many do today. This was why Jesus said, "Why callest thou me good?" (Matthew 19:17). The young ruler's knowledge was partial, external, and not full-orbed as ours is if we have obeyed the call of the Master. We live on this side of the cross, and know Him not after the flesh, but as the risen, glorified Son of God.

2. *He had strivings after a higher life.*

He had a strong, heart-hunger driving him irresistibly in all haste to the Source of true satisfaction. "What good thing shall I do, that I may have eternal life?" (19:16). There was never a more important question presented to Jesus. Eternal life is the most glorious prize in the universe to be gained. It embraces all the blessings of salvation in the world, and then a place in the family of God for ever. It is no wonder this young man *ran* to ask Christ this question. The wonder is that so few people ever do run to make the same inquiry. They run to seek earth's poor prizes, but are slow in their pace when they are seeking eternal life.

He was sincere when he asked the question out of the fullness of his heart, and an examination of his question reveals two things usually common in all seekers. *First,* there was dissatisfaction, and, because of inner, spiritual longings, came to Jesus on a purely religious quest. He did not come to Him for loaves and fishes, or to trap Him as the Pharisees did, or out of idle curiosity. There are two kinds of dissatisfied people, namely, those dissatisfied with what they have, and others with what they are. The majority, whether rich or poor, are in the first class, but the young ruler was dissatisfied with what he *was*. With all his wealth, possessions and commendable qualities, he was not at peace within his soul.

In the second place, he had a wrong conception, and asked, "What must I do?" Under the Levitical law, life was gained by doing, "This do and live" (Leviticus 18:5). However, eternal life is not gained by doing, but received by believing. It is a gift to be appropriated by faith (Romans 6:23; I John 5:11, 12). No sinner can be saved by works, but once saved, he must work like a slave for his Saviour. Eternal life cannot be secured by saying prayers, or fasting, or joining a church and being baptized in a certain way, or by giving liberally to religious and charitable causes, or by a round of religious exercises. It is a gift bestowed upon those who accept it by faith.

3. *He had morality.* "All the commandments I have kept from my youth up" (Matthew 19:18-20).

His reply to Christ's demand indicates his lofty morality. He was not an ungodly youth like the prodigal son, but "a hopeful young gentleman," wearing the white flower of a blameless life as far as the law was concerned. He only obeyed the mere letter of the law. He was ignorant of the living Spirit animating all its precepts. He had the law but not life. Although he never stooped to anything mean, despicable, contemptible, but was always doing good things and wanted to do another in order to possess eternal life, he sought a right blessing in the wrong way.

4. *He had youth.*

The phrase, "the young man," suggests that he might have been about the same age as Jesus. Youth attracts youth, and thus the young Prince of Glory and the rich young ruler were attracted to each other. "Remember now thy Creator in the days of thy youth" (Ecclesiastes 12:1). Why? Youth is the period of tender conscience, love, energy, aspiration, decision and glory. If one does not surrender to God in life's most beautiful time of youth, the probability is that if left to later years, such a surrender will be extremely difficult. This may account for very few people being saved when middle life or old age are reached. In the salvation of a young person, there is a double salvation, for the soul is saved and the life secured for the Saviour.

5. *He had a godly parentage.*

When he said that he had kept the commandments from his "youth up" (19:20), he implied that he had been nurtured in a religious atmosphere, and that his home was one in which God was honored. A godly home is indeed a priceless privilege, yet one can imbibe religion in such a way and not know what it is to be saved. And a lost eternity is all the more bitter for the person going there from a home where God was feared and loved.

6. *He had earnestness.* "He came running" (Mark 10:17).

He was desperate to reach Christ with the question of his heart before He passed out of His sight. But commendable though anxiety is, it cannot save. Only an unreserved commitment to Christ can make a person His.

7. *He had reverence.* "He kneeled to Him" (Mark 10:17).

This was the recognition of Christ's superiority, and that He was One worthy of the deepest reverence and allegiance he could give. We gain

nothing by dashing irreverently into the divine presence. Humiliation and a worshipful frame of mind and prayers, while they can create the right atmosphere within one, cannot in themselves save. Genuine repentance, faith and surrender are the only avenues of salvation.

8. *He had the look of Christ.* "Jesus beholding him" (10:21).

The original here implies a deep searching look. Jesus fixed His eyes upon him so as to read the young man's inner desires. The same penetrating heart-searching look is used of John the Baptist "looking upon Jesus" (John 1:36) and of Jesus as He "looked upon Peter" (Luke 22:61). We can never hide anything from Him. "Thou God seest me" (Genesis 16:13). What does He see as He looks within?

9. *He had the love of Jesus.* "He loved him" (Mark 10:21).

This is the only seeker after truth of whom it is said that Jesus loved him. Yet it is true that He loves all sinners. Some of the old Jewish expositors wondered why Christ loved one who was unprepared for His kingdom. So they belittle His affection by saying that it means He kissed or caressed the young man as Jewish doctors rise up and kiss the disciples they are pleased with. But the Bible says that "beholding him Jesus loved him." There was something in him that drew out His affection. He saw in him many amiable qualities, many elements of beauty of character which He knew could be made into great loveliness and power. Christ was drawn out to this young seeker with his pure heart, clean life and religious aspirations. He had learned how to restrain animal passions as his obedience to specific commandments clearly prove. He had a craving for the highest things. His soul was no cage of unclean birds. He was not like the prodigal son, unchaste, bestial and profane, and Jesus, taking cognizance of his noble qualities, loved him. He saw the possibility of an angel in the stone, and knew that a life least damaged by sin, and fully surrendered to Him would be a great asset in His service.

10. *He had position.* "He was a ruler" (Luke 18:18).

As a ruler of the synagogue, his high, ecclesiastical office was a testimony to his legal blamelessness. Education, culture, integrity and ability were his, and if only these virtues had been harnessed to the chariot of the Master what an effective witness he would have become.

11. *He had wealth.* "He was very rich" (Luke 18:23). "He had great possessions" (Matthew 19:22).

The language used to describe his affluence implies a vast abundance of material riches which he had possibly inherited. Yet, "rich, increased with goods, and in need of nothing," he was not satisfied. He lacked the riches of divine grace. He was destitute of the wealth of faith and sacrifice, and rejected the price of same. Alas! too many in our time have all that the world can give but are not content, and are not prepared to sing —

> With many dreams of fame and gold
> Success and joy to make me bold,
> But dearer still Thy faith to hold,
>   O Lamb of God, I come.

B. *Things Unpossessed.*

Having considered the good things the young ruler did possess, let us now think of the better things he did not have. His question to Christ, "What lack I yet?" was severely answered, "One thing thou lackest" — or come short of (Mark 10:21; Romans 3:23).

It is most profitable to watch our Lord's different treatment of sinners. He did not open wide His arms to welcome this young man with longings for a higher life, as He did when receiving the publican and harlots. He knew that the self-complacency of this youth must be shattered. Jesus did not flatter him and then leave him, but, giving him full credit for his good qualities, He sternly told him the truth — which hurt! Easy-going disciples are easily made — and lost. The abiding disciples are those who come by the way of a deep unreserved surrender to Christ.

This young man recoiled from the sharp test which Christ imposed. He wanted the prize but the cost was too great. He lacked the courage to fulfill his inner conviction. It may seem hard to condemn him for one thing, but that one thing was *everything*. What is the use of a beautiful watch if only one thing is wrong with it — a broken mainspring?

1. *The One Command* — "Go and sell all that thou hast" (Matthew 19:21).

For a moment the young man stood stunned as he heard this demand, then turned away silently as a prisoner who had heard his doom. The greatest hour of his life had come, with destiny hanging upon his decision, but he was found wanting. If we would have eternal life, all that comes between our soul and Christ must be surrendered. With the youthful ruler it was his gold. While Christ did not imply that all rich sinners must surrender their wealth, the principle involved is medicine for all. When the same crisis faces a sinner and his conscience is searched, and the command of a full surrender is heard, the Spirit of God reminds the anxious one, of, not what they have done, but of what they are unready to do. The fork of the road is reached and the nature of the future depends upon a personal response to the call of Christ.

2. *The One Lack* — "One thing thou lackest" (Mark 10:21).

Our Lord's answer to the young man's question is most instructive. What is the one thing which, besides all we can do for ourselves by obedience and cultivation of character, makes one a Christian? Character and destiny depend upon the answer given. A person may appear to be Christian — attend church, keep the commandments, love his family, be generous to the poor and needy, and live conscientiously in all things. If such a man should ask, "What lack I yet?" how would we answer him? Would we tell him to sell his house and all his goods and give to the poor, as the young ruler was told to do? No, he had to do it because his heart was attached to his wealth. This alone was his barrier to blessing. The "one thing" he failed to do was to take Christ instead of his material riches. With us, it may not be money, but worldly pleasures and pursuits, companions, ambitions, self-interests. The selling and giving are but parts of the essential decision to follow Christ.

3. *The One Result* — "He went away sorrowful" (Matthew 19:22).

The word used for "sorrowful" means "sad" and is applied to the sky and is translated "lowering" (Matthew 16:3). The stern request of Christ which the youth refused cast a gloom over his heart and shadowed his face. He did not become angry, or turn away careless, saying, "Oh! what's the use!" He went away with a soul as heavy as lead, and, turning from Christ with

such an acute feeling, must have added to dissatisfaction. Somehow the enjoyment of his possessions would now be spoiled because of his encounter with One who had surrendered all to save a lost world. He would not be able to walk the road of selfishness and love the world with the same zest again. A fanciful suggestion has been made that possibly the rich young ruler was Saul of Tarsus who became Paul the apostle. If this is so then we can appreciate what he had to say about counting all he had as dung for Christ's sake (Philippians 3:4-8).

4. *The One Treasure* — "Follow me" (Luke 18:22).

It is not enough to forsake that which hinders. One must forsake and *follow* the Saviour who calls us to Himself. The treasure offered the youth in exchange for his material wealth was the divine treasury, "filled with boundless stores of grace." And Christ was only asking him to follow His example. Suppose Jesus, in a past eternity, had said to God, "What must I do in order to bring eternal life to lost souls in the world below?" and received the reply, "Go, sell all that Thou hast in outward glory and majesty and go down and die," what would have been our lot had Jesus refused, turning from God sorrowful because of His glorious possessions? What a dark world this would have been if He had kept the riches of glory all to Himself. But the blessedness of the Gospel is that although rich, for our sakes He became poor, that through His poverty we might be made rich.

In many ways today young people are being urged to "sell" all they have, or to yield themselves utterly to the Saviour; and to "give to the poor" which implies willingness for their life to be spent in the Master's service wherever

He may direct. As a young man He gave His all for the young, and He expects *all* from them. For His best, our best must be surrendered. We can never possess His treasures unless our hearts are freed from lesser loves, and our hands emptied of fancied wealth. How appealing is the call to youth in the hymnist's verses —

> Just as I am, Thine own to be,
>   Friend of the young, who lovest me,
> To consecrate myself to Thee,
>   O Jesus Christ, I come.
> In the glad morning of my day,
>   My life to give, my vows to pay,
> With no reserve and no delay,
>   With all my heart I come.
> I would live ever in the light,
>   I would work ever for the right,
> I would serve Thee with all my might;
>   Therefore to Thee I come.
> Just as I am, young, strong, and free,
>   To be the best that I can be
> For truth, and righteousness and Thee,
>   Lord of my life, I come.
>   — Marianne Hearn

For Graduation or Baccalaureate Day

For Graduation or Baccalaureate Day

The Master of My Boat

I owned a little boat awhile ago
  And sailed a morning sea without
    a fear,
And whither any breeze might fairly
    blow
  I'd steer the little craft afar or near.
    Mine was the boat, and mine the
      air,
    And mine the sea, not mine, a
      care.

My boat became my place of nightly
    toil,
  I sailed at sunset to the fishing
    ground,
At morn the boat was freighted with
    the spoil
  That my all-conquering work and
    skill had found.
    Mine was the boat and mine the
      net,
    And mine the skill and power to
      get.

One day there passed along the silent
    shore,
  While I my net was casting in the
    sea,
A man, who spoke as never man
    before;

I followed Him — new life begun
    in me.
  Mine was the boat, but His, the
    voice,
  And His the call, yet mine, the
    choice.

Ah, 'twas a fearful night out on the
    lake,
  And all my skill availed not at the
    helm.
Till Him asleep I waken, crying,
    "Take,
  Take Thou command, lest waters
    overwhelm!"
    His was the boat, and His the sea,
    And His the peace o'er all and
      me.

Once from His boat He taught the
    curious throng,
  Then bade me let down nets out in
    the sea;
I murmured, but obeyed, nor was it
    long
  Before the catch amazed and
    humbled me.
    His was the boat and His the
      skill,
    And His the catch, and His, my
      will.

— J. H. Richards

MEDITATION FOR
GRADUATION OR BACCALAUREATE DAY

THERE GO THE SHIPS!
Psalm 104:26

Ships! What romances cluster around them! They are the creators of civilization, the producers of prosperity, and the inanimate traveling evangelists to all the world.

Ships! Why, they are conspicuous for the opposite ministry! They unite, yet divide. They carry life, yet belch out death. To a crowd on a dock they bring joy to some, anguish to others.

Ships! The history of the race is the history of its ships. Think of the ship that carried Paul to Europe! What precious cargo that was. Europe owes its Christianity and the democracy we hold so dear to that sea voyage.

Think of the ship that bore St. Augustine from France to England. Sent by Gregory, Bishop of Rome, that vessel brought to the old world, one whose ministry radically changed civilization more than 1500 years ago. From that ship we received our best Anglo-Saxon language, the great cultural centers of Oxford and Cambridge, and the historic religious shrines of Yorkminster and Westminster.

Think of the ship that carried Christopher Columbus on August 3, 1492, to his discovery of a vast continent! It has been said, "San Salvador became the Bethlehem of a new civilization."

Think of another ship that followed Columbus, almost a century and a half later, *The Mayflower*, which bore the Pilgrim Fathers from east to west. Carlyle was right when he declared that *The Mayflower* bore the most precious cargo of any ship that ever sailed the seas. The day came when they signed their compact in the cabin of their vessel — a compact Daniel Webster called "the seed corn of the Constitution." Think of that little Dutch ship, in whose hold was hidden away a shoemaker someone has called "the inspired cobbler," who as William Carey, became the father of modern missions.

Ships! There are all kinds. Ships are as varied as the seas they sail. We have warships, merchant-ships, discovery ships, passenger ships, fishing ships, life ships, missionary ships.

Ships! The Bible is full of ships from the one built by Noah, according to divine specifications, right on until you come to the costly merchant ships of Babylon, the doom of which John describes in the Revelation.

Ships! Yes, and what are we but ships that pass in a night. Here we are sailing out on the voyage from school or college into the unknown future. We have said Farewell to the classroom, and with moorings loosed, we have put out to the uncharted sea of coming years. Let us then consider the psalmist's nautical illustration (Psalm 104:26), as it applies to ourselves and the days ahead upon which we are privileged to embark.

As a ship puts out to sea, fervent prayers arise that the passage over the mighty deep will be a safe and an uneventful one. *Bon Voyage!* is the message we send to a departing friend. And a cable, indicating the ultimate arrival of the vessel, sets our mind at rest. As, however, there is a combination of forces responsible for a good journey, let us think of a few that we can apply to ourselves.

A. *The Tides.*

Ships are dependent upon tides. A low tide means delay for boats entering and leaving the harbor. And, as ships, we must watch for and work with the tides, the spiritual tides of the Spirit. To set sail without the tide will mean inevitable disaster before the year is much older.

B. *The Prosperous Gales.*

Ships can pursue their course pleasantly and well when beneficial winds are with them. The disciples found it difficult to navigate their ship, seeing "the wind was contrary" (Matthew 14:24). It is not without significance

that the Holy Spirit is symbolized as a ruling, mighty wind. And, if we are to have a prosperous journey we must set our sails to catch the breeze. The favorite poem of the late Bishop Taylor Smith, chaplain to Queen Victoria, who died in a ship and was buried in the sea he dearly loved, was:

> One ship drives North,
>   One ship drives South,
> By the self-same wind that blows;
>   It's the set of the sails,
>   And not the gales,
> That determines the way it goes.
>
>   One basks in the blaze
>   Of the Southern Sun,
> Beneath the Southern Cross;
>   The other is wrecked,
>   On some ice-bound coast,
> For ever a total loss.
>
>   One soul finds life,
>   One soul finds death,
> But the grace of God is the same;
>   For the one rejects,
>   While the other accepts,
> And trusts in the Saviour's Name.
>
>   One sets his face,
>   To receive God's grace,
> And walks in the light of the Lord;
>   While one turns aside,
>   Thro' the gate that is wide,
> And walks in the way that is broad.
>   — H. Maxwell Wright

C. *The Necessity of a Correct Compass.*

The absence of the visible sun and stars seriously hindered the ship carrying Paul to Rome. Having no compass was one reason why ships, at that time, did not venture out during winter. Now, perfect compasses and all kinds of nautical instruments insure a straight course.

Since we can be likened to ships sailing on the sea of life, our safe and only compass is the incomparable Word of God. Modernists may tell us that the Bible, as a compass, is defective, antiquated and unreliable. The Scriptures, however, are the church's sole source of guidance and direction. We can only avoid disaster as we believe and rest in God's infallible Compass, for its truths never fail to guide us aright.

D. *The Importance of having a Capable Pilot.*

Any ship must have someone well-able to command and steer her course. He must have a thorough knowledge of charts, and must also know where all the rocks, sand banks and dangerous reefs are. Everything on board — lives and cargo — are dependent upon him.

Well, we have an efficient Pilot in "The Master of ocean and earth and skies"! He has never lost a vessel — and never will!

> The Christ who stilled the troubled
>   wave on restless Galilee
> Is near, when at each tidal hour,
>   some barque puts out to sea.

And as we set sail, let Him have the bridge. Let us never question His command nor direction. He sailed through bloodier seas than He will ask you to cross, so trust Him implicitly, even though you may not know where He is guiding you. When the dark days come, and it seems as if your little ship is at the mercy of the cruel waves, remember that your Pilot is at hand, and that He controls all natural, material and satanic forces. Winds and waves must obey Him.

For the fogs of doubt and unbelief — the hidden sands of indifference and carelessness — the icebergs of formality — religious pirates in cap and gown to rob us of our faith, all alike await our voyage. Sinister forces will seek our shipwreck, but

> Tell not of wrecks and hidden rocks,
> Tell not of storms and winds that
>   mock,
> No ill can ever come to me,
> With Him, on land or any sea.

As a magnificent fleet of well-laden ships may we steam out with flying banners. May He who made the sea, grant us a prosperous voyage! Multitudes of souls in all parts of this storm-tossed world await the discharge of our cargo. May nothing hinder our journey of good will! Let us learn to travel well with pardon and peace and other heavenly merchandise. With *faith* as a sail to appropriate the power of God, *hope* as an anchor so that we will not drift from the Word of God, *love* as the helm in our completion of the will of God, all will be well.

Farewell, then, ship of destiny! We may not pass again on the wide sea of life. This, however, is our mutual confidence, that at daybreak our vessels will gather within the heavenly port, there to recount our exploits and receive our rewards for successful voyages. It is thus that we commend each other to God. With prayerful, loving hearts, vibrating with emotion we find ourselves wishing one another *Bon Voyage!* as we set sail upon a year which may prove to be one of the most momentous in our lives.

> My little craft sails not alone:
> A thousand fleets from every zone
> Are out upon a thousand seas;
> And what for me were favoring breeze
> Might deal another, with the shock
> Of doom, upon some hidden rock.
> And so I do not dare to pray
> For winds to waft me on my way;
> But leave it to a higher Will
> To stay or speed me; trusting still
> That all is well, and sure that He
> Who launched my barque will sail
>   with me
> Through storm and calm. He will not
>   fail
> Whatever breezes may prevail.
> To land me, every peril past,
> Within the sheltering haven at last.

For Children's Dedication Day

For Children's Dedication Day

Good Shepherd, who carriest the lambs in Thine arms, give Thy Spirit, we beseech Thee, to all those engaged in training the young; make them patient, grant them tenderness, sincerity and firmness, and enable them to lead the young hearts to Thee, for Thy name's sake. Amen.

— Anonymous

O Lord Jesus Christ, who didst take little children in Thine arms and bless them; bless, we beseech Thee, all children dear to us. Take them into the arms of Thy everlasting mercy. Keep them from all evil, and bring them into the company of those who ever behold the face of Thy Father which is in heaven, to the glory of Thy Holy Name. Amen.

— Prayer Book for Priests (1870)

The childhood shows the man,
As morning shows the day.

— John Milton

Christian child, all must be
Mild, obedient, good as He.

— Mrs. C. F. Alexander

MEDITATION FOR
CHILDREN'S DEDICATION DAY

A LITTLE CHILD IN THE MIDST
Mark 9:36

When the disciples were discussing the fact of who should be the greatest among them, Jesus, seeking to teach them the necessary lesson of humility, took a child and set him in their midst (Mark 9:36). In order to continue human society God places children in our homes and churches, and it is the solemn obligation of parents and of all who work with children to lead them, in their earliest years, to Him who urges us to suffer the children to come unto Him. Pharaoh's daughter, ignorant of the fact that the nurse chosen to rear young Moses was his mother, said to her: "Take this child away, and nurse it for me, and I will give thee thy wages" (Exodus 2:9). Bringing up children in the fear and admonition of the Lord is always rewarding.

The religious instruction of the young must have, as its objective, their salvation, for they need to be saved, and, thank God, can be saved. If little ones are to be led to the Saviour, it will not be by the recital of moral essays, but by parents, pastors and teachers coming down to their level and presenting the truth in a way that their growing minds can understand. If they ask for bread we must not give them a stone. The portion of the children's bread must be broken small enough for them to eat, and such is the nature of Christian truth that it can be simplified to present the claims of Jesus and the glory and beauty of life in Him. But if we would lead girls and boys to Him who became the Babe of Bethlehem, and steady younger and feebler feet when they falter, we ourselves must hold the unseen hand with firmer grasp.

Children are here and everywhere, and are the same yesterday and today. Wherever they are found they laugh and cry, smile and love, and, as real internationalists, ignore all social and race boundaries. Further, with every little child the world begins anew, giving to parents and pastors another opportunity of adding another member to the Body of Christ.

Jesus loves the children of the world.

215

All the children of the world;
Red and yellow, black and white,
They are precious in His sight;
Jesus loves the children of the world.

One of the most appealing of Bible children, whose story our children like to hear about is Samuel, of whom it is said that he "ministered before the Lord, *being a child,* girded with a linen ephod" (I Samuel 2:18). Simply told and illustrated, the record of this child minister, born of godly parents, Elkanah and Hannah, never fails to attract the attention of the young who love stories about other children. The first thing to emphasize is that the Bible can teach us that young hearts can love God, young lives can be surrendered to Him, and young hands can serve Him. The kingdom of heaven has a place for little children out of whose mouths God can perfect praise. Samuel was only a child, but he was not too young to love God and serve Him.

There's not a child so small and weak
But has his little cross to take,
His little work of love and praise
That he may do for Jesus' sake.
— Mrs. C. F. Alexander

There are so many little things that little folks can do. Of course, we know that consciously or unconsciously they can do much harm. In the report of a robbery it was said that the people living in the house thought they had guarded it securely with bolts on the doors and bars on the windows, but when the servants came down one morning they found all the gold and silver articles gone. Then it was discovered that just one very small window was unlocked. It was so tiny that the household thought there was no danger in it. However, the thieves saw their opportunity and put a very small boy through the tiny window. Once inside, he opened a larger window and the mischief was done.

On the other hand, little people and little things can do much good. What an interesting story that is of a lion who somehow got himself enmeshed in a net — the great king of the forest bound — but other animals hearing of his plight came to his help. An elephant appeared, walked around as majestically, yet as sad, as it could. A bear came and danced, and a tiger came on the scene and roared loudly. Hyenas and jackals and wolves found their way to the lion in the net, but they shook their heads as if to suggest that the lion should have been more careful. Thus it seemed as if the king of the jungle must die a miserable death in its net, but, when he was sadly bemoaning his fate, a little mouse came and asked if he could do anything to help. How absurd to think that he could set the lion free when the large powerful animals were helpless to assist!

The lion thought there was no harm in the mouse trying to do something, so the mouse crept up to the net and began to gnaw at it. Strand after strand of the rope was bitten through by the sharp little teeth. It was a long and wearisome task, but those little teeth worked on, and at last the rope was loosed and the despairing lion was freed. The *child* Samuel ministered unto the Lord, and while he could not undertake the solemn priestly functions of the temple, his small hands could pour oil into the lamp, trim the wick, keep the golden candlesticks clean, and put out the lamps at night. As all day long Samuel waited upon the old man Eli, he knew that he was a little staff for the aging priest to lean on. At sunrise little Samuel would draw aside the covering of skins, and the sunlight would flood the sanctuary with radiance. Children often bring sunshine and joy with them into the home, and, all unknown to them minister unto the Lord by their simple trust in Him. Out of the mouths of praise He can perfect praise.

Another aspect of the child minister is that he *was girded with a linen ephod*. Now the linen ephod was the dress the priest wore, but Samuel, although he was only a child, could not appear before the Lord without the proper robe. His mother made him a little coat and brought it to him, but this was not the one he wore as he ministered unto the Lord. He had to wear the robe appointed and commanded of God. Does this fact not teach us that we cannot minister to God in our own strength and our own goodness? All of us, even children, must have the right robe — the one washed and made white by the blood of Jesus. The ephod was fashioned of gold, purple, blue, scarlet and of fine twined linen, and girls and boys, as well as adults, must receive the heavenly robe and experience all the golden love and virtues it symbolizes before they can minister to the Lord.

A final word is necessary as to young Samuel's mother who made a *little coat* for her child, and worked into it all the love of her heart. Her son, given to the Lord, did not become too proud to wear the plain small coat his mother made for him. He did not strut about like a peacock when dressed in his brilliant ephod, and despise the homespun coat. He wore that too, and with gratitude to God for the godly, praying mother who had fashioned it. The colored ephod would remind little Samuel of his relationship to God and the worship of the temple — the little coat bound him to his home and loved ones, and kept his young heart in remembrance of his precious father and mother who had surrendered him to the Lord.

On this Decision Day, pray that girls and boys, hearing the call of God, will be ready to say with the child Samuel, "Speak, Lord; for thy servant heareth" (I Samuel 3:9), and then like him, grow "in wisdom and stature, and in favour with God and man" (Luke 2:52).

> Little children are remembered in the Saviour's promise,
> They may early share the blessings of redeeming grace;
> He is watching kindly o'er them, and His Word assures us
> That in Heaven their angels ever see the Father's face.

For Pastor's Ordination Day

For Pastor's
Ordination Day

There stands the messenger of the
    truth! there stands
The legate of the skies! his theme
    divine:
His office sacred, his credential clear;
By him, in streams as sweet
As angels use, the Gospel whispers
    peace.

By day and night strict guard to keep
To warn the sinner, cheer the saints,
Nourish the lambs and feed the sheep.

I have a fellowship with hearts
To keep and cultivate.

My album is the human heart,
Where tempests rage and tear-drops
    start,
    Without a ray of light;
To write the name of Jesus there:
To see the sinner bend in prayer;
To point to worlds both bright and
    fair,
    Is my supreme delight.

To other souls to be
The cup of strength in some great
    agony.

MEDITATION FOR
PASTOR'S ORDINATION DAY

In his three pastoral epistles, I and II Timothy and Titus, Paul offers to all preachers of the Word much sound, practical advice. Taken together, these three epistles present a threefold view of the preacher.

In I Timothy he is before us as a *leader*, with a charge to discharge; in II Timothy he is the *worker*, who must labor for the Master from "dawn till setting sun"; in Titus he is the *instructor*, responsible for tuition in sound doctrine.

A close study of Paul's first letter to Timothy reveals that it is made up of great, living, moral watchwords by which the preacher is to guide his life. After the apostle's close analytical reasonings and practical expositions of certain writings, we come across these unescapable watchwords. Take, for example, the summary Paul presents to Timothy in the challenge, "But thou, O man of God, flee these things; and follow after righteousness, godliness, faith, love, patience, meekness. Fight the good fight of faith, lay hold on eternal life" (I Timothy 6:11, 12).

A fivefold portrait is sketched for Timothy, this young preacher, by Paul, the veteran preacher. May grace be ours to conform to such a portrait!

A. *A Godly Designation* — "*O man of God.*"

Godliness and its cognates occur some ten times in these pastoral epistles, and is a term suggesting, as Archbishop Trench has reminded us, "a reverence well and rightly directed . . . the force of piety in the life itself, whether internal or external. It is not so much an inward, inherent holiness as a practical operative, collective piety." And, as our Christian faith is proven and self-evident by its fruits, may those of us who have been called to preach have a character molded more and more perfectly after such a heavenly model.

By comparing the two epistles we discover various titles or designations given to Timothy as he faced his career as a preacher. He is a *good soldier*, and as such must endure hardness (II

Timothy 2:3). He is an *athlete,* and must therefore play the man in the contest of faith (I Timothy 4:7; 6:12). He is a *physician,* and must be ready to recommend doctrine for sickly souls and combat those errors as destructive as gangrene (II Timothy 2:17). He is a *cunning hunter,* coaxing to life, out of the toils of the master-fowler, those who have fallen into snares (I Timothy 3:7; 6:9). He is a *wise banker,* who has a most precious deposit to guard (I Timothy 6:20; 2:1-12). He is a *patient husband-man,* and must practice hard work, remembering "no pains, no gains" (II Timothy 2:6). He is a *workman,* laying out in a straight line the highway of truth (II Timothy 2:15). He is a *slave,* under the necessity of exhibiting meekness (II Timothy 2:24). He is a *man of God,* whose designation is associated not so much with his office, but with his character. (Frequently used in the Old Testament, such a title for a preacher occurs only here, and in II Timothy 3:17). And, as used by Paul in addressing Timothy, it speaks of what he must *be* rather than *do.* Godliness of character is suggested by the term "man of God." It was practically another name for the Christian faith, as a new cult, which the convert had professed and adopted in contrast to the religions of heathenism around him.

Godliness, it will be found, is associated with:

1. The mystery of God (I Timothy 3:16).

2. The doctrine of Christ (I Timothy 6:3).

3. A form (I Timothy 3:5).

4. Is profitable unto all things (I Timothy 4:8).

5. Is of great gain (I Timothy 6:6).

6. Is worthy of earnest pursuit (I Timothy 6:11).

(The only other reference to the term in the New Testament is in II Peter 1:3, 6, 7 and 3:11).

As a *man of God* the preacher must see to it that his life does not belie the name he bears. A soldier by the name of Alexander was brought into the presence of Alexander the Great. Guilty of disgraceful conduct, he awaited the judgment of the monarch whose name he bore. "Is your name Alexander?" asked Alexander the Great of the soldier. "Yes, sir," was the timid reply. "Go, and either change your name or your character," was how the soldier was dismissed by Alexander.

B. *A Godly Renunciation — "Flee these things."*

As a godly man, there are several striking traits which Timothy's character must manifest. He must withdraw himself from certain people and things which are specifically mentioned in the previous verses of this chapter. As a preacher, Timothy must shun, must escape, the false ideals and aims of those around him. Army officers hate to rehearse their men in retreat, yet it is sometimes necessary to retreat in order to win. A successful retreating action can mean victory! Therefore we see Paul's twofold use of the word "flee" (II Timothy 2:22). Let us look for a moment at Paul's unfolding of "these things."

Timothy must shun

1. *The Peril of False Teaching.*

In verses 3-5 Paul outlines the features, character and results of unwholesome words from which his young preacher-associate will endeavor to escape. The twofold characteristic of false teachers is given as "pride" and "ignorance." They are "proud" or puffed up with their own knowledge.

Their minds are besotted and beclouded with conceit. They know nothing, in spite of their professed learning. They are incapable of understanding truth from the divine standpoint.

As to the character of these false teachers, "doting" fittingly describes them. The Greek word for "doting" is *sickly,* and this is the exact opposite to *wholesome* in verse 3. Idle disputes and verbal controversies are sickening. True doctrine creates robustness of character.

Coming to the results of error, Paul enumerates them as envy, wrath, strife, railings and evil surmisings. What a dreary catalogue! Obstinate contests, diatribes of a prolonged nature, in which neither side will give away, are common to those who teach error. Timothy must shun

2. *The Peril of Discontent.*

Paul would have Timothy know that godliness is a gainful trade. It certainly pays to be a Christian. "Godliness with contentment is great gain" (I Timothy 6:6). Some there are who strive to be godly, but they are not very content. Others have a contentment without godliness. But the ideal is godliness with contentment. Are we godly, and therefore content? Paul himself had learned to be content in whatever state he found himself. Are we content with whatever we may have? Are we satisfied and happy with things as they are? We have to confess, and that with shame, that we are so discontented with our circumstances. We grumble and complain about the weather and the least inconvenience. Preachers, above all, must not only preach but live the gospel of contentment. Timothy must shun

3. *The Peril of Money.*

Paul is found addressing three cogent reasons why Timothy should flee the love of money (verses 7-10).

1. The precarious nature of all earthly possessions (verse 7). Timothy brought nothing into the world, and he can carry nothing out. When a rich man dies, his will declares that he left so many thousands of dollars. Of course he left them! What else could he do? Alexander the Great requested that he be buried with his empty hand outside the coffin, signifying that he left the world as bare as he entered it.

2. Moral ruin awaits those who are bent on acquiring wealth for wealth's sake (verse 9). Timothy is to warn those who have a mind to be rich of the snares and lusts awaiting them. If they want to be rich, then let them be rich in good works; ready not to hoard, but to distribute (verse 18).

> There was a man, some thought him mad,
> For the more he gave, the more he had.

3. The Mischievous fertility of the love of money (verse 10). The love of money, Timothy must remember, is the root or parent of all evil, or all kinds of evil. It will be noted that Paul does not say that money is the root of all evil, but only the wrong love of it. Many a preacher has pierced his heart through with sorrows because of his love of money. Such a desire has torn his character apart and stripped him of his spiritual power.

C. *A Godly Pursuit — "follow after."*

To "flee" is retreat, but to "follow" is pursuit. Thus there are vices to expel and virtues to emulate. Fleeing is negative . . . following is positive. Forgetting what is behind, Timothy must reach forward to what is before. Paul now expands all that is implied by the designation — "man of God." A trinity of couplets, with their ethical beauty, throw into sharp contrast the evil features of false teachers and preachers. When he comes to his second epistle, Paul reminds Timothy that he is simply urging the young evangelist to follow his example (II Timothy 3:10).

It is essential for Timothy to have

1. *A Godly Character.*

"Righteousness" and "godliness" express the *outward* life. In the "righteousness" Paul exhorts Timothy to exhibit, we have the foundation of all wholesome doctrines. There must be faithfulness to the charge he had received, and gravity and dignity of life. In the "godliness" we have the godlikeness, so impressive amid surrounding ungodliness.

2. *Godly Principles.*

Timothy's life *upward* is indicated by the attributes of "faith" and "love." Faith must be held in the goblet of a pure conscience. Love, the girdle of perfection, must spring out of a pure heart.

3. *Godly Conduct.*

In the "patience" and "meekness" Paul exhorts, we have the *inward* life of Timothy. There must be a true temper within toward all foes without. Patience means endurance, or that steadfastness which has hope and victory as its keynote. Meekness is not weakness, but silence amid all gainsaying. Jesus endured the contradiction of sinners against Himself.

D. *A Godly Contest — "fight."*

As a true, successful preacher Timothy must "fight," as well as "flee" and "follow." He must fight the good fight of faith (verse 12). Later on Paul could write of his own work, "I have fought a good fight" (II Timothy 4:7). The word which the apostle uses suggests a wrestling match, with its strict conditions and tense agony of struggle — and a cloud of witnesses ready to cheer as the chaplet of reward is handed the victor.

E. *A Godly Reward — "lay hold on eternal life."*

Twice Paul uses the phrase "lay hold." In I Timothy 6:19 Timothy must lay hold on the life which is life indeed. In this verse we have the present installment of what is to come, but in 6:12 it is the future which Paul has in mind. In this verse he depicts the last act of the long contest. The wrestler may be faint, but he snatches finally, completely and forever, the prize for which he had striven. And, truly, such a moment will be worth a lifetime of pain, agony and endeavor. The "well done" of the Master at His appearing (6:14) will far outweigh all the afflictions of this life.

Like Mr. Standfast in the River of Death, we shall see:

The head that was crowned with thorns and the face that was spit upon for him.

Passing on like a kingly Arthur, Timothy, Paul's genuine son in the faith, must catch something of the splendor of the coming vision.

Then from the dawn it seemed there came but first
As from beyond the limit of the world,
Like the last echo born of a great cry
Sounds as if some fair city were one voice,
Around a king returning from his wars.

For Deacons', Elders',
Church Officers' Ordination Day

For Deacons', Elders', Church Officers' Ordination Day

O Holy and Eternal Lord Jesus Christ, Thou great Shepherd and Bishop of our souls, send down upon Thy servants, the chosen officers of Thy Church, Thy heavenly benediction. Grant unto them the spirit of wisdom and holiness, patience and love, zeal and watchfulness, that they may faithfully declare Thy will, boldly witness for Thee, and rightly and duly administer their responsibilities. Support them by Thy grace, and enable them through their tasks to turn many to righteousness that they may shine as the stars forever. In Thy own prevailing Name we present our petition on their behalf. Amen.

Deacons

Deacons similarly should be men of serious outlook and sincere conviction. They too should be temperate and not greedy for money. They should hold the mystery of the faith with complete sincerity.

Let them serve a period of probation first, and only serve as deacons if they prove satisfactory. Their wives should share their serious outlook, and must be women of discretion and self-control — women who can be trusted. Deacons should be men with only one wife, able to control their children and manage their own households properly. Those who do well as deacons earn for themselves a certain legitimate standing, as well as gaining confidence and freedom in the Christian faith.

— I Timothy 3:8-13 *Phillips*

MEDITATION FOR DEACONS', ELDERS', CHURCH OFFICERS' ORDINATION DAY

THE FIRST MARTYR — DEACON
Acts 7:55, 56

Service in the church of God is a responsibility which all within the church must loyally accept and equip themselves to undertake effectively. It is to be regretted that we do not think sufficiently about the glory of service in the Christian sphere. The word "service" is a much used — and abused — one, representing an overworked slogan in the business world. Firms compete with each other to give us "the best service." But service, as the Bible presents it, is devoid of pride, gain, or selfishness and is characterized by love, self-effacement and devotion. "The whole system of Christian religion is based upon God's stupendous act of service for the salvation of mankind."

When Jesus appeared, He came as the Son of Man, "not to be ministered unto, but to minister." To Him, service was the language of love and the service of consecrated men and women in His church continues His ministering activities and also proclaims a testimony of their faith to a grasping and greedy world. Therefore, because of the solemn task facing all who would truly serve the church, or better still, its heavenly Head, it is but fitting to have a special day when deacons, elders and/or church officers are set aside for the service their church requires of them. It is also incumbent upon all the members to pray for them as they assume office that they may be guarded by God, kept by His power, and enabled to serve Him with all joy and patience.

Paul makes no distinction between elders, presbyters and bishops, but regards them as holding offices equal and identical (Titus 1:5-7). The first occurrence of "elders" is found in Paul's exhortation to the church at Ephesus (Acts 20:17). He does seem, however, to draw a distinction between the interchangeable terms of elder and bishop meaning an "overseer" and a deacon which signifies a "servant" or "messenger" (Matthew 26:26; Philippians 1:1; I Timothy 3:1-13). Deacons had particular responsibility in matters of benevolence in the Christian congregation. The cause and manner of their appointment, as well as the necessary qualifications for their office are clearly defined for our guidance (Acts 6:1-9; I Timothy 3:8, 12, 13; Philippians 1:1). Conspicuous among the church's first deacons was Stephen who sealed his testimony with his blood.

Called to "serve tables" Stephen, whose name means, "a crown," and who ultimately received a martyr's crown, crossed over the limitations of his humble task and became a powerful preacher of the Word. His fearless and remarkable defense before the enraged Jewish leaders revealed how immersed he was in Old Testament teachings. So provoked were his religious foes that they cast him out of the city and brutally stoned him to death (Acts 6:5-9; 7:59; 11:19; 22:20). His tragic end, however, was overruled by God who can make the wrath of man to praise Him. Saul of Tarsus, who witnessed Stephen's terrible murder, was convicted of his need of the Saviour Stephen died for, and in turn became the mighty apostle.

For all who are called to serve Christ in His church, Stephen's character and confession are worthy of emulation. To assist the apostles in the administration of the practical affairs of the church it was decided to seek out "seven men of honest report, full of the Holy Spirit and wisdom" (Acts 6:3), and first among the chosen was Stephen who is the only one out of the seven delineated as "a man full of faith and of the Holy Ghost" (Acts 6:5). Other attributes are added by Luke in his report of Stephen's appearance before the Jewish council.

A. *He was a man of honest report* (6:3).

Phillips translates this passage, "of good reputation who are both practical and spiritually-minded." In his catalog of qualifications of elders and deacons, Paul says that they "must have a good report of them which are without . . . blameless" (I Timothy 3:7, 10). Among those outside the church — *them which are without* — it was necessary for deacons to have a good reputation. Behavior has to correspond to belief. Thus, wearing the jewel of consistency, deacons would magnify their office and likewise recommend their Lord. Stephen was such a deacon. There was no contradiction between his character and his confession. There was no divorce between profession and practice.

B. *He was a man full of wisdom.*

Stephen's conspicuous wisdom was not *attained* by effort but *obtained* by faith from above. It was the wisdom God gives liberally to all who are willing to claim it (James 1:5). The Holy Spirit of wisdom and revelation inspired this early deacon, not only to be wise in the care of neglected widows, but also to outwit his enemies until they were unable to resist the wisdom by which he spake (Acts 6:3, 7). He manifested "great boldness in the faith which is in Christ Jesus" and purchased for himself thereby, "a good degree" (I Timothy 3:13).

C. *He was a man full of the Holy Spirit.*

Infilled by the Spirit, Stephen knew what it was to be "full of power" (Acts 6:5, 8; 7:55). Ability was his both to serve and suffer. Before Jesus left his disciples He promised them that they should receive power from on high, and that power became theirs at Pentecost when the Spirit came upon them. Stephen's power, then, was not something but Someone. He received power, the Holy Spirit coming upon him (Acts 1:8). It was because of this unction of the Holy One, that Stephen manifested spiritual force as he performed miracles among the people.

D. *He was a man saturated with Scripture.*

In his address to the council when his theme was the unbelief of Israel, Stephen summarized in a most remarkable way the history of Israel from Abraham to Christ. Such a masterly, irrefutable defense stung the unbelieving Jews to fury and, grinding their teeth, they demanded the death of the noble witness (Acts 7). By the power of the Spirit, the Word, as it left the saintly lips of Stephen was "quick, and powerful, and sharper than any two-edged sword" (Hebrews 4:12). Capable though he was, in the discharge of his practical duties, Stephen excelled himself in handling the mighty Word of God, and being full of the Spirit and full of Scripture, how irresistible a witness he was for Christ.

E. *He was mantled with heavenly courage.*

Stephen had to be a stranger to fear when he spoke of his accusers as being "stiffnecked and uncircumcised in heart . . . betrayers and murderers" (Acts 7:51, 52). He was not snared by the fear of man. Fearing God, he feared no other. He feared no foe knowing that Christ was at hand to sustain and bless. The queen whom John Knox the Reformer was not afraid to rebuke, confessed that she feared his prayers more than an army of soldiers.

> Sure I must fight, if I would reign;
> Increase my courage, Lord;
> I'll bear the toil, endure the pain,
> Supported by Thy Word.
> — Isaac Watts

F. *He was full of grace.*

Some versions give us "full of grace" for "full of faith" in Acts 6:8. Stephen was not only saved by grace and, therefore, qualified to serve his Saviour in His church as a deacon. Along with gifts of the Spirit, he likewise exhibited His graces and so was gracious in all his ways. What a more effective Christian witness would be ours if only, as those saved by matchless grace, we acted more graciously in our homes, and in our dealings with others. Is grace being poured into our lips? (Psalm 45:2).

G. *He was a man with an angel face.*

The testimony to Stephen's angelic countenance came from the religious leaders who had condemned him of uttering "blasphemous words" (Acts 6: 13-15). As they looked intently upon him "they saw his face as it had been the face of an angel" (Acts 6:15). They saw a radiancy divine, a serenity, a heavenly glow not of earth. Doubtless, like Moses, Stephen "wist not that the skin of his face shone" (Exodus 34:29). This godly deacon, prayed for and commissioned for his task by the apostles (Acts 6:6), had a glory-face even in the presence of his enemies because there was glory in his soul (Acts 7:56).

H. *He was a man Christ-like in forgiveness.*

Whether or not Stephen was present at Calvary and heard the crucified Saviour pray, "Father, forgive them; for they know not what they do" (Luke 23:34), he was certainly borne along by the Calvary spirit when, as he was being brutally stoned to death, he could pray for his murderers, "Lord, lay not this sin to their charge" (Acts 7:60). Thus he not only had an angel-face, but he had an angel-spirit. As he drew his last breath, he emulated the confidence of the Lord he loved when He died, and calling upon Him said, "Lord Jesus, receive my spirit" (7:59, 60) and then "fell asleep."

Are we not impressed with Stephen's

utter indifference to the hatred of the Jewish leaders, and to their determination to murder him? How awesome are his vision and statement — "But he [Stephen], being full of the Holy Ghost, looked up stedfastly into heaven, and saw the glory of God, and Jesus standing on the right hand of God, And said, Behold, I see the heavens opened, and the Son of man standing on the right hand of God" (Acts 7:55, 56). Is not the position of Jesus significant? He was not *seated* on "the right hand of the Majesty on high" (Hebrews 1:3), but *standing*. Isaiah says that, "The Lord standeth up to plead, and standeth to judge the people" (Isaiah 3:13). Can it be that Jesus whom Stephen had so sacrificially served, rose from His seat to welcome the courageous deacon as he entered the gates of glory to take his place among other martyred saints? Rising to greet Stephen was certainly a token of honor.

In his last moments, Stephen had his eyes fixed, not on the faces of hate in the council chamber where the persecutors had condemned the Spirit-filled deacon to die, but on heaven. The record says that he looked steadfastly *into* heaven, and became indifferent to the cruelty he was about to endure because he saw first of all "the glory of God" which his angel-face reflected, and then the newly risen Saviour with His wounds "still fresh and visible above." No wonder his foes could not bear such a sight nor could they listen to what Stephen saw through those opened heavens. We read they "stopped their ears" and then "stoned" the deacon, but one Pharisee at least could not smother the testimony of all Stephen saw. It was the young man, Saul, who, seeing how a saint can die, was not long in filling the gap which Stephen's martyrdom caused.

For Lay Sister or Deaconess Ordination Day

For Lay Sister or Deaconess Ordination Day

In her expressive poem *Her Creed*, Sarah Knowles Bolton reminds us how women can follow and serve their Lord —

She stood before a chosen few
With modest air and eyes of blue;
A gentle creature, in whose face
Were mingled tenderness and grace.

"You wish to join our fold," they said;
"Do you believe in all that's read
From ritual and written creed,
Essential to our human need?"

A troubled look was in her eyes;
She answered, as in vague surprise,
As though the sense to her were dim,
"I only strive to follow Him."

They knew her life, how oft she stood,
Pure in her guileless maidenhood,
By dying bed, in hovel home,
Whose sorrow she had made her own.

Oft had her voice in prayer been heard,
Sweet as the note of any bird,
Her hand been open in distress;
Her joy to brighten and to bless.

Yet still she answered, when they sought
To know her inmost, earnest thought,
With look as of the seraphim,
"I only strive to follow Him."

Gracious Saviour, Thou who didst condescend to be born of a woman, mercifully undertake for all consecrated women who minister unto Thee of their substance. For all who serve Thy church, visit the poor and suffering, the needy and the distressed wherever found. Grant that they may be guarded and kept by Thy power, and constantly inspired to labor for Thee with joy and patience. In Thy name and for Thy glory. Amen.

MEDITATION FOR LAY SISTER OR DEACONESS ORDINATION DAY

A MODEL DEACONESS
Romans 16:1, 2

It is clearly evident that there were certain commendable women in the early church who held office alike to that of deacon. Paul mentions many of them by name (Romans 16:1-15; Philippians 4:2, 3). We cannot infer from these references, however, that we have any historical record of an Order of Deaconesses, or that women held any official position in the church ministry. While a few prophetesses are named in Scripture, there were no females in the apostolate or among the elders. That there were successful career women who supported the church and its officers is evident from the mention of Lydia. Early Christianity owed a great deal to spiritually-minded women, and as the church expanded some form of female service became necessary. The advent and teaching of Christ resulted in the emancipation of womanhood. From His cradle to His cross, He was dependent upon women, and they never failed Him. This is one reason why we find in Paul's catalog of his valued helpers several Roman female names which is somewhat striking when we remember the low position of women in heathenism. Let us single out one of these, namely, Phebe the helper.

A. *Her Character.*

Because of her direct association with the Apostle Paul, and also her own character and repute, Phebe claims our special attention as a model female laborer in the vineyards of the Lord. From the portrait given we gather five facts about this notable woman.

1. *She was a convert from Paganism.*

Her name suggests her spiritual transformation. "Phebe" was a name generally used among women of Greek birth in the early Roman empire, and stamps Paul's associate as a former heathen. The name itself was originally derived from the heathen deity, Appollo, a sun god of heaven and earth. It is related to "crescent moon," and means shining or pure. Phebe's ancestors were sun-worshipers, but seeing that she herself is spoken of as a "sis-

233

ter," she must have been converted
from her paganism and led to worship
the Son of Righteousness. Although
her life was transformed, she yet retained her old name which was a common custom among early Christian
converts.

2. *She was a light amid darkness.*

We are told that Phebe lived in
Cenchrea, an Eastern seaport of Corinth, a few miles from the city itself.
Such a port, like most seaports, was
corrupt, providing soil in which goodness was hard to grow. To be a Christian in a place like Cenchrea was no
light task, but Phebe was a sparkling
diamond in the gutter of sin. It is quite
probable that when Paul visited Corinth
that Phebe was brought under the influence of the Gospel, and came to experience its emancipating, ennobling
power. Hidden immoralities were engaged in by both sexes at Cenchrea,
but now as a trophy of grace, Phebe
became an example of true womanhood. The darker and more difficult
the community, the greater the need of
light.

3. *She was a sister in Christ.*

Paul gave her the affectionate term
of "sister," which she was, not by nature, but in grace. She was his own
sister in the faith. If the apostle had
been the means of her conversion, then
we can understand him loving Phebe
in the Lord. Such a relationship implies
regeneration and adoption into the
family of God (John 1:12, 13). Jesus
said of a woman obedient to His Word
and Will, "The same . . . is my sister"
(Mark 3:35). Eternity alone will reveal what Christianity owes to its
spiritual sisterhood.

4. *She was a servant of the Church.*

As a "sister" we have Phebe's experience of salvation, but as a "servant"
we have her obligation toward her

Lord and His church. Thus, she
learned early that she had been saved
to serve (I Thessalonians 1:9, 10),
and actually became a deaconess, or
servant, as the term implies, in the
church at Cenchrea. Evidently she held
a recognized official position in her
local church being active among its
women and needy. Nothing was more
in harmony with the will and practice
of Christ and His apostles than the full
use of the consecrated gifts of those
women who were able to labor in the
Gospel. True to her name, "shining"
then "pure", Phebe shone for her Lord
because she was pure in heart. How
tragic that not all who are saved shine
for the Master as they should in this
dark world of sin.

5. *She was a succorer of the needy.*

While "succorer" is a beautiful word,
as it stands, this English form fails to
express the whole sense of the original. "Succor" is used in various ways,
but employed by Paul it indicated one
who stood forth as a patroness of the
unprotected and despised — a champion, or "one who stands by another" —
a designation sweetly true of this
mother in Israel. It may be that the
word conveyed a graceful allusion to
the request that the Roman believers
"stand by" Phebe, as she had stood by
many a needy and suffering Christian.
Breaking up the phrase, let us think of
her first of all —

1. *As a succorer.*

Describing the gifts of the Spirit
to the church Paul speaks of *helps*
(I Corinthians 12:28), and Phebe's
constant ministry had been one of help
— a gentle ministry befitting a woman's
heart and coming most graciously
from her hands. We have reason to
believe that this saint of Cenchrea
was a person of rank and substance.
She can be compared to the great

woman of Shunem who showed such gracious hospitality to the prophet Elisha. How full the world is of those in need, and how formidable is the army of female helpers who come as angels of consolation! Somehow nature has bestowed upon woman the more delicate perception and intuitive understanding of sorrow than man. Man is apt to be somewhat clumsy in the art of comfort, and hurts where he means to soothe and sympathize. Woman, on the other hand, is more gifted in binding up the wounded spirit, and in the drying of tears.

2. *A succorer of many.*

Phebe had a large heart, and cared for all who came her way for help. Hers was a life of devotion and of gracious ministrations of material and spiritual assistance. She lived in a world of unmentioned kindnesses with heart-sympathy accompanying her gifts to relieve the needy. So many of the women of the Bible represent a large amount of brave and active service for God and humanity. Phebe is a striking example to all of her sex who have a passion to promote the cause of Christ in practical ways.

3. *A Succorer of Paul.*

While Phebe helped all and sundry she found on life's highway, the apostle particularizes and says that she was a succorer "of me also." How she cared for Paul we are not told. It may be that she sheltered and nursed him in times of sickness and weakness. Here we encounter that warm feeling, giving great charm to Paul's intercourse with his friends. Gratitude was one of the marked features of his character, and its manifestation is seen in the way he remembers the kindness of his fellow-workers. As Phebe left her home and church she carried with her a letter of gratitude for all he owed her, and

must have had a profound appeal to the Roman Church as they read the apostle's letter to receive Phebe and aid her to the limit of their power. The acknowledgement of favors is the least return we can make for those who treat us with kindness, and whenever the book of Romans is read her Christ-like goodness to Paul is told for a memorial of her.

B. *Her Commendation.*

Why Phebe had to journey to Rome is not stated. It may have been a business trip, contact with governmental authorities, or some legal matter. This we do know, that Paul commended her to the brethren at Rome, assured that their influence would stand her in good stead. If, as some expositors suggest, Phebe was the bearer of the Roman epistle, the same would gain for her immediate recognition. The whole-hearted commendation of Paul was in the form of a threefold request.

1. *Receive her in the Lord.*

This characteristic phrase which Paul uses denotes a community of interest under Christ and indicates that all the saints belong to Him. It also implies a cooperation of the same kind in spiritual service — a fellowship in which all were of one faith. Think of the union that knit together Paul, a Jew, Phebe, a Gentile and all the Roman readers of the book of Romans! All had been fused together by Christ, whose love had won their hearts and made them as one in Him. The entreaty to receive Phebe *in the Lord* is expressive with the fact that women owe not only their emancipation from the slavery of sin to Jesus, but also the removal of the stigma of inferiority. In Christ, there is neither male nor female.

2. *As becometh saints.*

As Christians, the believers in Rome were exhorted to welcome Phebe as a fellow-Christian. Does not this phrase merit our prayerful and careful attention? It is not easy to decide whether it means that Phebe be received in such a manner as she deserved or the way becoming the profession of the saints in Rome. Perhaps both thoughts are implied. What a happier place this world would be if only all professed Christians were more *Christian* in the treatment of each other. How grievous to Christ the estrangements, jealousies, and bitterness between His avowed followers must be!

3. *Assist her as she may require.*

Phebe was to be given not only a friendly and worthy reception, but also furnished with all needed assistance in the errand bringing her to Rome. Paul asked help for one who had been helpful to many and a blessing to his own heart, and his plea was not in vain. We should always be ready to help others, for the day may come when we ourselves will require assistance in some form or another. "He that watereth shall be watered also himself" (Proverbs 11:25). Two final lessons can be adduced from our meditation of Phebe, the model deaconess.

First of all, the world needs Pauls who are strong and fearless in the denunciation of sin and earnest in the proclamation of the saving Gospel. It also requires the less conspicuous Phebes who trudge life's pilgrimage helping those in need. To Christ, all service is acceptable if it is one in essence and actuated by the same motive. Paul and Phebe were one in their desire to serve the Lord and were one in reward. Whether our gifts are conspicuous or otherwise makes little difference. Faithfulness to God in the use of what we have is to form the basis of reward in eternity (Revelation 2:10).

Another thought is that Phebe little dreamed that her unnoticed deeds of kindness would be remembered by succeeding generations. What an inspiration the witness of Phebe has been to Christian women of all ages! What an encouragement she is to those who serve the Master in unknown, unnoticed areas. Day in and day out they scatter sunshine, receiving little attention or praise. Sometimes they are chilled by the ingratitude of those they serve, yet on they toil. "The Master praises, what are men?" Their sacrificial help is recorded by the angels, and because they lived and labored for the glory of God their deeds will be proclaimed before the Father and His holy angels (Philippians 4:3).

> Go, labor on; your hands are weak,
> Your knees are faint, your souls cast down;
> Yet falter not; the prize you seek
> Is near, a kingdom and a crown.

For Communion Day

For Communion Day

Almighty and most merciful Father, we are about to commemorate the death of Thy Son Jesus Christ, our Saviour and Redeemer. Grant, O Lord, that our whole hope and confidence may be in His merits and Thy mercy. Enforce and accept our imperfect repentance, make this commemoration available to the confirmation of our faith, the establishment of our hope, and the enlargement of our love, and make the death of Thy dear Son Jesus Christ effectual to our redemption. Have mercy upon us, and pardon the multitude of our offenses. Bless our friends. Have mercy upon all men. Support us by the Holy Spirit throughout our life, and receive us at last into everlasting happiness, for the sake of Jesus Christ our Lord. Amen.
— Dr. Samuel Johnson (1709)

MEDITATION FOR COMMUNION DAY

THE VESPER SIGH OF MEMORY
I Corinthians 11:25

It was Thomas Moore, the eighteenth century poet who gave us the line — "Memory breathes her vesper sigh to thee," and of all services connected with the worship of the Christian Church, the Lord's Supper is not only the most solemn, impressive and instructive one, but also the most commemorative. As we gather in His name, in His ordained way, our minds are taken back to the cross upon which He died so long ago.

When divested of all the forms, ceremony and trappings with which tradition has clothed the Supper, how attractive it is in its naked simplicity as a memorial of His sacrifice on our behalf.

In the Upper Room that night when Jesus abolished the Jewish Passover Feast was the blood. It commemorated a deliverance from death through the shed blood of lambs sprinkled upon the doorposts and lintels of the households of Israelites in Egypt. At the Feast they ate the lambs and continued such an act until Christ established the Christian Feast, proclaiming as it does, the Passover sacrificed for sinners everywhere. All who partake of the Feast are those, or should be those, sheltered by the blood He so freely shed. Participation implies salvation.

A. The Request — "This do."

Behind these two simple words — This do — we have a directive as to the order of the memorial Feast begun and commanded by our Lord (Luke 22:1-30). The breaking and handling of the bread, and the drinking from the cup are simply means of reminding us of His unique death for us. Knowing how apt we are to forget, He supplied us with these sacred emblems as loving mementoes, to keep ever-fresh in our weak, forgetful memories, His death upon the tree.

1. The Command of a Lord.

This do! We have no option but to obey. Observance is not a matter we can accept or refuse. Obedience is imperative. Paul adds solemn emphasis to the command when he wrote

"I have received of the Lord" (I Corinthians 11:23). There are those who teach that the Table is not necessary and who make no provision for it. Our obligation, however, is not to be influenced by the theories and explanations of men, but to take the command as it stands.

While we have no specific command as to how often we should participate, the weekly custom of the apostles is worthy of emulation. Yet we must be careful lest the very frequency of participation begets a familiarity resulting in a cold, dead formalism. Paul's injunction reads, "As oft as ye eat and drink." He did not say how often. Frequency is not the all-important matter, but the spirit in which we approach the hour of remembrance.

Furthermore, we must not engage in such a holy service merely because we are commanded to. Loving our Lord, we love to obey, realizing that obedience to any dear command of His results in spiritual blessing. Obedience is robbed of power if love is absent.

2. *The Request of a Friend.*

Before He left His own, Jesus called them "friends" (John 15:15), and we prefer to see in the words — "This do" — the dying request of our heavenly Friend. A lock of hair brings back the memory of the love and goodness of a departed friend. A little shoe hidden away in a drawer, recalls to the heart of a parent the death of a babe, untarnished by practiced sin. Gifts, valueless in themselves, costing only a few cents, are yet cherished and are priceless in that they recall those who, although dead, yet speak to our hearts.

A young man, while in conversation with a friend, drew a letter from his pocket received from his sister in the far-away home. Within the letter was pressed flowers and a few dried blades of grass. With deep emotion the young man said: "These are from my mother's grave."

The bread and wine are cheap and valueless in themselves, yet priceless because they remind us of Him who died that we might be forgiven. The elements, so emblematic, take us back to Calvary, to our Saviour's grave. Slavish obedience can cripple spirituality. But when we look upon our presence at the Table as compliance with the request of a loving, dying Friend, what adoration is ours! It was as if He said, "My body will soon be broken for you, and when I am gone, do not forget Me. Come together as often as possible, and as you eat and drink remember Me and all My pains." As our Lord He commands remembrance, but as our Friend, he desires remembrance, and lovingly we comply.

> Remember Thee and all Thy pains,
>   And all Thy love to me:
> Yea, while a breath, a pulse remains,
>   Will I remember Thee.
>   — James Montgomery

B. *The Remembrance — "In remembrance of me."*

As it is His Presence that makes the Feast, let us think more fully of Him, who is the sole Object of our remembrance. We are exhorted to remember not merely His words, doctrines, ways, miracles, but *Himself*. We are not to fix our thoughts about the Table itself and think more of the Feast than the Friend — more of the Supper than the Saviour. We must make more of "The Lord of the Feast" than "The Feast of the Lord." Remember *Me*, Jesus asked of His own.

1. *Me — The Lowly Nazarene.*

What thoughts must have filled the minds of the disciples as they gathered in the chamber Jesus had chosen! How they would think of His life and labors in the days of His flesh! Had He not been fashioned in the likeness of a man (Philippians 2:7)? Did He not come as bone of their bone, flesh of their flesh; and had they not witnessed evidences of His humanity? Was He not One so human yet divine? Would not the Feast remind them that there was to be one Mediator, the Man Christ Jesus? And does not the bread tell us that He had a real, living body like yours and mine? And does not the wine indicate that He possessed warm, red blood like that coursing through our veins, only untainted by sin?

2. *Me — The Crucified Saviour.*

The center of the Lord's Supper is the cross. All associated with the institution of the Supper revolves around the work He accomplished when He died as the Lamb of God. Broken bread suggests the sorrow and shame heaped upon His sacred body, ultimately pierced by cruel nails. The outpoured cup symbolizes the blood He shed for our redemption.

3. *Me — The Victorious Redeemer.*

It was an early custom to link together the Lord's Day and the Lord's Table, which supplies us with a two-fold aspect of the Christian Passover.

The Lord's Day calls us to remember that although Jesus died, He did not remain dead. The Day called Sunday is the Resurrection day — the day declaring that He rose again and is alive forevermore.

The Lord's Table is a constant reminder of His "free grace and dying love." It is eloquent with the truth that He paid the price of our redemption.

4. *Me — The Ascended Lord.*

In apostolic times, when the church gathered around the Table to engage in the holy, love feast, how vivid would the recollections of those disciples be as they meditated upon those last days they spent with the Saviour. They had also witnessed the stupendous miracle of His translation to heaven, and great joy would be theirs as they realized that the One who had ascended on high, leading captivity captive, was yet with them presiding over the Feast.

5. *Me — The Interceding Advocate.*

We cannot partake of the elements He prescribed to commemorate His death, without looking up to worship Him as our great High Priest. The Table bids us remember His priestly intercession for us with the holiest of all (Hebrews 7:25). The cross is the foundation of His present ministry in heaven, for His five bleeding wounds pour effectual prayers on our behalf. As we remember Him here on earth, He remembers us in heaven before the Father's face. Christ is in glory, and by His Spirit seeks to make more effectual in our lives here the past work of Calvary.

6. *Me — The Coming Bridegroom.*

The Table covers the journey of the Saviour from His cross to His crown — from the tree to the throne. As we are commanded to remember the shadows of dark Calvary, the glory of the future bursts upon us in all its splendor. We eat and drink "til He come" (I Corinthians 11:26).

Between the calling out of the Jews by Moses to the First Advent of Christ we have a Feast — The Passover associated with the miracle of the Red Sea. Between the calling out of the church at Pentecost to the Second Advent of Christ we have another Feast —The Lord's Table speaking of deliverance from the bondage of sin. So as the Feasts come and go, we learn to cultivate more perfectly the forward look, the glory gaze. The Table has

two fingers — one pointing back to the
crucified Saviour — "The Lord's death"
— the other pointing forward to the
coming Bridegroom — "Till He Come."
Thus faith can sing with Horatius
Bonar:

Feast after feast thus comes and
        passes by,
    Yet passing points to that great feast
    above;
Giving sweet foretastes of the festal
        joy,
    The Lamb's great bridal feast of
    bliss and love.

For Critical National Days

For Critical National Days

Once to every man and nation comes
    the moment to decide,
In the strife of truth with falsehood,
    for the good or evil side;
Some great cause, God's new Messiah,
    offering each the bloom or blight,
Parts the goats upon the left hand and
    the sheep upon the right,
And the choice goes by forever, 'twixt
    that darkness and that light.

Count me o'er earth's chosen heroes —
    they were souls that stood alone,
While the men they agonized for
    hurled the contumelious stone;
Stood serene, and down the future saw
    the folden beam incline
To the side of perfect justice, mastered
    by their faith divine,
By one man's plain truth to manhood
    and to God's supreme design.

'Tis as easy to be heroes as to sit the
    idle slaves
Of a legendary virtue carved upon our
    fathers' graves;
Worshipers of light ancestral make the
    present light a crime —
Was the Mayflower launched by
    cowards steered by men behind
    their time?
Turn those tracks toward Past or
    Future that make Plymouth Rock
    sublime?

        — James Russell Lowell

MEDITATION FOR
CRITICAL NATIONAL DAYS

I Chronicles 12:32

At a time like this, when the nations of the world are perplexed and distressed, it is incumbent upon us to ascertain the reasons of the world's unhappy plight, and then discover and declare the only infallible remedy for its disorder and dread.

The men of Issachar, the sacred historian tells us, had an understanding of the times, knowing what the nations ought to do (I Chronicles 12:32). Going back to Genesis 49:14, 15, we discover a most interesting insight into the characterization of the tribe of Issachar. Issachar, as a strong ass, crouched down between two burdens; Issachar was willing to dig or die. Tillage and tribute formed his lot. The territory he occupied was the most fertile in Canaan, and hardy, patient labor brought much success. Being land workers, those of this tribe were naturally adverse to war. More or less pacifistic, they became subject to invaders.

In Issachar as a tribe we see Israel as a nation, content to be slaves of the Gentiles. As a passive slave, each preferred the yoke of hard bondage to the doubtful issues of war. Industrious Issachar had to bear the burden of taxes, but he could be firm, constant and courageous when occasion demanded brave action. Deborah praised Issachar as being valiant and invincible in war (Judges 5). Thus, whether in work or war, the men of Issachar played their part. Well, we are children of Immanuel, and parallels are obvious! Let us apply these two features of Issachar to ourselves.

A. *An understanding of the Times.*

The men of Issachar had an understanding of their own times, seeing that they got behind the times. External crises were judged by internal circumstances. Issachar realized that the hour had dawned for the whole kingdom to become David's. Knowledge on the part of this tribe led to action. Some there are who have knowledge, but little action. Others, again, have plenty of action, which, however, is not founded upon true knowledge. May we be found among the number who, knowing the right, will not be afraid to act!

With the aid of a Bible Concordance, it is highly profitable to trace out various "times" we should endeavor to understand. For example, we have —

1. *Perilous Times.*

"In the last days perilous times shall come" (II Timothy 3:1).

What a descriptive verse of this present, war-torn world this is! Perils confront us no matter where we turn. There are moral, physical and spiritual perils, perils for every age, perils reaching from the skies, on and under the seas, and on the earth. Like Paul, we are "in perils oft," as sin and death stalk the earth. There are perils in abundance for the Jew, the Gentile and the church of God. Many, like those whom Jeremiah mentions, secure their bread with peril (Lamentations 5:9). It is blessed to realize, as Paul indicates, that no kind of peril can separate us from Christ (Romans 8:35).

2. *Latter Times.*

"In the latter times some shall depart from the faith" (I Timothy 4:1).

These particular "times" are identical with "the last time" mentioned by John (I John 2:18), and cover the period from the apostles until the return of Christ for His church. The characteristic feature of these times is the "apostasy" which was beginning to rear its ugly head in Paul's day. Now that we are almost at the end of these times, departure from the faith is even more pronounced. We are constantly hearing of young men being ordained for the ministry who scarcely believe any of the foundational truths — the doctrines of our faith. The saints, however, know this time, and realize that "it is high time to awake out of sleep: for now is our salvation nearer than when we believed" (Romans 13:11).

3. *The Times of the Gentiles.*

"Until the times of the Gentiles be fulfilled" (Luke 21:24).

Since the captivity of Judah under Nebuchadnezzar, Jerusalem has been under Gentile overlordship. The "times of the Gentiles" began when Daniel said to Nebuchadnezzar, "Thou, O king, art a king of kings" (Daniel 2:37), and will end with Christ returning to earth to fashion the Gentile kingdom into his own world-kingdom (Revelation 11:15; 19:16). And the present shaking of the nations reveals that Gentile dominion is hurrying to its death.

4. *Times of Refreshing.*

"When the times of refreshing shall come from the presence of the Lord" (Acts 3:19).

Seeing that this verse is sometimes used as the basis of a "revival" sermon, it is imperative to understand what Peter had in mind when he spoke of such times. Dr. C. I. Scofield quotes H. A. W. Meyer's comment on the verse. These refreshing times are "seasons in which, through the appearance of the Messiah in His kingdom, there shall occur blessed rest and refreshment for the people of God." The phrase "times of refreshing" indicates a "breathing space or respite," and can be identified with the national repentance of Israel. And what a revival such will be!

5. *Times and Seasons.*

"It is not for you to know the times or the seasons which the Father hath put in His own power (Acts 1:7; I Thessalonians 5:1).

The narrative makes it clear that the "times" in question cover the restoration of the kingdom to Israel. When

Christ is to appear for His church and regather the Jews, has not been revealed. The facts of both are certain: the times of their realization is uncertain. For the church, Christ is coming as the Bridegroom — for Israel, He is coming as a thief in the night.

6. *Times, Times, and Half a Time.*
   "Until a time and times and the dividing of time" (Daniel 7:25).

Prophetically, a "time" means a year; "times," two years; and "dividing of times," half a time. The whole makes forty-two months of 1260 days, which is three and one-half years, covering the last half of the Great Tribulation. Daniel's division is repeated by John in Revelation 12:14 where it is related to Israel's persecution by Satan. During this latter half of Daniel's seventieth week, however, Israel, the woman, is nourished and protected by God.

7. *An Acceptable Time.*
   "In an acceptable time" (Psalm 69:13; II Corinthians 6:2).

This "acceptable time" is this present season of grace, or day of salvation. It is called "acceptable" in that it is the time in which God waits to be gracious unto men. All who would be saved from the penalty of sin and the guilt of their sin should notice that this is the day when they can call upon the Lord and be delivered from their lost condition.

8. *My Times.*
   "My times are in thy hand" (Psalm 31:15).

Here are "times" to which each of us are definitely related. The question is: Do we understand these personal times? Surely this is a verse applicable to any age and to any life. My times — whether they are glad or sad, prosperous or poor, joyful or grief-laden — my times are in His hands. And truly, we triumph in life when we can trust Him at *all* times.

> Our times are in Thy hand —
> O God, we will them there;
> Our lives, our souls, our all, we leave
> Entirely to Thy care.
> Our times are in Thy hand —
> Why should we doubt or fear?
> A Father's hand will never cause
> His child a needless tear.

9. *The Rest of His Time.*
   "That he no longer should live the rest of his time in the flesh to the lusts of men, but to the will of God" (I Peter 4:2).

In this chapter Peter gives us three aspects of time. In this first reference he has a word for your heart and mine in these critical days. These are death-laden days, and what is happening among the nations indicates that Christ is not far away. And this means that we cannot have long on the earth. Is it our passion to live the rest of our time, not in the flesh to the lusts of men, but to the will of God? May He grant that the little time left to each of us may be characterized by intense devotion to His cause! The time is short, and we must redeem it (Psalm 89:47; I Corinthians 7:29; Ephesians 5:16).

10. *The Time Past.*
    "The time past of our life" (I Peter 4:3).

This is the part of our time that we do not care to remember, seeing it was a time of alienation from the will of God. But the past is under the blood, and now many we had fellowshipped with will think it strange that we no longer run with them in the same riotous living.

11. *The Time Is Come.*
    "The time is come that judgment must begin at the house of God" (I Peter 4:17).

If Peter thought the time was ripe

for judgment of the church in his day, when it was not more than thirty or forty years old, what judgment does it now deserve with all its departure from apostolic standards and ideals? If civilization is to be saved from total eclipse, it must have a revival of first-century Christianity, and before that revival can come, judgment must begin at the house of God. The church must banish its modernism, materialism, indifferentism, if she is to become as terrible as an army with banners.

B. *Knowing What Israel Ought to Do.*

It was the determination of the nation to give David his coronation. "The rest also of Israel were of one heart to make David king" (I Chronicles 12: 38). David had just come from Hebron "to turn the kingdom of Saul to him, according to the word of the Lord" (12:23), and each tribe knew the part it had to play in such a crisis. David, of course, came into his own by degrees. There was his private anointing as king by Samuel; his partial anointing by Judah; his perfect anointing by the men of Israel.

Here is a phrase, however, capable of various applications. For example, understanding and discerning our own times, do we know what God requires of His own and others? We have come to the most critical period of the world's history, and behind the events of the hour there is a divine call to action.

Understanding the times, do we know what Israel should do? Well, this is certainly a season of anguish for God's ancient people. Through the scourge of Nazism, the plight of the Jews was terrible. What must such a persecuted people do? Why, turn to the Messiah they have so long rejected! Here and now in grace they must look on Him whom they pierced, and mourn over their own sins. Let us pray for the immediate salvation of the Jews, so that there may be widespread joy in Israel.

Understanding the times, do we know what the nations ought to do? The prophecy of Haggai is certainly being realized in our time, "I will shake all nations" (Haggai 2:7). Volcanic forces have shaken the foundation of civilization. What distress there is among the nations! Slaughter, bloodshed, destruction, famine and universal sorrow have overtaken the earth. But do the nations know that God has a quarrel with them? As nations, they have forgotten God, and He is permitting them to have a foretaste of hell. What must the nations do? Repent of their national sins and turn to the Lord in all humility.

Understanding the times, do we know what the church ought to do? The pitiable condition of the world presents the church with the greatest challenge of her career. The end of World War II, with the Allied Nations victorious, gave the church one of the greatest missionary opportunities it had ever faced; but she failed to evangelize a war-torn world? It would seem that Peter's word, already considered, about the time being opportune for judgment to begin at the house of God, is one that the church must consider, for she confronts the unhappy condition of the world so destitute of power. Modernism, politics, worldliness, orthodoxy plague our church today and leave her dead and barren. Lamentable divisions have robbed the church of the influence she once had to turn the world upside down. She must remember from whence she has fallen, and, repenting, do the first works.

Understanding the times, do we know what we, as individuals, ought to do? Have we realized that these serious times constitute a call to personal holiness and the dedication of all we are and have? Returning to the narrative where our basic text is found, there are one or two characteristic features of some of the tribes which we can apply to our own heart and life. We read, for instance, that those of Zebulun were not of "double heart" (I Chronicles 12:33). They went forth to war with singleness of purpose. Fifty thousand of them could keep rank. These warriors marched in step. Possibly you are out of step with God and man. You do not have a single eye for God's glory. And then we read of men of war belonging to several tribes who had a "perfect heart" to make David king over all Israel. Is yours the heart, that is, the heart that knows no rival to your heavenly David? The rest of Israel, we are told, were of "one heart" (12:38) to crown David as king over the entire nation. There were no dissenting voices. How tragic that so often our heart is not one. We have conflicting desires and motives. Our heart is not united to serve and satisfy the Lord. We do not praise Him with our whole heart.

The name "Issachar" itself means "there is reward," and if he emulate the outstanding qualities of this tribe, the reward of the judgment seat will be ours. From Genesis 49 we learn that Issachar crouched between two burdens. Have we a double burden in these last days? What do we know about the burden of the Lord and the burden of souls? Issachar saw that rest was good. In a restless, feverish age, is ours the rest of faith? Issachar bowed his shoulder to bear. Are we bearing Christ's yoke? Issachar became a servant unto tribute. Can we say that we are heaven's love-slaves? Paul called himself a slave of Christ. Are we glad vessals of a Saviour's throne?

Beloved, let us not misunderstand our times! They are so heavy with prophetic significance. Let us seek that Spirit-inspired knowledge of current events and crises, and then give ourselves without stint or reserve to the accomplishment of God's redemptive plan as the midnight hour of judgment approaches.

Stir me, oh! stir me, Lord, for I can see
Thy glorious triumph-day begins to break;
The dawn already gilds the eastern sky:
Oh, Church of Christ, arise, awake, awake;
Oh! stir us, Lord as heralds of the day,
For night is past, our King is on His way.

— Mrs. Albert Head

For the Opening of an Evangelistic Crusade

For the Opening of an Evangelistic Crusade

Evangelize

Go forth, go forth and win the lost,
Evangelize, whate'er the cost;
The Gospel preach in ev'ry land,
Go forth, it is the Lord's command.

Evangelize in ev'ry tribe,
The Gospel none must be denied;
Go forth and tell of how He died,
Go, tell of Christ the Crucified.

Go forth and tell of how He rose
And lives triumphant o'er His foes;
Of how He's coming back again
In pow'r and majesty to reign.

He's coming back to take His Bride
For ev'ry kindred, tongue and tribe;
He's coming back to usher in
The day of judgment for man's sin.

Go forth, the Message must be told,
Go, bring them to the Saviour's fold;
The Master calls, O then arise,
Evangelize! Evangelize!
— Oswald J. Smith

Oh, for a passionate passion for souls!
  Oh, for a pity that yearns!
Oh, for a love that loves unto death,
  Oh, for a fire that burns!
Oh, for a prayer power that prevails,
  That pours itself out for the lost;
Victorious prayer in the Conqueror's
    Name,
  Oh, for a Pentecost.
— Anonymous

MEDITATION FOR THE OPENING OF AN EVANGELISTIC CRUSADE

THE SAVIOUR OF SOULS
Hebrews 7:25

Universally, Christ is honored as being unique and superb, mighty and majestic. There has never been One like Him. While here among men He revealed himself not only as the Man Christ Jesus, but as very God of very God. Jesus stands in a category all His own — solitary yet sublime. His greatness is the dominant fact of Holy Writ. He is the First and the Last, and all in between. In these apostate days, modernists deny the uniqueness and supernatural character of His Person, cripple His omnipotence, and reduce Him to the level of ordinary humanity. With blatant impudence they declare Him to be a good man, but only a man, and not God in the flesh.

It is clearly evident that our conception of His magnificence datermines the quality of life. Low opinions of His worth often lead to low living. Faith in Him as the preeminent Lord results in a preeminent life. Also, the acceptance of His Lordship delivers us from the anxieties and fears of life.

The thought of Him as the all-sufficient One destroys all doubt as to the meeting of all our needs. All undue concern is slain as we rest in the declaration of Job, "I know that thou canst do everything" (Job 42:2). The grasp of the truth of the sovereignty of our Redeemer destroys the fear of men and things, and inspires us to look away from all outward circumstances, from puny men, from sin and Satan to Him to whom all authorities and powers are subject.

In no realm is Christ so preeminent, however, as that of salvation from the guilt and power of sin. Beside Him there is no Saviour. None is like Him in the pardoning of iniquity. He is matchless, incomparable in extricating sin-cursed lives from the clutches of the monarch of hell. Does not the New Testament justify the claim that He alone is the Saviour of all men, especially of them who believe? Think of these manifestations of His saving grace and power!

A. *He Can Save Any Number.*

There is no restraint with Christ to

253

save by many or by few. Omnipotence never stops at numbers. As heaven's arithmetic is different from ours, the greater includes the lesser as the Bible proves. Our Lord believed in and practiced personal evangelism, and so saved men *one by one*. Some of His most remarkable utterances were made to individuals, as in the case of Nicodemus. He also had power to save *many at the same time*. At the well of Sychar in a personal conversation with the woman who had come there, He won her to Himself, and as a result, many of the Samaritans believed. With the same ease He can save *a multitude all at once*, as He did on the day of Pentecost when some 3,000 were gloriously saved. During the history of the church there have been similar displays of His power, as for instance, the African Pentecost through the ministry of the late Dr. Charles Inwood when 2,500 souls were bowed down under the power of the Spirit at one time. With equal power, Christ is able to save *a nation*, for we read that a nation is to be born anew in a day. The prophetic word reminds us that He will move upon His scattered people, the Jews, and refashion them in a day, making them a nation unto honor.

B. *He Can Save Anywhere.*

Christ is no respecter of places, even as He is no respecter of persons. Omnipresent, as well as omnipotent, He can save anywhere. He fills all space, and is the center and circumference of all planets. He saved one man *under a tree* for that is where he found Zacchaeus. He saved another at *a custom house* for that was where He met Levi, the tax-gatherer, who became Matthew the apostle. He saved others at *the seaside*, for it was there that He called Peter and others to follow Him. He often saved *in a house*

as He did when He healed and forgave the paralytic. He was able to save *in the middle of a road* as Saul of Tarsus experienced, who, when he became Paul never forgot that he was an open-air convert. He could save *in a temple*, for it was in such that the man of Bethesda found the healing mercy of the Saviour. He can save *in the heart of a desert*, for that was where He found the Ethiopian eunuch. He can save *in a prison* as the jailer at Philippi came to believe. He can save *on a cross*, for it was at Calvary that the dying thief repented in his last hour. "Whither shall I go from thy spirit?" (Psalm 139:7). It makes no difference where men are, He is able to meet them where they are and save them with an uttermost salvation. As the good Samaritan came to where the wounded traveler lay, so Jesus seeks to meet us where we are.

C. *He Can Save at Any Time.*

Because the Saviour never slumbers nor sleeps, He is always on the alert to save souls. Beholding the need of the Christless, His hands are always ready to deliver from sin. He does not judge His movements by the hands of a clock. He is not restrained by time. What the unsaved must be warned against is that they cannot be saved just when they like and in their own time, but only in God's time, which is *now*. "Now is the day of salvation" (II Corinthians 6:2). That His saving grace is not bound by time is evident from the following facts. The 3,000 at Pentecost were saved at the *third hour of the day*, or about 9 o'clock in the morning. Saul was converted at *midday*, or the noon hour. The thief was saved from the *sixth to the ninth hour*, or from twelve noon to three in the afternoon. John met Christ *at the tenth hour*, or four o'clock in the afternoon. Nicodemus found Jesus at *the evening hour*, and the jailer was saved *at the midnight hour*. Thus, from midday to midnight, Jesus seeks the lost. At all hours of day or night, souls burdened with the load of their iniquity can hear His voice saying, "Come unto Me and rest." Whenever or wherever the lost call upon Him, He is at hand to save them from sin.

D. *He Can Save at Any Age.*

The Bible also indicates that Jesus Christ is able to save at all ages. From the first dawn of conscious action until life's last hour He is able to manifest His power to snatch souls as brands from the burning. He can adopt His truth to meet the needs of all, no matter what their age. He can save *children*. As a child, Samuel heard His voice and remained His all through his honored life. Did not the Saviour Himself say, "Suffer little children to come unto me" (Mark 10:14)? There is a double salvation for those who come to Him in life's fair morning, for not only is the soul saved, but the life is also secured for the Master. He can likewise save *youth*. The rich young ruler became concerned about his spiritual welfare but was not prepared to pay the price of a complete, unreserved surrender to the claims of Christ. The first disciples were comparatively young men when they heard His call and rose up and followed Him. Then, He can save *the old*. Nicodemus who said to Jesus, "How can a man be born when he is old?" (John 3:4), learned this. All who labor for the souls of men know how few aged people respond to the appeal of the Gospel. Yet old as they may be, the promise is for them. "Him that cometh to me I will in no wise cast out" (John 6:37). In life's latest hour, Jesus can save. It was at the eleventh hour that the dying

thief at Calvary became a new creature in Christ Jesus.

E. *He Can Save Anyone.*

The disciple asked, "*Who* then can be saved?" and the answer is, all who are willing to repent and believe. Our blessed Lord is no respecter of persons. He pays no attention to the superficial divisions of society. To Him there is only one clan — "All have sinned, and come short of the glory of God" (Romans 3:23). He is able to draw *all* men to Himself. He saved *a harlot* like Rahab, that sin-stained soul of Samaria. He can save *the demon-possessed* like Mary Magdalene, and young girl controlled by the spirit of divination. He can save *a moral man* like Nathanael — save *a religious man* like Nicodemus — save *a rich man* like Zacchaeus. While it is true that "not many wise men after the flesh . . . not many noble are called" (I Corinthians 1:26), some are, and with their wisdom, gifts, culture and wealth become conspicuous trophies of divine grace. Christ can save *the poor* as He made clear in the salvation of Lazarus, the sore-covered beggar. Riches or poverty are no criterion, for He saves men from what they are and not because of what they have or lack. He can save *fishermen* for this was the occupation of His first disciples. He can save *doctors*, of whom Luke, the beloved physician is an example. He is able to save *a prime minister*, for this is what the eunuch was whom Philip met in the desert. He was a black man from Ethiopia, but the Saviour pays no attention to the color of a man's skin. It is the blacker condition of the heart He seeks to change. He can save *a tent-maker*, as He did Priscilla and Aquila and Saul of Tarsus — save *a tax-gatherer* as He did Levi — save *a lawyer* as He did Zenas — save a *busi-*

ness man or woman, as He did Lydia, the seller of purple — save *a jailer* as He did at Philippi — save *a thief* as He did when He died. Thus, whether vicious or virtuous, princes or paupers, Christ is able to reach them and make them His very own.

> While grace is offered to the prince,
> The poor may take their share;
> No mortal has a just pretense,
> To perish in despair.
> None are excluded hence, but those
> Who do themselves exclude;
> Welcome the learned and polite,
> The ignorant and rude.

With this confirmation of Christ's ability to save all kinds and types of sinners, we have the solemn obligation of proclaiming far and wide that Jesus can save anyone, at any time, at any age, and under all circumstances. It is still true as it was in the days of His flesh, "They came to him from every quarter" (Mark 1:45).

For a Funeral

For a Funeral

Sunset and evening star,
　And one clear call to me!
And may there be no moaning of the
　bar,
　When I put out to sea,

But such a tide as moving seems
　asleep,
　Too full for sound and foam,
When that which drew from out the
　boundless deep
　Turns again home.

Twilight and evening bell,
　And after that the dark!
And may there be no sadness of fare-
　well,
　When I embark;

For tho' from out our bourne of Time
　and Place
　The flood may bear me far,
I hope to see my Pilot face to face
　When I have crossed the bar.

— Alfred Tennyson

MEDITATION FOR A FUNERAL

THE KEY OF THE GRAVE
Revelation 1:18

As a pastor is always near death in his church and community, there is constant need of suitable material for funeral messages. Much help can be found in the writer's volume, *The Funeral Sourcebook*, published by Zondervan Publishing House, Grand Rapids, Michigan.

Hearts are tender and receptive when in the presence of death, and the wise preacher will take the advantage of pressing home the solemn facts of the brevity of life, of death, and of eternity. Often the death of a loved one is the gate of life to unsaved relatives and friends, as emphasis is given to the truth that "the sky, not the grave, is our goal." As to the certainty of an after life, our Lord gives no proof. He presupposes that existence. What He did was to dispel the banks of clouds and let the future life shine forth. He did not create immortality by His words or resurrection; He brought it to light, just as the telescope brings to light the stars unseen by the naked eye. And His doctrine on the world beyond is all His own. "It is too fresh and original," says Professor Stalker, "to have been obtained secondhand. He speaks as One who has been there, and the statement of the New Testament is literally true, that he brought life and immortality to light by the Gospel."

It would take volumes to set forth all that Jesus taught, not only in parable, precept, proclamation and promise, but also in His Person regarding the eternal world. Canon Knox Little says — "Our Lord revealed it:

"By His example, by the manner in which He subordinated the claims of this present world to the thought of a life beyond;

"By the whole tenor of His teaching, the precepts of which require for their adequate fulfillment a life beyond the narrow boundary of time;

"By direct statement — 'God, not the God of the dead, but of the living'; the 'many mansions'; 'Abraham's bosom'; the 'Coming-Again'; the 'shining forth of the righteous in their

Father's Kingdom'; He revealed it, and guaranteed the truth of His Godhead and, therefore, His right to reveal, by the stupendous miracle of the resurrection. He carried on His revelation by His ascension into glory, and by the coming of the Holy Spirit."

One would wish to linger over the parables of the virgins; Dives and Lazarus; over the Transfiguration; over the raising of the dead; over all the teaching of the eternal Word on His Second Coming, but as His resurrection according to Paul's resurrection-message is the pledge and pattern of ours, let us confine ourselves to a brief consideration of this miracle. "If a man die, shall he live again?" (Job 14:14). And the empty grave of Jesus answers, "Yes!" Because He lives, we shall live also. "If the Spirit of him that raised up Jesus," etc. (Romans 8:11).

Dr. J. D. Jones puts it beautifully when he says, "Men argued for years about the possibility of there being a new world out yonder toward the west . . . Columbus sailed out toward the sunset until he discovered land. Then, coming back, he was able to say, 'There is land out yonder; I have been there'. Jesus is our Columbus . . . He has travelled beyond the sunset, and He has come back to say that beyond the grave and gate of death."

> There is a land of pure delight,
>   Where saints immortal reign;
> Eternal day excludes the night,
>   And pleasures banish pain."
>   — Isaac Watts

It is not true any longer that the other side of death is also an undiscovered country, a "bourne from which no traveller returns." Jesus has come back. Thus by the resurrection, we are taught to say:

> We bow our heads at going out, we think,
> And enter straight another golden

chamber of the King's,
> Larger than this we leave, and lovelier.

To quote Canon Knox Little, "The apostles one and all taught what Christ had revealed, and now the whole Church throughout the world, however externally divided through human frailties, still, as God's family, proclaims with one living voice in the catholic creeds, 'I believe in the resurrection of the body, the life everlasting, the life of the world to come'."

If space allowed, one would like to touch on every contribution made to this important doctrine by Peter, Paul, James, John and Jude, showing how each writer was inspired by the Holy Spirit to add his quota to the truth of our life beyond the grave.

Genesis 1:1 and Revelation 22:21 not only open and close the divine revelation, but form the two poles of the deathlessness of man. For as the existence and nature of God bespeak our immortality, so in the closing verse of the Bible the resurrection of the saint to blessedness, as well as the resurrection of the sinner to condemnation, are both wrapped up in the prayer for the coming of Jesus. These two verses are the first and last pearls on the string of immortality. What a multitude of precious gems there are in between, especially in the epistles and the Revelation!

Let us note four figures setting forth the new conception of death, as given in the New Testament.

A. *Death is a Sleep.*

"Our friend Lazarus sleepeth" (John 11:11).

"Them also which sleep in Jesus" (I Thessalonians 4:14).

Sleep indicates the absence of terror and the presence of repose. Thus, the old Christians called their cemeteries "Cubicula" — sleeping places. Germans call their graveyards "God's Acre." Martin Luther says, "A man who lies asleep is much like one who is dead. Therefore, the ancient sages said, 'Sleep is the brother of death'." So, also, death and life are pictured and signified in the revolutions and transformations of day and night, and of all creatures. Sleep is verily a death, and equally death is a sleep. Our death is nothing but a night's sleep. In sleep, all weariness passes away and we rise again in the morning, joyous, fresh and strong.

This term, however, must not be stressed to teach the unconscious theory some teachers declare. It is a word applied to the body and not the spirit. Our bodies sleep or rest in the grave until the resurrection morn. An old English author says, "Sleep is death's youngest brother, and so like him, that I never dare trust him without my prayers." So far, however, as the image is expressive of consolation, it belongs to Christianity alone. It is true of both body and soul, although not in the same sense, that until the time of the resurrection, they "sleep."

Sleep brings rest to man's body, and so death does to the believer's body. Then the grave is his "long home," and a "quiet resting place." There is repose also for the soul. The rest of the spirit, however, does not take the form of unconsciousness; there is no sleep of the soul in this sense. The Bible asserts at once the clear consciousness and the continuous activity of the soul after death. "Absent from the body," says Paul, "present with the Lord" (II Corinthians 5:8).

B. *Death Is a Departure.*
"The time of my departure is at hand" (II Timothy 4:6).
This word "departure" literally means to pull up anchor and set sail. This is what death is as revealed by Jesus Christ. In this world we are anchored to material things; in death, the anchor is pulled up and we set sail for the golden port. At the funeral of Dr. John Neal, of whom Archbishop Trench said, "He is the most profoundly learned hymnologist of our church," his friends sang a special favorite with him, for its music's sake, the first verse of which runs —

Safe home, safe home in port!
  Rent cordage, shatter'd deck,
Torn sails, provisions short,
  And only not a wreck;
But oh! the joy upon the shore
To tell our voyage-perils o'er!

Something of the same picture is drawn by Tennyson in his lovely poem we have quoted, *Crossing the Bar*, where death is likened to one putting out to sea.

C. *Death Is an Exodus.*
"They spake of his decease" (Luke 9:31)

The word "decease" means "exodus" or "a going out." It is a term taking us back to the book of Exodus, where the people of Israel are seen going out of Egypt. It was "a going out," of bondage into liberty; from a land of sorrow and affliction and want into a land "flowing with milk and honey." And so death is our "way out" from the partial to the perfect; from the old gloom into the full day.

That great Frenchman, Victor Hugo, wrote, "For half a century I have been writing my thoughts in history, prose, verse, philosophy, drama, romance, tradition, satire, ode and song. I have tried all, but I feel that I have not said the thousandth part of what is in me. When I go down to my grave, I can say, like so many others, 'I have finished my day's work'; but I cannot say I have finished my life. My day's work will begin again the next morning. The tomb is not a blind alley; it is a thoroughfare; it closes in the twilight, to open with the dawn."

And so death means an exodus or going out from all those influences shackling our powers and gifts, and an entrance into the land of promise, where it will be a joyful privilege to realize fully in our individual lives the divine plan.

D. *Death Is a Removal.*

"If our earthly house of this tabernacle were dissolved" (II Corinthians 5:1).

Here Paul likens death to the exchange of a tent for a house. Life below is a pilgrimage, an abode like a fragile tent. It is not meant to be a permanent residence. So death is the pulling up of the tent pegs, the folding up of the canvass, and moving into our permanent residence above. We enter into the many mansions, or abiding places, in the Father's home, where thieves can never break into and steal. This, then, is the Christian view of death. It is the passing out of an order whose purpose is probation, whose distinction is the opportunity of attaining a higher and nobler life. It is an exodus from the wilderness into a life of fuller energy, happier fellowship, pure joy, unflawed peace. It is, above all, the short, swift passage to a life with Christ forevermore. Death is thus a gate into a holy city, a falling asleep to awake to an endless life, a quick journey home to God. Such as the revelation that brings the chant to a believer's life — "O death, where is thy sting? O grave, where is thy victory?" (I Corinthians 15:55).

How different is all this to the ordinary conception of death! Men talk about the "great beyond," the unknown, the unexplored land, the unseen, a leap in the dark, but such is not the language of Scripture. Says Professor Clow, "Every reader of the New Testament is disconcerted by the contrast between expectancy and desire of the primitive church and the bewilderment and shrinking of Christian men today. Stephen sees heaven opened; Paul longs to depart and to be with Christ; Peter exults in an 'inheritance incorruptible, undefiled, and that fadeth not away.' The early believers might be pictured as looking stedfastly up into heaven. Even a generation or two ago, devout men and women died with a psalm of desire on their lips. We still read, beside the bier of the dead, the wondrous words which proclaim the Resurrection." But we are now being told by some of our theologians that all this talk about heaven is a "pie-in-the-sky" hope irrelevant to these times with their pressing social problems. Alas, for most men the veil of sense hangs darkly between this life and the next. Agnosticism has crushed the reality of those things, unseen and eternal. Did not our Lord tear the mask away from the cruel face of death and rob it of its power to smite the heart with fear, and enable us to embrace death as a friend leading us from a vale of tears to the summer-land above where eyes are never wet with tears? "Precious in the sight of the Lord is the death of his saints" (Psalm 116:15), because it takes us into His immediate presence for ever.

For Bible Day

For Bible Day

This Holy Book, on every line
Marked with the seal of high Divinity,
On every leaf bedewed with drops of
    love
Divine, and with the Eternal heraldry
And signature of God Almighty
    stamped,
      From first to last.

                    — Robert Pollok

The Bible is —

  A companion to the lonely.
  A staff to the weak.
  A light in the darkness.
  A breaker of fetters.
  A lifter of burdens.
  A solver of problems.
  A banquet to the hungry.
  A well to the thirsty.
  A drier of tears.
  A cleanser of hearts.
  A distributor of riches.
  An anchor in the storm.
  The compass on the ocean.
  A finger-post to the traveler.
  The airplane of the spirit.
  The wrecker of false hopes.
  The upsetter of human plans.
  The smasher of vain ambitions.
  The breaker of idols.
  An exposer of unreality.
  A revealer of hypocrisy.
  An unveiler of deceit.
  A voice against sin.
  The devil's greatest foe.
  The sinner's greatest terror.
  The penitent's greatest friend.
  The ammunition of the soldier.
  The guarantor of victory.
  The pioneer's tonic.
  Oil for the lamp, the face, and the
    wounds.
  The studio of the ever Blessed
    Trinity.
  A divine library.
  Our chart.
  The revealer of Christ.
  God's greatest and grandest gift
    to man.
  The revealer of man.
  God's masterpiece.
  The revealer of man's fall and
    failure.
  The unveiler of the remedy for
    the recovery, regeneration and
    renewal of man.
  The assurer of eternal bliss to
    God's own.

*Can any other book show such a
record?*

                    — George Dempsie

MEDITATION FOR BIBLE DAY

WHY WE CAN BELIEVE THE BIBLE
II Timothy 3:16

It is both necessary and profitable to have a day like this when we can call attention to the beauty, power, value, and indispensability of God's most precious Word — The Holy Bible — the world's best seller. Supreme in the realm of literature, its worth has been lauded by the most outstanding men in every walk of life. It would take a volume as large as the Bible itself to record all the tributes to the perennial influence of its teachings.

Napoleon, who failed to live by the principles of the Bible, yet wrote of it, "The Bible is no mere Book, but a Living Creature, with a power that conquers all that oppose it."

Abraham Lincoln, in all sincerity declared, "I believe the Bible is the best gift God has ever given to man. All the good from the Saviour of the world is communicated to us through this Book."

W. E. Gladstone, renowned British statesman who wrote *The Impregnable Rock of Holy Scriptures* affirmed,

"I have known ninety-five of the world's great men in my time, and of these eighty-seven were followers of the Bible. The Bible is stamped with a speciality of origin, and an immeasurable distance separates it from all competitors."

Queen Victoria, who reigned over an empire upon which the sun never set, was familiar with the Bible and said of it, "That Book accounts for the supremacy of England."

John Ruskin, who wielded a powerful influence as an art critic confessed, "Whatever merit there is in anything that I have written is simply due to the fact that when I was a child my mother daily read me a part of the Bible and daily made me learn a part of it by heart."

Charles Dickens, the British novelist, who remains a giant among English writers, said that, "The New Testament is the very best Book that ever was or ever will be known in the world."

Sir Isaac Newton, the scientist famous for his formation of the law of gravitation, had no hesitation in affirming that, "There are more sure marks of authenticity in the Bible than in any profane history."

At a time like this when the authority and value of the Bible are being persistently attacked by religious, as well as secular writers, it is incumbent upon us to reaffirm why we believe the Bible to be God's infallible Word. Its claim, as a divine revelation holding authority over reason and conscience, is being challenged by those who reject its inspiration and authority. The Bible is relegated to a place among sacred books of religious systems, but its teachings have a loftier level seeing they are no human production. What saddens us most is the way some theologians discredit the supernatural element found in the Bible. Miracles, if not mythical, can be explained on natural grounds. How are we to meet this adverse criticism of the inerrant Scriptures?

While the regenerated heart has its reasons for accepting the Bible in its entirety as the revelation of the mind of God, critics of this affirmation are not convinced. It carries no conviction to their minds to listen to the fact that our own inner consciousness says, "I know the Bible is all it says it is." Nor is it sufficient to invoke the authority of tradition handed down through the ages. We must be prepared to furnish arguments justifying our faith and establishing our claims as to the veracity of Holy Writ. Before listing unassailable evidences that the Bible is the Word of God, there are two introductory thoughts to bear in mind.

The first is that a divine revelation is possible.

When God created man He endowed him with faculties to receive His communications. He did not close all avenues to Himself as the Creator. As human minds can have intercourse and act upon each other, is it not likewise possible for the mind of God to convey its thoughts to the mind of man? No earthly father could maintain perpetual silence among his offspring. How cruel it would be for our heavenly Father not to offer light and guidance to His own children! As I am speaking to your mind through these words from my mind and hand, so in the Bible we have the thoughts of the divine mind which holy men of old wrote down for our enlightenment and edification.

The second thought is that a divine revelation must bear its own credentials.

It must prove its divine origin by being worthy of its Author in the realization of all that is written. Its contents must coincide with all we know of His character — holy, wise and good. It must meet the deepest needs of man, and lead him to mastery over evil. Its incomparable superiority in the realm of literature depends upon its greater influence over nations and men. Here, then, are our evidences that the Bible is the world's masterpiece.

A. *Because Of Its Claims to Be the Word Of God in All Its Parts, and the Direct and Authoritative Revelation Of His Will.*

These claims are specific and carry with them the authority of a royal decree or act of parliament or congress. That it speaks in the name of God is testified to in the declaration, repeated hundreds of times, "Thus saith the Lord." If this and similar utterances do not constitute a claim to divine authority, then language has no meaning. If the human writers did not set down what the Holy Spirit inspired them to do, as they confessed they did, they are branded as blatant liars and wilfull deceivers. From this viewpoint they would have been evil men, and it would have been utterly impossible for deceitful men to write such a marvelous Book. There is no other explanation for the unique Psalms which David wrote than the one he himself gave, "The spirit of the Lord spake by me" (II Samuel 23:2).

B. *Because of the Nature of Its Contents.*

The glorious truths found in the Bible touch the secrets of man's inner life, and also its external aspects and thus influences both character and conduct. Within its sacred pages we have outlined the course of human history from its origin to its final destiny. Here, as nowhere else, the veil is lifted hiding the unseen from view, and where the torch of reason fails the Bible sheds a clear, true light upon mysteries of life and of eternity. It covers the entire field of divine and human thought and action.

Where have we a complete conception of the Godhead apart from the Bible? Here alone can we see and know God as the Creator, Governor, Father and Redeemer.

Where have we a record of creation so explicit as that to be found in the opening chapter of Genesis? How purile alongside of this chapter are the surmisings of evolutionists!

Where can we find an authentic account of man's origin, nature, sin, salvation and immortality outside the pages of the Book which reveals the Son of God becoming the Son of man that He might make the sons of men the sons of God?

Where else in any system of religion or philosophy is sin dealt with as in the Bible? What a faithful exposure of its source, pollution, tragedy and doom it gives us! It is yet full of entreaty for the sinner to repent of his sin and find peace with God.

Where is it possible to read of God's redeeming grace in the findings of philosophers? The central truth of Scripture is the love of God for a lost world revealed in the death of His Son.

Where can we discover, in any other book, moral perfection of contents and moral truths and precepts comparable to those presented in the Holy Bible?

Where have we intellectual supremacy which this masterly Book represents? As Jesus is supreme as a Man among men, so the Bible is pre-eminent as a Book among books. There is none like it. It has a majesty all its own.

Where can we find historical veracity such as the Bible contains? Its records have been challenged often, but the spade of archaeology is proving the reliability of what men wrote centuries ago.

Where is there another volume abreast of the latest scientific discoveries like the Bible? While it does not exist to teach science, its scientific accuracy can't be disputed.

C. *Because of the Unity of Its Contents.*

Although a period of something like 1,500 years separated Moses from John, and about forty different men from all walks of life wrote under the greatest variety of circumstances, yet the sixty-six books they composed under divine inspiration form one Book. While it contains a progressive revelation, unity of thought about God, sin, repentance, redemption and judgment is preserved. What one writer adds does not contradict what a previous one has said. If stones were gathered together from different quarries, but when fitted together presented the figure of man, we would be forced to conclude that one mind conceived the plan. It is thus with all the writers employed to complete the Bible. There was the overruling guidance of the Holy Spirit prompting men to present God in the Person of the Man Christ Jesus. This is only one feature making the Bible the most fascinating book in the world to read and study.

D. *Because of Its Adaptation to, and Power Over the Human Soul.*

Coleridge said that he valued the Bible because "it found him." How true is the dictum, "He who made my heart made this Book." A key fitting the complicated mechanism of a lock proves that both lock and key were designed by the same mind. It would take volumes upon volumes to record all the triumphs of the Bible. Wherever it travels, and its truths are received, man experiences deliverance from the thraldom and pollution of sin. Countless multitudes owe all they are and have to the transforming power of Him whom the Bible extols. The best evidence of the veracity of Scripture is the outliving of its truths in your daily life and mine. In Christ, these truths became flesh and dwelt among men. He *lived* the Old Testament, which was the only part of the Bible He possessed. May our beliefs and behavior harmonize!

E. *Because of Its Influence Upon the World.*

Ezekiel reminds us that life and blessing followed the river from the temple. It is so with the Bible, for everything lives wherever it flows. The testimony of history is that where the truths of the Bible are believed and acted upon, civilization is greatly enriched. Slaves are liberated — the downtrodden emancipated — the needy cared for — justice prevails — society is elevated — evil practices die. The American Constitution was founded upon the precepts of the Bible — which is yearly printed in millions of copies in hundreds of languages. Statesmen and some of the world's greatest men have all alike testified to the remarkable influence of the Bible upon nations and human society. A sceptic who found himself in a heathen part of the world came upon a one-time cannibal chief reading his Bible. Sneeringly he said to the chief, "Surely you don't believe the fancies and myths of such a Book?" Quietly the transformed man-eater replied, "Do you see that large pot over there? You would have been in it before this if the Book you scorn had not been true." The darkness of the world is appalling, but it would be far worse if it were not for the Bible shining as a light in a dark world.

F. *Because of Its Prophetic Element.*

Peter, who wrote of the Bible as "the more sure word of prophecy" (II Peter 1:19), gives us many striking evidences of man's ability, by the Holy Spirit who came to show us things to come, to forecast the future. We know that the Bible is the infallible Word of God because predictions against contemporary nations like Tyre, Babylon, Nineveh and Egypt, given when these nations were at the zenith of their power and grandeur, were literally fulfilled. Old Testament predictions of Christ were fulfilled in the New Testament. He, Himself, said of these Scriptures, "They testify of me," (John 5:39). Then predictions regarding the past, present and future of the Jews receive a like fulfillment. When Frederick the Great asked the court chaplain for one argument in favor of the Bible's authenticity, the minister replied, "The Jews, Sir." And the fulfillment of manifold prophecies is an unassailable proof of the divine origin of the Bible.

G. *Because of the Verdict of Christ.*

A striking feature of the gospels is the way in which Christ set His seal upon the authenticity and authority of the Old Testament. Facts which are assailed by critics today, He declared as truth. He believed Adam and Eve and Jonah were actual persons and not myths. He likewise confirmed the historicity of events such as Lot's wife. How dishonoring it is to affirm that Jesus accommodated Himself to the ignorance, prejudices and superstitions of His time! He loved, and lived in, Old Testament Scriptures and was forever quoting them. They were the Word of God to Him, and in them He saw Himself (Luke 24:27, 44). Is not ours the solemn obligation of treating Scripture as reverently and obediently as Jesus did?

If we receive the Word as from God, and hold the same implied trust and confidence in it as the Master did, we shall not be long in discovering its power in our life and witness. One of the ministries of the Holy Book is to make us *holy*, hence, the decision of the psalmist, "Thy word have I hid in mine heart that I might not sin against thee (Psalm 119:11). It is, therefore, the responsibility of the saint to imbibe the precious truths of Scripture and allow them to become flesh and dwell among men. As for sinners, they can only cleanse their ways as they take heed to the solemn warnings of the Bible and get right with God, who is its Author.

H. *Epilogue — Banning the Best.*

When a noted orator once asked Charles Dickens, "What is the most pathetic story in all literature?" the master novelist answered readily, "The story of the Prodigal Son."

Whan Samuel Taylor Coleridge was asked, "What is the richest passage in literature?" the poet answered, "The first sixteen verses of the fifth chapter of Matthew."

When Daniel Webster was asked, "What is the greatest legal digest?" he replied, "the Sermon on the Mount."

And an internationally known figure has said, "No one has equalled Moses in law, David in poetry, Isaiah for vision, Jesus for way, truth, and life, Peter for holy zeal, Paul for logic, or Apollos for fiery oratory."

In view of these high tributes from recognized masters it seems foolish to say that a study of the Bible marks a backward step in education.

Yet some very powerful individuals and some very influential organizations are devoting full time to the single task of barring Bible teaching from all public schools.

Of course, the opposition of these enemies of Bible teaching is based upon their unwillingness to see religious instruction introduced into the schools. But while opposing religious instruction they are seeking to exclude from the schools the world's greatest compendium of moral philosophy and the greatest collection of literary masterpieces that the world has ever seen.

For a Day of National Mourning

For a Day of National Mourning

When King George VI — the sovereign who had greatness thrust upon him because of the abdication of his brother, Edward VIII, the present Duke of Windsor — died in 1952 at the age of 56, a nation who admired him mourned his passing. In his honor, Oswald J. Smith penned the poem:

The King Is Dead

An Empire mourns, an Empire vast
   and great,
The hearts of millions turn from strife
   and hate;
A world stands still, forgetful of its
   fate —
      The King is dead.

A nation weeps, a nation brave and
   strong,
Across the sea the bells toll loud and
   long;
The Father of the Empire now is
   gone —
      The King is dead.

The glory fades, the pride of conquest
   wanes,
And o'er the air the organ's mournful
   strains
Remind us all that he no longer
   reigns —
      The King is dead.

It is not loneliness of soul,
Nor grief nor tears that sternly bring
The pall that rests on broken hearts,
But shattered hopes and bleeding
   wounds
Of mind and spirit, slow to heal.
And gentle souls will never weep
When Death's cold ruthless hand lays
   hold
The silver cords of love and life.
      — James Hervey Hyslop (1915)

MEDITATION FOR A DAY OF NATIONAL MOURNING

A NATION WITH DRAWN BLINDS
Exodus 12:30

The senseless assassination of John F. Kennedy, in 1963 — the fourth American president to be murdered — shocked and saddened the entire world. In the streets of the nation strong men paused and wept as the news of such a diabolical deed was broadcast. Wales also became a land of tears on the fatal day when the mountain of pit-slap at Aberfan moved and almost 150 children were buried alive. Such a tragic catastrophe turned a nation of song into one of sobs. Turning to the Bible we find it unique, incomparable in the realm of literature in its approach to life from different angles. History, drama, tragedy, philosophy, psalmody and prophecy — they all are within the covers of the majestic Book.

As a record of national tragedies it has few equals. The Flood, the destruction of Sodom, the slaughter of Hebrew males under Pharaoh, the massacre of innocent babies under Herod, the martyrdom of early Christians, and the destruction of Jerusalem, are among the Bible's records of universal woe. Egypt became a nation with drawn blinds the day the last plague of judgment overtook it and the firstborn in all Egyptian homes, from sovereign to slave, and all the firstborn among cattle were smitten with sudden death. What tragedy and pathos are packed into the phrase, "There was not a house where there was not one dead" (Exodus 12:28-40). What an ocean of tears flowed that day in the land of Egypt! Meditating upon this grim record we note the following features —

A. *The Midnight Hour.*

The historian tells us that it was at "midnight" when the Lord smote all the firstborn in Egypt (Exodus 12:29). How the black hour of the night must have magnified the tragic circumstances! We can imagine what national consternation prevailed. Is there not something significant about the time of this divine visitation at the least expected and the least prepared hour of the night? Midnight indicates the darkest possible period when the black-

273

ness of night reaches its limit. Does this not describe the state of the world? Are we not living in the midnight hour of world history? Have we not come to the Saturday night of the week of God's eternal purpose? Midnight also depicts the condition of the unsaved soul who lives in the darkness of sin. Nicodemus came to Jesus "by night," and found Him who is the Light.

We read that "Pharaoh called for Moses and Aaron by night" (Exodus 12:31). It was at midnight that the cry was raised, "Behold, the Bridegroom cometh" (Matthew 25:6). As the darkest hour is before the dawn, all who rest in Scripture as God's light in a dark place can rejoice in affirmation that the night is far spent. It was at midnight that Paul and Silas prayed to God and praised Him. We, too, can rejoice for the breaking of the day will soon be upon us.

What an avalanche of anguish overtook the land! What a vast sepulcher Egypt became at that grim hour as the land was filled with corpses and cries! Hopes were shattered as all heirs of Pharaoh down to his humblest servant were caught up in the holocaust of death. As the destroying angel passed over the land not one home or field was missed as darkness and death prevailed. Proud, defiant Egypt became a nation of mourners as every house buried its dead. Is not the world as a whole a valley of moans and miseries, sobs and sorrows, tears and tragedies? In peaceful times, but more particularly when war rages, there are broken hearts and lives in every land. Think of the river of tears daily shed over sin and suffering and the separations in life! The terrible cry going up all over the Egypt of this world would kill us, if our ears were tuned to hear it.

Do we ever pause to think of the accumulation of groans, moans, cries and curses reaching the ear of God every day? An agnostic said to a believer, "If I could see and hear all that God sees and hears, my heart would break." The believer's reply was, "God's heart did break at Calvary." And the cross alone is heaven's remedy for the moans of earth. The healing of the blood is always efficacious for the deep sores of humanity. Are we in sympathy with God as He listens to the cry of millions still in heathen darkness? Do we not have to confess with shame that our ears are deaf to the sighs of mankind; that we do not weep o'er the erring one as we ought? A greater wail will be heard when the last moment of the day of God's sufferance comes. "All kindreds of the earth shall wail because of him" (Revelation 1:7). Then there will be "weeping and gnashing of teeth" exceeding that of the cry of Egypt. In hell, there is no solace. Perdition is the scene of perpetual anguish. Would that we could hear all over our land the cry of contrition and sorrow because of sin, with the penitent turning to the Saviour!

B. *The Mourning Nation.*

Another poignant passage in the record of Egypt's midnight hour of judgment reads, "There was not a house where there was not one dead" (Exodus 12:30). Such a divine act proved God's supremacy and that, as the Creator, He was able not only to impart life but also to withdraw it at will. Our breath is in our nostrils, and at any given moment God can cause it to cease. Our time and times are in His hands. Therefore we should be right with him so that whether the death angel visits us at midday or midnight, a blessed future is assured. There is a threefold application of the national bereavement when a corpse lay in every Egyptian home.

1. *The Universality of Sorrow* — Death of the Body.

There is not a house in which there is not a broken circle, an empty chair, a vacant place. Sovereign and subject alike experience the cruel partings death produces. The king of terrors is no respecter of persons. Today I have merriment, you have moans. Tomorrow the gladness will be yours, and the grief mine. If our house is set in order then it matters little when death attacks. If we are Christ's, then death is gain.

2. *The Universality of Sin* — Death of the Spirit.

Paul speaks of those who are dead as they live (I Timothy 5:6). Sin has left its mark upon every home. Even in the most respectable and seemingly happy household, a skeleton can be found in the cupboard — a member of the home whose prodigal ways bring so much heartache. Houses are few in which there is not one within who is dead in trespasses and sin. Prayers arise from many godly homes that all the family may be gathered into the fold.

3. *The Universality of Separation* — Death of the Saint to the World.

God's eye is always upon the house in which, although the majority respect Him, there is one at least who has surrendered to His claims. These lonely saints are dead to sin with a life hid in God. Dead to the ways of the world which their home may follow, their courageous separation always leaves its impact upon the atmosphere of the home. It is not easy to maintain an isolated witness among those we live with, but strength is ours as we remember that the blood is over the lintel of life and that consequently we are saved from eternal death.

C. *The Message Declared.*

The message which the people of Israel longed to hear came as the stench of dead men and dead cattle polluted the air, "Get you forth . . . go serve the Lord" (Exodus 12:31). At last, Pharaoh yielded as he looked into the face of his own firstborn. The twofold aspect of divine deliverance are implied by the two words *Get . . . Go.* The people were brought out of the land of bondage that they might be brought into the land of promise. Severed from sin, we should be found serving our Deliverer. We can imagine how glad Egypt was when Israel departed. Do we so live for God as to make the devil anxious to quit troubling us? Our Lord was always a source of annoyance to the devil. This was why his agents besought Him to depart from their coasts. Are we a trouble to the devil? It is to be feared that the majority of Christians do not cause our satanic foe to be nervous.

An aspect of Pharaoh's liberation of Israel is the fact that he was letting a people go whom he had no right to retain. They were God's people, not his. It is thus with ourselves whether, Christian or otherwise. Satan has no right whatever, even to the control of a sinner who is God's property seeing He created him and gave His Son to die for his salvation. But for us all Pharaoh's pertinent command must be obeyed.

Get Forth. We must turn aside from our sin, worldly company, and all entanglements resulting in spiritual bondage. Bridges must be burned behind us.

Go Serve. Leaving Egypt means separation from all that is alien to God. "Go serve" indicates separation unto

Him. The emancipated life is fully yielded to the Deliverer for use in His service. Saved, we must serve. The expansion of the church is hampered by those who claim to be saved, but fail to serve the Saviour.

D. *The Mixed Multitude.*

Do we grasp the full import of the fact noted by the sacred historian that "a mixed multitude went up also with them"? (Exodus 12:38). Many Egyptians, scared by the display of God's omnipotence, felt it better to follow Him, and so outwardly abandoned their idols. Although they left Egypt as a place, it was still in their hearts, and it was the atmosphere of Egypt that they took with them that caused so much trouble and delay in the wilderness. We read, "It is a night to be much observed unto the Lord for bringing them out from the land of Egypt" (Exodus 12:42), but it is tragic to know that they took some of Egypt with them. Among the mixed multitude there were not only frightened Egyptians, but also Israelites who had come to love the provisions, and when the trials of the wilderness overtook them, wished they had never left Egypt with its fish, cucumbers, melons, leeks, onions and garlic (Numbers 11:1-6).

In church life today, progress is retarded because of a mixed multitude. The door into membership is very wide, and unregenerated men and women mingle with those who are truly born again and who seek purely spiritual aims. Conflict often arises in a church where unspiritual members seek to introduce worldly and carnal methods to further the interests of their church. Because they are religious but not Christian, or Christian but not spiritual, such members are a positive hindrance to the true spirituality of their church. If we have been taken out of the world, as the sphere of sin, we must be sure that the world is taken out of us. Lot's wife left Sodom, but Sodom was in her heart and looking back she perished. "Come out from among them, and be ye separate, saith the Lord" (II Corinthians 6:17). Does not separation mean that what we turn from must be expelled from within us. If our desires or company are mixed, how can we serve the Lord acceptably? Any effort to mix the spiritual and the carnal makes the Christian life a distortion. Are we among the numbers mercifully delivered out of the Egypt of this godless world? Then may grace be ours to live as those whose hearts are wholly possessed by Him who was not of this world.

For a National Election Day

For a National Election Day

O Almighty Lord and Heavenly Father, we beseech Thee to guide and govern the minds of Thy people in wisdom, sincerity, and judgment, that they being called to elect just legislators and faithful counsellors for our country, on behalf of all conditions of men in many nations, they may understand both the sacredness of the trust which Thy providence commits to each of them, and also the greatness of the interests which thereon depend for Thy world and Church, for virtue and Thy true religion. To Thee, O Lord, we commend this whole land, for which Thou hast done so many great things of old. Abolish all mean desire and unworthy motive; let none be deceived through wilfulness or vain words. Cleanse all thoughts, uplift all minds, enable them to consider all things diligently, and in singleness of heart to fulfill Thy will: through Jesus Christ our Lord. Amen.

— Archbishop Benson (1829)

Govern, O Lord, the minds of all who are called to choose faithful men into the great council of the nation, that, considering their sacred trust and the great issues thereof, they may exercise the same in all godliness and honesty; through Jesus Christ our Lord. Amen.

— Diocese of Southwark (1910)

MEDITATION FOR
A NATIONAL ELECTION DAY

THE CANDIDATE OF OUR CHOICE
Acts 1:26

In the apostolic band a vacancy occurred because of the sin and suicide of Judas, and the apostles adopted a simple yet effective method of filling the gap. Two godly men were eligible for the position, and the apostles met together and prayed and then voted. "They gave forth their lots; and the lot fell upon Matthias" (Acts 1:26). The important lesson to be gleaned from that ancient election is that, faced with two candidates, the apostles prayed *before* they voted and doubtless prayed *as* they voted. At a time of national election in the modern world what a different atmosphere would prevail if only all candidates and voters resorted to prayer. How equally necessary is such a prerogative in all other political elections, whether of a local, regional or state nature. This is also true in the religious realm in the election of a church leader, pastor, or office-bearer! Then, as we are to see, the personalities and methods involved in an election can be given a spiritual application.

A. *The Choice of a Candidate.*

When an election is planned it is usual for several aspirants for office to present themselves before the electorate with each presenting his own qualifications and platform. Much efficient organization, effort and money go into the election with each party doing its utmost to entice the mass of voters who often find themselves confused by the counter claims and promises of opposing candidates. Too often those who are fortunate enough to be elected are not able to perform what they promised. A clergyman of the seventeenth century, Charles Churchill by name, wrote of —

> Those who would gain the votes of British Tribes,
> Must add to force of merit, force of bribes.

Sir Charles J. Darling, an outstanding judge born in 1849, said that, "To convince a poor voter by the common argument of promised reforms is merely to corrupt him with hope."

Turning to the spiritual realm there are candidates diverse in character

279

and purpose bidding for the vote of the soul. Two groups with three candidates in each present themselves, namely, the "trinity of hell," and the "trinity of heaven." In the first trinity we have the world, the flesh and the devil, who use all subtle means to gain the vote of the will. The promises they offer are a package of lies, and all who decide in their favor are deluded. And if they persist and die in their delusion, they die damned. The other trinity, composed of the Father, the Saviour and the Holy Spirit, likewise offer themselves for our choice. They promise to deliver us from sin, cleanse the heart, ennoble the life, enrich character and grant us life forevermore. And having promised, they are faithful in fulfillment. "There failed not aught of any good thing which the Lord had spoken . . . all came to pass" (Joshua 21:45).

What a solemn choice, then, faces each one of us — a choice as to whether Christ or the devil is to govern our life and determine our eternal destiny!

> Once to every man and nation, Comes the moment to decide,
> In the strife of truth with falsehood, for the good or evil side;
> Some great cause God's new Messiah, offering each the bloom or blight,
> And the choice goes by forever 'twixt that darkness and that light.
> — James Russell Lowell

B. *The Value of the Vote.*

Whenever a local or national election comes around, how the populace is urged to get out and vote. "No matter who your candidate is, turn up at the polling station and vote," is the exhortation we read and hear. Apathy or indifference on the part of those who have the right and privilege to vote may endanger their country's welfare. Oliver Wendell Holmes (1809-1897)

had the importance of the personal vote in mind when he wrote —

> The freeman, casting with unpurchased hand,
> The vote that shakes the turrets of the land.

We find ourselves in disagreement with those religious people who affirm that we should not involve ourselves in the government of our city or nation. Surely if it is our obligation "to pray for all that are in authority" (I Timothy 2:1-3), we have an equal responsibility to vote prayerfully that the right kind of men, able to "lead us to a quiet and peaceful life in all godliness and honesty," may be chosen.

We can understand the sentiment of Edmund Burke, the renowned British statesman (1729-1797) that —

> Politics and the pulpit are terms that have little agreement. No sound ought to be heard in the church but the healing voice of Christian charity . . . Surely the church is a place where one day's truce ought to be allowed to the dissensions and animosities of mankind.

But surely church going people need to be given the Christian aspect of their social, as well as their spiritual responsibilities. This does not mean dragging politics into the pulpit or influencing the voting right of members in communal or national affairs, but guidance as to the choice of those candidates whose lives and standards are compatible with christian ideals.

There are several features of the vote in democratic countries where liberty of choice and conscience still prevail that we can spiritualize.

1. *The Vote Is Secret.*

In polling stations great precautions are taken to preserve the secrecy of balloting, so that no one else in the world can know how we voted unless we whisper our choice of a candidate. Of this we are confident, that many useless, industrial strikes would never take place if only a secret ballot of workers was allowed. Often the choice of Christ as Saviour and Lord of one's life is taken in secret, but though the inner decision is hid from the gaze of the world, the results of that personal choice soon become evident to all.

2. *The Vote Is Personal.*

Each person on the voter's "roll" in a community must register his or her own vote. No one can vote for them. One by one, voters go to the polling booth and place a X against the name of the candidate they feel is worthy of their choice. Is it not thus when it comes to a decision for Christ? No one can believe or choose for us, nor can we be saved by proxy. Certainly, we can be lovingly persuaded by others to cast our vote on the Saviour's side, just as in elections we are influenced by the electoral speeches and literature of a condidate. But, ultimately, salvation involves a personal choice, "Choose *you* this day whom *ye* will serve" (Joshua 24:15).

3. *The Vote Is Voluntary.*

Although we are urged to realize the importance of any issues confronting a nation or a community at election time, and we are reminded of the necessity of recording our personal vote, in a democratic country like ours in which liberty of action and conscience are respected, we are not forced to go to the poll. Failure to vote does not mean punishment as it does in some totalitarian countries. Is it not also true that in matters concerning the government of our life, the decision is voluntary? No heart is ever forced by God to yield to His claims. If a sinner is to be emancipated from sin and transformed into a child of God, there must come the voluntary surrender of heart and life to the Saviour.

The same principle can be applied to servitude to Satan. No one is compelled to cast a vote in his favor. Multitudes are his slaves because they *will* to be so. The tremendous issue is that a person can choose heaven or hell, or *will* their salvation or damnation.

4. *The Vote Is Representative.*

When election time comes around in the country or our own home town, we have certain ideals we are anxious to see realized, and if the candidates presenting themselves for office are in agreement with our idea of just government, we vote for them and they become our representatives. Our votes declare the kind of men we want to see in office. Under Communism, where there is no freedom of choice — no opposition party, this is not so. Compulsory voting is all in the one direction whether the populace like the candidates or no. But in a democracy, if the people feel that a politician no longer represents their wishes, the ballot can register their rejection of his services to the country or community.

One of the most pathetic sentences in Sir Winston Churchill's volumes on *The Second World War* appears in Volume 1 on "The Gathering Storm." It reads —

> On the night of the tenth of May, 1940, at the outset of this mighty battle, I acquired the chief power in the State, which henceforth I wielded in ever-growing measure for five years and three months of World war, at the end of which time, all our enemies having surrendered unconditionally or being about to do so, I was immediately dismissed by the British electorate from all further conduct of their affairs.

Rightly or wrongly, the British people felt that while this great man nobly represented them in time of war, he was not the kind of representative they wanted in a time of blood-bought peace.

In the things of the Spirit, the decision we make indicates our inner desire, the kind of life-control we feel is profitable. Who is our representative? If it is Satan, then we reveal by our choice, our state of heart, and that we want no other to reign over us. But if we have yearnings for holiness of life then Christ is our true Representative. He is the only One who can meet the deepest longings of the soul, and fulfill our aspiration for eternal peace. In a general election pamphlet, printed in 1910, there is the expressive prayer —

> Raise up, O God, politicians who will fear Thee and Thee alone, and will Thy will, and work Thy work, fearless and faithful unto death in the Name of Jesus Christ. Amen.

In Christ, we have the Ruler who perfectly fulfills all of these requirements which we covet for ourselves, and who is likewise able to realize them in and through us.

Whether the candidates we vote for win or lose, let us bear in mind the paragraph Jonathan Swift gives us in *Voyage To Laputa* —

> He gave it for his opinion, that whoever could make two ears of corn or two blades of grass to grow upon a spot of ground where only one grew before, would deserve better of mankind, and do more essential service to his country than the whole race of politicians put together.

BIBLIOGRAPHY

Golladay, Dr. R. E., *The Challenge of a New Day* (Columbus: Lutheran Book Co., n.d.)

Hardy, Thomas G., *The Year With Christ* (London: A. R. Mowbray Co., 1935)

Lindemann, Paul, *Festival Days* (Minneapolis: Augsburg Publishing Co., 1935)

Keble, John, *The Christian Year* (London: Basil M. Pickering, 1877)

Sangster, W. E., *At Feast and Festival* (London: Epworth Press, 1960)

Warren, Neil, *This Is the Day* (Grand Rapids: Zondervan Publishing House, 1937)